Digital Approaches to Inclusion and Participation in Cultural Heritage

This edited book brings together best examples and practices of digital and interactive approaches and platforms from a number of projects based in European countries to foster social inclusion and participation in heritage and culture. It engages with ongoing debates on the role of culture and heritage in contemporary society relating to inclusion and exclusion, openness, access, and bottom-up participation.

The contributions address key themes such as the engagement of marginalised communities, the opening of debates and new interpretations around socially and historically contested heritages, and the way in which digital technologies may foster more inclusive cultural heritage practices. They will also showcase examples of work that can inspire reflection, further research, and also practice for readers such as practice-focused researchers in both HCI and design. Indeed, as well as consolidating the achievements of researchers, the contributions also represent concrete approaches to digital heritage innovation for social inclusion purposes.

The book's primary audience is academics, researchers, and students in the fields of cultural heritage, digital heritage, human-computer interaction, digital humanities, and digital media, as well as practitioners in the cultural sector.

Danilo Giglitto is a researcher working at Sheffield Hallam University, UK. His work falls in the areas of heritage studies, sociology, and human-computer interaction, with a particular focus on digitally mediated and social-innovation compatible community-led cultural heritage projects.

Luigina Ciolfi is Professor of Human-Computer Interaction in the School of Applied Psychology, University College Cork, Ireland. She researches the human experience of and practices around digital technologies, with a particular focus on the cultural heritage domain and on participatory and co-design methodologies.

Eleanor Lockley is a Research Fellow at the Culture and Creativity Research Institute at Sheffield Hallam University, UK. She works across and within sociology, media, human-computer interaction, and cultural studies. Her research focuses on digital media and the sociology of communication as well as aspects of digital inclusion, and digital and media literacy.

Eirini Kaldeli is a senior researcher at the Artificial Intelligence and Learning Systems Laboratory of the National Technical University of Athens. Her most recent work focuses on the development of frameworks and tools that make use of cutting-edge digital technologies for data management, creative reuse, crowdsourcing, and engagement in the field of cultural heritage.

Digital Approaches to Inclusion and Participation in Cultural Heritage

Insights from Research and Practice in Europe

Danilo Giglitto, Luigina Ciolfi, Eleanor Lockley, and Eirini Kaldeli

Routledge
Taylor & Francis Group
LONDON AND NEW YORK

First published 2023
by Routledge
4 Park Square, Milton Park, Abingdon, Oxon OX14 4RN

and by Routledge
605 Third Avenue, New York, NY 10158

Routledge is an imprint of the Taylor & Francis Group, an informa business

British Library Cataloguing-in-Publication Data
A catalogue record for this book is available from the British Library

ISBN: 978-1-032-23438-0 (hbk)
ISBN: 978-1-032-23439-7 (pbk)
ISBN: 978-1-003-27760-6 (ebk)

DOI: 10.4324/9781003277606

Typeset in Times New Roman
by MPS Limited, Dehradun

Contents

Figures

Tables

Contributors

Ilgım Veryeri Alaca is an Associate Professor at Koç University and the Director of Artistic Research Studio and its subgroup Picturebook Studies. Her articles appeared in *Bookbird*, *Leonardo*, the *International Journal of Child-Computer Interaction*, and the *International Journal of Education Through Art*. She contributed to *The Routledge Companion to Picturebooks* and *The Routledge International Handbook of Early Literacy Education.*

Charlotte Armstrong was the postdoctoral research associate on the AHRC-funded project 'The Internet of Musical Events: Digital Scholarship, Community, and the Archiving of Performance' (InterMusE). The project is investigating new ways of capturing and linking different forms of data around musical events to form a dynamic, open-access digital archive. She gained her PhD from the University of York in 2020 with a thesis examining the representation of disability and pre-Fascist discourses of 'degeneracy' in the operas of Franz Schreker and Alexander Zemlinsky. Charlotte now works as the Communications Coordinator for the European Network on Statelessness.

Christina Bashford is a Professor of musicology at the University of Illinois at Urbana-Champaign, USA. Christina works in the sphere of cultural musicology, examining the functions and meanings of music, music-making, and its associated activities in the nineteenth and early twentieth centuries. Her focus is on Britain and its relationships with other nations, and her research explores a range of themes, including the tensions between the sacralisation of music and its commodification, changing intersections of class, gender, and national identity, and the role of music in situations and times of war.

Elisa Bonacini is an Archaeologist, with a BA in Classics (2001) and another in Enhancement of Archaeological Heritage (2010); she specialised in Classical Archaeology (2005). She has a PhD in Humanities and Cultural Heritage (2014) and another in Lenguas y Culturas (2022). She is an expert in digital cultural communication and digital enhancement and co-creative participatory storytelling through heritage communities.

Since 2016, she is the coordinator of the #iziTRAVELSicilia project, focused on creating participatory multimedia audio guides for museums and tours on izi.TRAVEL. She published many papers and books and is currently working as a consultant.

Rinella Cere is Associate Professor in Media and Cultural Studies at Sheffield Hallam University (UK). Her publications include *An International Study of Film Museums* (Routledge, 2021). She is the co-editor of *Postcolonial Media Culture in Britain* and has introduced postcolonial theory in the study of film and media in *Postcolonial and Media Studies: A Cognitive Map* (2011). She has contributed to *Postcolonial Studies Meets Media Studies. A Critical Encounter* (2016) and has published extensively on a variety of media coverage from anti-immigration discourses to Brexit. She is currently collaborating on the research project Polyvocal Interpretation of Contested Colonial Heritage (PICCH).

Luigina Ciolfi is Professor of Human-Computer Interaction in the School of Applied Psychology, University College Cork (Ireland). She researches human practices and experiences of digital technologies in everyday settings, with a focus on collaboration, participation, and placemaking. Her work connects computing, social sciences and design, with cultural heritage being one of her core domains of expertise. She is an Associate Editor of the *CSCW Journal*, and a scientific referee for many conferences and journals in her field. She is a senior member of ACM SIGCHI and member of EUSSET – the European Society for Socially Embedded Technologies and of the British Psychological Society.

Rachel Cowgill is Professor of Music and University Research Theme Champion for Creativity at the University of York, UK. Her research focuses on music in cultural history, encompassing Mozart; opera studies; British musical cultures; musical internationalism, diplomacy and commemoration; performance and reception histories; and music, gender and identity. She is Principal Investigator of the AHRC-funded project "The Internet of Musical Events: Digital Scholarship, Community, and the Archiving of Performance" (InterMusE) and of the UKCRF-funded StreetLife project, which includes a community digital archive based on The Willow Cantonese restaurant and nightclub formerly in York's Coney Street.

Cristina Da Milano holds a degree in Archaeology (University of Rome) and a MA in Museum Studies (University of Leicester). She has been involved in several projects and studies at local, national and European levels related to cultural access, participation, and audience development. Expert in European cultural policy and programmes, since 2010 she is president of ECCOM-European Centre for Cultural Organisation and Management and a member of the Commission for the National Museum System of the Italian Ministry of Culture. From 2015 to 2021, she has been a member of the board and vice president of Culture Action Europe.

Anna Näslund Dahlgren is Professor of Art History at Stockholm University, Sweden. She has written extensively on different aspects of photography, visual culture, historiography, the digital turn, archives and museum practices. Recent publications include *Fashioned in the North. Nordic Histories, Agents and Images of Fashion Photography* (2020), *Travelling Images. Looking Across the Borderlands of Art, Media and Visual Culture* (2018), and *Representational Machines. Photography and the Production of Space* (2013). She recently guest edited a special issue on the "Politics of Metadata" for the *Journal of Digital Culture & Society* (2020) and is currently working with the anthology *Critical Digital Art History* under contract with Intellect (2023).

Betül Gaye Dinç is a researcher recently graduated from Erasmus Mundus International Master in Children's Literature, Media, and Culture at the University of Glasgow. She obtained her BA in Archaeology and Art History with a double major in English Language and Comparative Literature and received her MA in Design, Technology, and Society from Koç University. She presented at European Network of Picturebook Research – The 7th International Conference and the 25th International Research Society for Children's Literature Congress. She contributed to the edited volumes, *Verbal and Visual Strategies in Nonfiction Picturebooks* (2021) and *VEKAM Cultural Heritage Studies for Children* (0-18) Workshops (2020). She published in *Drawing: Research, Theory, Practice*, *Studies in Comics* and the *Journal of Graphic Novels and Comics.*

Alan Dix is Professor and Director of the Computational Foundry at Swansea University and is Professorial Fellow at Cardiff Metropolitan University, in both roles working across disciplines to encourage fundamental research that makes a difference to real people. Alan's own career has included seminal work in human-computer interaction, including a core textbook in the area, foundational work on formal methods and user interaction, and the earliest academic papers on mobile interfaces, on privacy and on gender and ethnic bias in machine learning. He also walked a thousand miles around Wales, an exploration on the nature of community technology at the margins.

Sara Eloy is Assistant Professor at the Department of Architecture and Urbanism at Iscte (University Institute of Lisbon), where she teaches Architectural Computer-Aided Design, Drawing, and new technologies applied to Architecture and Research Methodologies. She is currently the director and fellow researcher at the Information Sciences Technologies and Architecture Research Center (ISTAR-Iscte). She graduated in Architecture (FA, Technical University of Lisbon, 1998) and has a PhD in Architecture (IST, Technical University of Lisbon, 2012). Her main research areas are applications of digital technologies, namely virtual and augmented reality, shape grammars, architecture design and heritage preservation applied to colonial architecture. Within the scope of cultural heritage and digital humanities, Eloy has organized several exhibitions such as "School of Chicago: digital skyscrapers" (2012), "Artificial Realities: Virtual as an aesthetic medium in architectural ideation" (2019), and "As Roças em São Tomé e Príncipe – O Lido e o Fotografado" (2022).

Elisabetta Falchetti holds a degree in Natural Sciences (University of Rome). She was a researcher and collaborator in national and European cultural projects for educational-cultural and didactic activities, previously within the Civic Zoological Museum of Rome and later within ECCOM. Her main fields of expertise are museum professional training, scientific-sustainability education and communication, socio-cultural inclusion, accessibility and intercultural dialogue. She participated in national and European projects for the training of cultural mediators and museum professionals and was the author of a number of contributions and books in her fields of research.

Tom Flint is an Associate Professor in the School of Arts and Creative Industry at Edinburgh Napier University, UK. Dr Tom Flint is a creative technologist whose work concentrates on people and their relationships with technology. Tom's research interests focus on cultural heritage, the creative industries and digital technology's role in these disciplines. His work explores the use of digital media and computing technology to communicate art collections and visitor attractions. Tom has collaborated with the sculpture park Jupiter Artland since 2011 to build numerous digital interventions.

Vendela Grundell Gachoud is a researcher, teacher, and photographer focused on diversity in digital contexts. Her PhD in art history (2016) explored how digital interfaces shape spectatorship and how this process is revealed in glitch art online, an interest in critical creative practices and user experiences that continued in her postdoc on visually impaired photographers (2018-2020). Output includes around a dozen scholarly publications, twenty press features and thirty exhibitions since 1998. She works in international, interdisciplinary and socially engaged settings from her base at Stockholm University where she currently holds a position as project leader for the Art & Research program at the artspace Accelerator.

Danilo Giglitto is a Researcher working at Sheffield Hallam University (SHU) on the PICCH project, exploring how archival material created in a colonial mindset can be re-appropriated and re-interpreted to become an effective source for decolonisation. He has several years of experience in researching at the intersection of cultural heritage and digital technologies. He holds a PhD in sociology from the University of Aberdeen, United Kingdom. His research interests include among others, qualitative research methods, research design, intangible cultural heritage, digital heritage, community engagement, bottom-up approaches, wikis, and decolonisation practices.

Tanis Grandison is a lecturer in the School of Computing, Engineering and Built Environment at Edinburgh Napier University (UK). Her area of interest is how digital media can complement critical heritage and creative placemaking in order to unpack geographies of meaning with children. Central to Tanis' research is the use of psychogeography and tangible computing to elicit and share stories from young participants. Tanis has undertaken her research in partnership with a local arts organisation and three primary schools in Edinburgh to co-create interactive talking maps of their community.

Karin Hansson is an Associate Professor in Media Technology at Södertörn University in Sweden and is currently the project leader of the research project "#MeToo activism in Sweden" and part of the "Metadata culture" research group at Stockholm University. Her research focuses on participatory research methods and online participation. She has recently co-edited: *Information & Culture, Special Issue: Datafication and Cultural Heritage* (2022); *Computer Supported Cooperative Work (CSCW), Special Issue: Materializing Activism (2021)*; *Digital Culture & Society, Special Issue: The Politics of Metadata* (2020); and *CSCW, Special Issue: Crowd Dynamics: Conflicts, Contradictions, and Cooperation Issues in Crowdsourcing* (2019).

Kirstie Jamieson is a researcher and lecturer in creative methods, critical heritage studies and interpretation design. Her research addresses heritage, representation, equality and diversity in the public realm. Most recent publications include *Exploring Deaf Heritage Futures through Critical Design and Public Things* (2020) and *The Deaf Heritage Collective: Collaboration with Critical Intent* (2021). She is currently working with curators and deaf researchers on the first co-produced draft of a national Deaf Heritage Archive at the National Library of Scotland. She is also developing a project that brings together feminist interpretation design with social justice, in the memorialisation of Scotland's accused witches.

Eirini Kaldeli is a senior researcher at the Artificial Intelligence and Learning Systems Laboratory of the National Technical University of Athens. She holds a PhD from the University of Groningen on the use of Automated Planning in the field of Web Services and an MSc in Artificial Intelligence from the University of Edinburgh. Her most recent work focuses on tools that make use of cutting-edge digital technologies for data management, creative reuse, crowdsourcing, and engagement in the field of cultural heritage. She has worked as a developer, technical manager, and expert in a number of European and national projects.

Eleanor Lockley is a Research fellow at Sheffield Hallam University in the Centre for Culture Media and Society and has a track record of working on interdisciplinary research projects, including commercial consultancy through knowledge exchange and works across and within sociology, media, human-computer interaction, and cultural studies. She holds a PhD about the social impact of mobile devices and has since focused her research on digital media and the sociology of communication: the impact of technology and digital media on individuals, and groups; as well as aspects of digital inclusion, and digital and media literacy. Lockley has more than 10 years of experience in designing and implementing research studies and she has published over 40 peer-reviewed articles and book chapters.

Pascuala Migone is a sociologist specialised in qualitative research and management and evaluation of projects in the cultural field. Her professional experience has focused on issues related to cultural heritage, migration, citizen participation, and local development. In the public sphere, she worked for the School Libraries program of the Ministry of Education of Chile, in charge of planning and coordinating studies for the promotion of reading in Chilean public schools. She has developed several research projects related to cultural heritage, including a comparative research project for the Dutch Center for Intangible Cultural Heritage on the intangible cultural heritage policies in Italy, Colombia and Netherlands using a participatory perspective. She also deals with facilitating participatory processes. Pascuala is part of the ECCOM research and project development team.

Valentina Nisi is a tenured Associate Professor at IST, University of Lisbon (Portugal), Adjunct Faculty at the HCI Institute Carnegie Mellon University (USA) and founding researcher at the Interactive Technologies Institute (ITI LARSyS). Her research encompasses Interactive Digital Storytelling, Gaming, and HCI, bringing awareness and care to pressing social and environmental issues. Spanning from Fine Arts, to Design and HCI, Valentina's research contributes to an interdisciplinary view on societal challenges combining a Research-through-Design approaches with post-humanistic concerns.

Ross Parry is a Professor of Museum Technology at the School of Museum Studies, University of Leicester. He leads the international research consortium "One by One UK-US: Building Digitally Confident Museums". He is a Principal Fellow of the Higher Education Academy, Board member for Attenborough Arts (Leicester), and Trustee of the Jodi Mattes Trust. Currently, Professor Parry serves as a member of the UK Research and Industry's Steering Committee of its £19mn digital cultural heritage initiative "Towards a National Collection". He is the founding co-editor of the Routledge book series *Critical Perspectives on Museums and Digital Technology*. Previously he has been: Director of CAMEo (the Research Institute for Cultural and Media

Economies) (2020); Deputy Pro-Vice-Chancellor (Digital) (2016–2019); and Academic Director of the College of Social Sciences Arts and Humanities (2013-2016) at the University of Leicester. In 2018, he was listed in the Education Foundation's "EdTech50", listing the fifty most influential people in the UK education and technology sectors.

Lara Perry is the Associate Dean for Education and Student Experience in the School of Humanities and Social Sciences at the University of Brighton, UK. Trained as a historian with a background in working with museum professionals, artists and art, her research mainly concerns the history of museums and in particular gender equity issues relating to collections and displays – an interest which has now extended to encompass digital collections and interpretation. Her publications include a number of studies of feminism and curatorial practices including two volumes edited with Elke Krasny and forthcoming from Routledge in 2023: *Curating as Feminist Organizing* and *Curating with Care*.

Daniela Petrelli is Professor of Interaction Design at the Art, Design & Media Research Centre at Sheffield Hallam University, UK. She has a broad range of research interests including user interfaces for multimedia digital libraries and multilingual information retrieval, language-based intelligent interfaces, interaction with digital heritage and personalisation for cultural heritage, data visualisation and visual analytics, and personal and family memories. She has over 20 years of experience in user-centred design, field studies, co-design, co-creation and creative practices applied in a range of different domains. Prof Petrelli has published over 100 peer-reviewed papers, led a number of collaborative projects and received 12 awards and recognitions from academia and industry.

Stefania Stellacci is an Integrated researcher at the Information Sciences Technologies and Architecture Research Center (ISTAR-Iscte, University Institute of Lisbon) and an Invited Professor at Iscte. She is an architect with an MSc in Architecture (University of Ferrara, 2006), a Built Conservation postgraduate degree (Roma3 University, 2007), and a PhD in Architecture (Iscte, 2018). Her research spans across critical heritage studies, multiple-criteria decision analysis, digital transformation, and sustainable heritage management.

Özge Subaşı is an Assistant Professor at the College of Social Sciences and Humanities at Koç University (Turkey) and is the director of Futurewell, a research group dedicated to justice and equity-oriented design. Their research is on the co-creation of new services and designs with under-valued populations, based on fieldwork in community settings, usually with crafty artefacts.

Acknowledgements

The work supporting the preparation of this edited book has been supported by funding from the European Union's Horizon 2020 research and innovation programme under grant agreement No. 770158. The sole responsibility of this book lies with the editors. The European Union is not responsible for any use that may be made of the information contained therein.

1 Introduction: digital approaches to inclusion and participation in cultural heritage

Danilo Giglitto, Luigina Ciolfi, and Eleanor Lockley

Cultural heritage is no longer seen solely as a safeguarding effort or an educational outlet but also as a form of civic and cultural representation and engagement that can contribute to social cohesion. Digital ecosystems are a long-established facet of heritage practice in supporting informal learning, interpretation, and engagement, and increasingly shape the dynamics between organisations (including museums and other GLAM institutions as well as academic institutions) and communities, leading to new models of collaboration, interaction, and communication around heritage and culture (Parry 2010, Waterton and Watson 2013, Ciolfi et al. 2017). Furthermore, cultural heritage is an essential part of debates on social inclusion and exclusion, difficult histories, and ideological contrasts, and digital platforms play a key role in conveying views and representing ideas as well as in mobilising heritage-related activism (Gröppel-Wegener and Kidd 2019, Black 2020). The field of Human-Computer Interaction (HCI) has also developed a growing concern for the social, societal, and cultural impact of digital technologies, also in the heritage sector (Hornecker and Ciolfi 2019), advocating for humanistic and critical approaches to reflect on the impact, legacies, and values that digital tools carry (Bardzell and Bardzell 2016). This rich and complex context linking heritage, institutions, communities, and digital tools and platforms sees several themes for reflection arising. These are particularly lively in the current context, with migration flows (towards Europe and within Europe), colonialist legacies and "difficult" heritage, debates on national and European identity (particularly after Brexit), and risks and forms of possible exclusion and marginalisation such as social class, education, disability, race and/or ethnicity, and sexuality (Galani et al. 2020).

Beyond academia, activists and grassroots cultural groups are campaigning to highlight the contested (and often divisive) political and social dimension of heritage such as public memorials. Furthermore, with an increasing number of digitised collections and archives available to the public, the digital arena can represent forms of exclusion as well as enable wider participation and polyvocality (Schofield et al. 2019). Policies and white

DOI: 10.4324/9781003277606-1

papers have made it clear that inclusion and inclusivity in heritage are of paramount importance in fostering "social inclusion, intercultural dialogue and cultural diversity" (European Commission 2017, p. 7), resonating with global calls for greater diversity and representation in heritage (UNESCO 2001). Such issues shape curatorial approaches and digital skills strategies (Parry 2018), push debates on legacies of inclusion and exclusion in existing museums and other cultural institutions and on how they should be tackled and motivate a wave of grassroots initiatives dedicated to representing diverse voices, memories, and perspectives.

In this context, digital technologies not only underpin contemporary fora where such issues are made visible and discussed, but also have great potential to mediate dialogue, debate, and participation in the heritage context and in relation to stakeholders (Schofield et al. 2019, Galani et al. 2020). By recognising the importance of practice-focused and inductive approaches that are widely adopted in HCI and critical heritage studies, this book explores how digital technologies can underpin a variety of cultural heritage initiatives by supporting greater inclusion of different communities in heritage and culture (see Chapters 2 and 4), envisioning more open and inclusive cultural heritage institutions (Chapters 5, 6, and 7), decolonising, questioning, and challenging the representation promulgated by established digital archives (Chapters 8 and 10), and pursuing digital innovation to foster educational, artistic, or archival values (Chapters 3, 9, and 11).

The chapters in this book detail work on projects involving several countries (e.g., the United Kingdom, the United States, Sweden, Italy and Turkey) and territories that are linked by complex legacies (e.g., São Tomé and Príncipe). Examples and practices of digital and interactive approaches and platforms from European-wide large consortiums aimed at fostering social inclusion and participation in heritage and culture (see Chapter 2, 5, and 8) are also brought together in this volume. Whilst there are limitations in geographical and cultural scope and we do not claim to report on a global scale, the significant examples provided within this volume illustrate innovative approaches in a research space that is still under development, and they are important in defining such space and in seeding a new transdisciplinary frame. Different types of cultural institutions (archives, museums, civic bodies) feature, and so do different publics and stakeholder groups. Relatedly, ecologies of relationships between various stakeholders and institutions emerge and point to the need of reflecting on the kinds of partnerships that can underpin such projects.

With an aim of providing an original set of insights, all the chapters engage with ongoing debates about the role of culture and heritage in contemporary society relating to inclusion and exclusion, openness, access, and bottom-up participation, exploring angles such as the engagement of marginalised communities, the opening of debates and new interpretations around socially and historically contested heritages, and the way in which digital technologies may foster more inclusive cultural heritage practices.

The contributions address key facets of these themes by reporting on cutting-edge theory and practice and by reflecting on future opportunities and challenges. Together, they illuminate a new space of research and reflection bridging heritage studies, social innovation, and human-centred digital innovation.

Following this Introduction, Chapter 2 provides an overview of the EU-funded project "MEMEX – Memories and Experiences for inclusive digital storytelling" (2019–2022), aimed at promoting social cohesion and inclusion through collaborative tools that provide inclusive and creative access to cultural heritage. MEMEX uses digital storytelling as an effective tool to engage people at risk of exclusion in the creative narration and reinterpretation of cultural heritage, promote social and cultural participation, and develop multiple skills. The results converge in a prototype of a smartphone app that allows users to create, share, and visualise geo-localised stories in augmented reality, where personal memories and experiences intertwine, allowing users to experience a multicultural and dynamic perspective of cultural heritage.

Focusing on the *roças*, a widespread system of cocoa and coffee plantations established in São Tomé and Príncipe by Portuguese colonisers, Chapter 3 shows how e-learning tools can be an important driver of systemic cultural overhaul, sustainable heritage management, global peacebuilding, and social cohesion, provided that broad communities, including descendants from formerly colonised countries, are actively involved throughout the critical design process of reinterpreting those sites.

Chapter 4 describes the co-creative and participatory methods adopted in a case study named #iziTRAVELSicilia, carried out in Sicily, Italy, on the global platform izi.TRAVEL. The project dealt with the topic of participatory strategies in multimedia audio-guide co-production, a co-creative process within a regional-scale with local stakeholders. Overall, the project involved more than 4,000 people from the local heritage communities. Many sub-projects have been carried out with students, some of them with learning difficulties, all engaged as "digital Ciceroni" (i.e., expert guides), able to develop their own digital narrative projects, bringing cognitive, relational, motivational, and skills enhancement benefits to local Sicilians.

Chapter 5 describes the EU-funded project "CultureLabs: Recipes for Social Innovation" (2018–2021), which developed an online platform that aims to streamline and facilitate the collaborative organisation of cultural heritage-oriented and social innovation-compatible participatory projects. Through the platform, users can discover helpful resources ("ingredients") and combine them to form "recipes" for social innovation. The aim of the project is to connect institutional practices, cultural heritage, and digital technology in a way that can leave a legacy for the broader cultural sector and society at large.

Chapter 6 reports on a series of digitally delivered projects designed to promote social inclusion and undertaken in 2020 and 2021 by the project partners: the Royal Pavilion and Museums Brighton and Hove (United Kingdom); the DeLaWarr Pavilion in Bexhill on Sea (United Kingdom); and the Peale in Baltimore, Maryland (United States). Their experiences are analysed under three different themes: optimising technology choices for greater accessibility by a range of audiences; the benefits of supporting inclusive content in enhancing accessibility; and the organisational implications of expanding digital provision as a mechanism for driving inclusivity in locally focussed cultural heritage institutions.

Chapter 7 describes the Digi-Mapping project, which ran in partnership with an arts organisation named WHALE Arts, based in Wester Hailes, Edinburgh, United Kingdom, and participants aged between 8 and 11 from three local primary schools. As part of a bottom-up creative placemaking project, Digi-Mapping allowed children to challenge dominant negative narratives of the local area by assigning them the role of expert. The chapter demonstrates how Digi-Mapping privileged marginalised voices and advanced an inclusive approach to creative placemaking.

Chapter 8 reports work on the EU-funded PICCH (Polyvocal Interpretation of Contested Colonial Heritage) project. Although many museums and archives are currently addressing their colonial past as institutions and as "guardians" of objects of dubious and often violent provenance, how to deal with images (films and photographs) has not been addressed yet. This research proposes a framework for decolonising anthropological films held in digital archives and obtained within colonial relationships. The chapter illustrates a re-usable process of re-appropriation and re-interpretation by analysing characteristics and patterns of a sample digitised anthropological films from the collection of the Pitt Rivers Museum in Oxford, United Kingdom.

Chapter 9 explores the Internet of Musical Events: Digital Scholarship, Community, and the Archiving of Performance (InterMusE) project, which, by modelling new approaches to the open-access presentation of music-historical research based on digitally enabled collaboration, adopts a collaborative and egalitarian approach to working alongside musical communities to understand and preserve their heritage. The chapter explores community archives of musical ephemera as sites of co-produced, "post-custodial" collecting, and preservation that can radically transform approaches to digitisation, community music-making, and archival value(s).

Focusing on Sami images in the online archive of the Swedish National Heritage Board, Chapter 10 presents a study of how metadata shapes the conditions of cultural heritage representation. The study uncovers how different metadata structures and practices facilitate different narratives that both hide and highlight Sami markers. It also identifies means to resolve or bypass limitations to the spectrum of perspectives expressed in image descriptions: omission, abstraction, translation, and hyperbole. The chapter illustrates how metadata affects diversity by governing image searches online textually and visually.

Chapter 11 examines how an interactive picturebook prototype can facilitate children's exposure to a museum collection of artworks presenting cultural heritage in Istanbul, Turkey. In line with critical heritage studies, this research prototypes an interactive picturebook for the Suna and İnan Kıraç Foundation's Orientalist Painting Collection tested by seven children in Pera Museum. The results challenge the status quo in how educational materials in museums can be tailored in more contextualised ways to inspire children for a deeper understanding of diverse heritages.

In the Afterword (Chapter 12), Ross Parry reflects on the collective contributions of this volume by contextualising it into the current "metamodern" discourse on digital practices and priorities in museums. Parry illuminates an "emotional turn" whereby affect and people (and not just processes and platforms) are currently a core concern of digital change in museums. He proposes "code switching" as a term for discussion to provoke and kickstart a debate on the various discourses underpinning museum and cultural heritage technology and how they can be both bridged and critiqued.

This range of efforts documents both the lively space of research and practices on themes of heritage, digital innovation, and social inclusion and some important findings achieved by projects engaging a variety of institutions, groups, communities, and types of heritage. They provide foundational insights to inform the further exploration of these topics and spark reflection on their impact.

Following from these insights, we propose important open questions and issues that need addressing. Firstly, cultural heritage projects aiming at fulfilling social innovation objectives generally need to mediate between a variety of stakeholders and beneficiaries, which may often translate into a tension of different sets of values, expertise, and motivations. More work is needed to establish best practices and frameworks that consider the ambitions of various institutions and communities and to identify areas of overlapping concern and contrast. Evidence shows how managing stakeholders and participants in social innovation via cultural heritage projects remains an open challenge (Giglitto et al. 2019, Giglitto et al. 2021). Some chapters of this book report on very large and multifaceted projects that use different approaches in order to pursue wide-scale benefits while needing to reconcile widely different perspectives. For instance, the #iziTRAVELSicilia project (Chapter 4) demonstrates how a proper articulation of motivations and benefits can lead to the involvement of a variety of public and private institutions as well as grassroots associations. On the other hand, the experience in the CultureLabs project (Chapter 5) shows how establishing well-thought-out and dedicated research activities, tailored to different types of stakeholders and beneficiaries, may better inform a complex technology design process.

Secondly, issues regarding the politics of technology design and cultural representation also need to be critically examined. Despite the fact that archives have been gradually losing their authoritative stance on history and heritage (Flinn 2012), helped by the possibilities opened up by the advancement of digital technologies (Flinn 2010), it still is not common for established digital archives to actively challenge biased narratives. This is particularly true for European archives that either feature historical media representations produced from within colonial-based relationships or that are fully or partially built around the practices, culture, and folklore of ethnic minorities. In light of the new cultural heritage paradigm that promotes bottom-up engagement and counter-hegemonic perspectives (Robertson 2012), monovocal interpretations and long-standing narratives may need to be complemented or even challenged. While the sensitivities towards dissonant or traditionally excluded voices are increasing, will still lack a corpus of best practices that light the way. Some of the chapters in this book explore ways to question the ethical foundations of digital archives and the way in which they preserve and present instances of cultural representations. For instance, Chapter 10 looks at the online archive of the Swedish National Heritage Board and how certain Sami markers can be either hidden or emphasised through different structures and practices for metadata. It then proposes four workaround strategies as a means to circumvent the limitations embedded in image descriptions. Chapter 8 takes a different approach, based on epistemology, that critically examines the relationship between colonialism and anthropology to produce an analytical framework to uncover colonial legacies in audiovisual material from the colonial era. These works contribute to an ongoing shift that, however, still requires more effort to engender polyvocality in archives.

Finally, more work is needed to reflexively identify and apply methods and processes that might facilitate work at the intersection of such complex terrains and discourses, and various configurations thereof (Chapter 12). Several chapters in this book show examples of innovative methodological synergies, such as the "creative placemaking" art-informed approach described in Chapter 7, and the various uses of digital prototypes as part of multi-method processes, from being used to complement pedagogical interpretations of heritage (Chapter 11), to providing a means for multicultural dialogue (Chapter 2). As the concerns for social inclusion become more prominent in the cultural heritage discourse, innovative processes might include further skillsets, epistemologies, and forms of knowledge. As research at the intersection of these topics progresses, maintaining a reflexive outlook on how it does so is absolutely necessary.

To conclude this introduction, the team of editors of this book have come together at the intersection of disciplines and approaches: museum and heritage studies, human-computer interaction, systems development, communication and media and cultural studies. Our experience has been not only about bringing together a group of contributors to speak to these topics, but also about defining and articulating a space to discuss these issues in a transdisciplinary yet coherent way, with the hope that it will thrive.

References

Bardzell, J., and Bardzell, S., 2016. Humanistic HCI. *Interactions*, 23 (2), 20–29.

Black, G., 2020. *Museum and the challenge of change: old institutions in a new world*. New York: Routledge.

Ciolfi, L., *et al.*, 2017. *Cultural heritage communities: technologies and challenges*. London: Routledge.

European Commission, 2017. *Mapping of cultural heritage actions in European Union policies, programmes and activities*. European Commission, Report Number (where relevant).

Flinn, A., 2010. Independent community archives and community-generated content: "Writing, saving and sharing our histories". *Convergence: The International Journal of Research into New Media Technologies*, 16 (1), 39–51.

Flinn, A., 2012. Archives and their communities: collecting histories, challenging heritage. In: G. Dawson, ed. *Memory, narrative and histories. Critical debates, new trajectories*. Brighton: University of Brighton, 19–35.

Galani, A., Mason, R., and Arrigoni, G., 2020. *European heritage, dialogue and digital practices*. London: Routledge.

Giglitto, D., *et al.*, 2019. Bridging cultural heritage and communities through digital technologies: understanding perspectives and challenges. In: *Proceedings of the 9th International Conference on Communities & Technologies – Transforming Communities*. New York: ACM Press, 81–91.

Giglitto, D., Ciolfi, L., and Bosswick, W., 2021. Building a bridge: opportunities and challenges for intangible cultural heritage at the intersection of institutions, civic society, and migrant communities. *International Journal of Heritage Studies*, 28 (1), 74–91.

Gröppel-Wegener, A., and Kidd, J., 2019. *Critical encounters with immersive storytelling*. London: Routledge.

Hornecker, E., and Ciolfi, L., 2019. *Human-computer interactions in museums*. San Rafael: Morgan & Claypool Publishers.

Parry, R., 2010. The practice of digital heritage and the heritage of digital practice. In: R. Parry, ed. *Museums in a digital age*. Abingdon: Routledge, 1–10.

Parry, R., 2018. Socially purposeful digital skills. In: *Connecting digital practice with social purpose: let's get real 6*. Report from the sixth Culture24 Action Research Project, 34–35.

Robertson, I.J.M., ed., 2012. *Heritage from below*. Farnham: Methuen.

Schofield, T., *et al.*, 2019. Design and plural heritages: composing critical futures. *In*: *CHI'19: Proceedings of the 2019 CHI Conference on Human Factors in Computing Systems g*, 4–9 May 2019 Glasgow. New York: ACM Press, 1–15.

UNESCO, 2001. *Universal declaration on cultural diversity*. Paris: UNESCO.

Waterton, E., and Watson, S., 2013. *Heritage and community engagement: collaboration or contestation?* London: Routledge.

2 Digital storytelling, cultural heritage, and social inclusion: the MEMEX project

Cristina Da Milano, Elisabetta Falchetti, Pascuala Migone, and Valentina Nisi

Culture and social inclusion in the EU perspective and policies

Cultural participation is universally considered a human right since the 1948 *Universal Declaration of Human Rights* (United Nations 1948), acknowledging that active and creative participation in cultural pathways and events promotes a complete development of human personality. The guidelines for the Lifelong Competences for the 21st century of the Council of the European Union (2018a) push for the construction of higher-order, transversal, and soft skills, promote the cultivation of problem-solving and emotional skills such as empathy, imagination, curiosity, the ability to perceive and appreciate diversity, and openness towards different solutions and possibilities. Among these, creativity and imagination are considered the "top" skills for our century (Carnwath and Brown 2014, Anttonen *et al.* 2016).

The report "From social inclusion to social cohesion. The role of culture policy" (European Union 2019) indicates that around 113 million Europeans (over 20%) are at risk of poverty or social exclusion, and 15% of them experience material deprivation. These conditions prevent socio-cultural and leisure opportunities, hinder real cultural participation, and impact social cohesion. The 2019 Eurostat – Culture statistics (European Commission 2019b) shows a direct correlation between cultural participation and income, with 82.5% of the EU-28 population (aged 16 or more) in the highest income bracket taking part in cultural activities, in comparison to 43.6% in the lowest income bracket. In 2017, 40% of Europeans surveyed felt that Member States were distant in terms of shared values. Culture topped the list of factors most likely to create a feeling of community, ahead of history, geography, and religion. However, more than a third of Europeans said that they did not participate at all in cultural activities. From the Standard Eurobarometer 87 (European Union 2017) it emerged that what creates a feeling of community among European Union are culture (31%), history (25%), values (24%), economy (21%), and geography (21%), confirming the impact of culture. Disparities and inequalities can create marginalisation and exclusion, mainly among the most vulnerable people.

DOI: 10.4324/9781003277606-2

The deprivation of cultural participation reduces the opportunities to construct higher-order skills, not only impacting on individuals' quality of life, but also reducing access to social and work opportunities. Culture plays an empowering role also in community relationships and growth. Through cultural participation, people interiorise knowledge, traditions, beliefs, and values, such as respect and appreciation of ethnic and cultural diversity, freedom, citizenship, social responsibility, and democracy, as well as improve social skills. As the EU White Paper (Council of Europe 2008) claims, intercultural dialogue is a key to social comprehension and peaceful relationships in a multicultural Europe, and intercultural dialogue is affected and improved by the creative and equal participation of citizens in cultural activities. In fact, cultural activities constitute a unique and special context to overcome social conflicts, give space and opportunities to marginalised people or minorities, promote reciprocal comprehension and appreciation, and foster dialogue among diverse generations and ethnic groups (see, e.g., Heritage Contact Zone 2018).

Cultural activities impact not only the quality of life and the future of individuals, but of communities and the planet, which is why culture has been identified as the "fourth pillar of sustainability" (United Cities and Local Governments 2010, Sabatini 2019), as "a bridge" *with and among* the three historical pillars: economy, society, and environment (see also European Commission 2018b). Participation in cultural and educational activities is a crucial strategy to tackle the environmental, social, and economic challenges of our and next century.

In this line, the European Community attributes a specific role to Cultural Heritage (CH) in achieving the goals of the European Strategy 2020 for "smart, sustainable and inclusive growth", for its social and sustainable impact (European Commission 2010), and for the goals of "Sustainable Europe by 2030" (European Commission 2019a, ICOMOS 2021). After the 1972 *UNESCO Convention on Cultural and Natural Heritage* (UNESCO 1972) and the 2003 *Convention for the Safeguarding of Intangible Heritage* (UNESCO 2003), governments and institutions began to consider the meaning and use of CH from a multifaceted perspective. The value of CH has been expanded to a series of benefits that go beyond the already acknowledged cultural enrichment and economic impact of tourism. In the last few years, many European studies have confirmed the power of CH in improving the quality of citizens' lives. Many research studies show the impact and stimuli of CH on personal development, identity, employment, creativity and innovation, economic development, education and lifelong learning, social cohesion, and cooperation (CHCFE Consortium 2015).

The *Faro Convention* (Council of the European Union 2005) and the *Florence Declaration* (ICOMOS 2014) have enriched CH with a new paradigm and community-based approach: its role in the construction of peaceful and democratic societies, in the processes of sustainable development and in the promotion of cultural diversity and intercultural dialogue.

CH is a catalyst of creativity and inspiration and directly or indirectly contributes to supporting creative industries and the prosperity of our societies. A communication from the Commission to the European Parliament (European Commission 2014) promotes an "integrated approach" to CH which interests many sectors of public life as education, social cohesion, environment, tourism, research and innovation, and local economy. In fact, Europe acknowledges that CH increases social capital, stimulates civic participation; improves individual and community quality of life; promotes a sense of belonging, inclusion, and intercultural dialogue, comprehension, and respect; reduces social disparities; offers opportunities to develop knowledge, skills, creativity, and innovation; contributes to formal, informal education and lifelong learning. Moreover, CH is a driver of local development and economies through cultural tourism, creative industries and the requalification of cities and rural environments (ICOM and OECD 2018). In the same document, the European Union recommends promoting long-term political models and research programmes on CH based on all these multiple aspects and goals, engaging in partnerships with public institutions, agencies, and civil organisations.

The European Union recognises the potential role of culture – and CH in particular – in constructing a stronger, democratic, inclusive, cohesive, and healthy Europe and in reinforcing a European collective identity. Europe also recognises the vital impact of culture on the economic and innovative-creative sectors, for their intrinsic values, but also because innovation is a necessary process in our post-modern societies and innovative skills must be cultivated among the young generation for giving rise to new ideas, different outputs, methods, products, and values (European Commission 2018a). The new *European Agenda for Culture* (European Commission 2018b) and the *Council's Work Plan for Culture* (Council of the European Union 2018b) indicate these goals and suggest policies; programmes such as Creative Europe support the implementation of these strategies.

The MEMEX project: digital storytelling for social and cultural inclusion

It is in this context, under the strong belief in the potential of culture for individual development, social cohesion, and inclusion, that the MEMEX project was designed, with the goal of experimenting with the synergic impact of digital technologies, CH, and storytelling for cultural and social inclusion. MEMEX – Memories and Experiences for inclusive digital storytelling is an ongoing three-year project (2019–2022) funded by the Horizon2020 European programme, born from the collaboration of eight partners with socio-cultural and technological profiles and expertise: Italian Institute of Technology Foundation (Italy; project coordinator), Interactive Technology Institute – LARSyS (Portugal), Ernst & Young (Italy), Noho Limited (Ireland), Ca 'Foscari University of Venice (Italy), CNRS – Center

National de Recherche Scientifique (France), Michael Culture Association (Belgium), Dédale (France), Interarts (Spain), Mapa das Ideias (Portugal), and ECCOM (Italy).

MEMEX promotes social cohesion through the use of digital tools, with the aim of providing inclusive access to tangible and intangible CH and facilitating encounters and interactions between communities at risk of social exclusion. To achieve these goals, MEMEX tests a smartphone app offering an augmented reality experience – co-designed by technical and socio-cultural partners – based on digital storytelling (DS), that provides a new paradigm for interaction with CH. Participants create, visualise, and share their geolocalised digital stories, in which personal memories and experiences intertwine with the heritage that surrounds them. These tools provide languages and spaces to collectively generate and make visible creative, inclusive, and plural narratives, emphasising the active role of the participants in re-interpreting existing CH. The communities chosen to test the MEMEX tools through pilot projects are three: migrant women in Barcelona; inhabitants of the 19th district of Paris; and first, second, and third generation Portuguese migrants living in Lisbon, where participants are actively and creatively engaged in the implementation of personal storytelling inspired by local CH.

This chapter presents the concept and strategic framework employed in the development of the project. It reflects on the approach and methodologies implemented in MEMEX, which combines different themes and strategies – DS, CH, and technologies – to promote cultural participation and social cohesion and the inclusion of communities that do not usually have access to cultural participation. These themes and strategies represent experimental fields in the framework of Audience Development (AD), which is one of the pillars of European cultural policy and programmes, aimed not only at fostering cultural access and participation but also to promote a shift of cultural institutions/organisations towards a deeper understanding of the social role of culture (European Commission 2017). The first part focuses on the concept of AD, as well as the strategies used for the diversification of audiences. Then, the methodology of digital storytelling is introduced from a cultural and technological perspective as a powerful tool for personal and social empowerment and the main tool employed towards the goal of engaging excluded audiences; to finally delve into the main AD strategies applied within the framework of the MEMEX project: the use of digital, co-creation and analysis of data.

Audience development: definitions and strategies

Both the use of DS and the design of the app fall within the framework of AD, defined as a strategic and dynamic process enabling audiences – understood not only as visitors, but individuals and communities – to actively participate in cultural life. The *Study on Audience Development. How to place audiences at the centre of cultural organizations: final report* (European Commission 2017) aimed at providing successful approaches and methods in the area of Audience Development to the European Commission, identified a model with two main aims addressed to current audiences: widening already active audiences while deepening their experiences and diversifying the present audience to new target audiences. Responding to this conceptual distinction, the study renamed the three main audience categories using intuitive labels: Audience by Habit, Audience by Choice and Audience by Surprise.

- "Audience by habit" correspond to people who usually attend and/or participate in cultural activities, whose barriers to access are relatively easy to overcome, and towards whom different strategies are possible, such as audience education to attract similar audiences not currently participating; and taste cultivation to increase and diversify content and attendance. "Habit" in this framework means that those audiences are familiar with the same idea of being an audience, therefore cultural experiences are not just something they are used to do, but much more a part of their identity and self-perception.
- "Audience by choice", in turn, are people who are not used to participate for reasons of lifestyle, lack of opportunities, or financial resources; those for whom participating is not a habit, or who rarely choose to attend a show or a concert, but do not have any particular social or cultural disadvantage. To engage them, different strategies are possible, such as extended marketing but also education and participatory approaches.
- Finally, "audience by surprise" are individuals that are hard to reach/indifferent/hostile, who do not participate in any cultural activity for a complex range of reasons, related to social exclusion factors, education, and accessibility. Their participation could hardly be possible without an intentional, long-term and targeted approach.

MEMEX focuses on the AD goal of diversification of audiences: through DS and technology, the pilot projects aim to tackle the issue of cultural participation and engagement of diverse groups who, in general, belong to the broader family of "Audience by surprise", as suggested by preliminary data (Da Milano *et al.* 2021). This is a flexible category aimed at helping organisations to better understand their audiences; they are tools to be used in relationshipship with the strategies of widening, deepening, and diversifying audiences and with the key action fields. There are many strategies and tools to pursue different audience goals, and they can be classified in many ways. Far from being rigid categories, these instruments are the prevailing action assets for developing new kinds of relationships with target groups:

- Place refers to those projects and cultural organisations' strategies strongly relying on the "place factor", creating links and building relationships based on a physical site and aimed at fostering ownership towards a cultural and physical space.

- Capacity building refers to those projects and cultural organisations' strategies strongly relying on the "people factor": the empowerment of the staff and the development of their skills, competences, and leadership are key factors for different experiences and recognising the need for change inside the organisation in order to modify audience behaviour.
- Co-creation/active participation refers to those projects and cultural organisations' strategies strongly relying on the "participatory factor": the need to involve the audiences in a more interactive, purposeful, and meaningful way, where the public is activated and made part of creative processes, to contribute to the implementation of specific projects or tasks and/or to be fully integrated into the life of the organisation. These are also particularly interesting in terms of their impacts on the organisation.
- Partnership, to the capacity to reach new and diverse audiences and to target specific communities lies also in the ability to create networks, partnerships, and collaborations with a wide range of potential stakeholders, such as NGOs, educational, cultural, and social operators and facilitators, artists, private companies, and media.
- Digital refers to those projects and cultural organisations' strategies strongly relying on the "digital factor", as a key aspect to reach audiences and foster engagement.
- Data analysis, to collecting and analysing quantitative and qualitative data in a productive way is crucial for assessing the actions, activities, and goals of cultural projects and organisations, to understand, support, and improve a broad range of AD goals.

Before delving into how these AD strategies have been implemented in MEMEX, it is important to explain the choice of DS both from a cultural and a technical perspective, as it is the main tool employed in the project and is transversal to the aforementioned strategic approaches to AD.

Storytelling for cultural heritage

All human languages, cultures, and communication codes include storytelling. It is a common expressive feature of all human beings, whose minds collect and interpret sensory information, events and emotions, and organise them in the form of stories. Logical-scientific and narrative thinking are the fundamental ways in which all human beings organise their understanding of the world (Bruner 1997). Taking multiple forms, cultures in every place and time have produced explicative models of reality in the shape of cosmogonies, legends, myths, and fantastic stories with universal symbols. We construct our cultural roots and beliefs, our immediate experience, and our lives in the shape of tales.

Stories have then a great individual and social value, playing a great role in language learning, in the construction and exchange of knowledge, in shaping educational processes, and in sharing moral and ethical rules, values, and traditions. They contribute to shaping and reinforcing personal identity and self-esteem; all individuals, in fact, identify themselves in a process of "narrative creation of the self" (Bruner 2003), through both individual/personal stories and stories about their families, communities, and cultures of origin. The shaping of an individual identity also allows understanding others and helps create or consolidate social identities and shared cultures. In turn, these shared, community cultures enrich narrative thinking with their stories, traditions, languages, and educational practices, thus building the symbolic, cognitive, and expressive features of the different peoples in different times and places. Narration and storytelling have a key role in human communication, education, knowledge construction and learning, creativity and imagination and intercultural dialogue, social cohesion and the definition of individual and collective identities (Graesser and Ottati 1995, Bruner 2003, Demetrio 2012, Falchetti 2015).

Today, the time is ripe to talk about participatory culture with a view to sharing and co-creation processes that gives participants an active role not only in the enjoyment but also in resignification CH. Stories play a fundamental role not only at the individual and social level, but also in the recognition, conservation, and resignification of CH. Due to its epistemological, pedagogical, and social acceptance, storytelling has established itself as an effective tool for the valorisation, mediation, and communication of CH in museums. Many have implemented narrative strategies to promote cultural accessibility, under the premise that storytelling can facilitate the understanding of exhibitions and engage visitors more intensely, as compared to explanatory or descriptive strategies. Storytelling in museums makes communication more accessible also to people less used to formal culture and engages people in empathic relationships; it encourages inspiration and creativity, which in turn nurture new ideas, stories, meanings, and new cultural paths (Falchetti and Guida 2019, Falchetti *et al.* 2021).

The production of stories by the public has become an essential part of educational programmes, such as intercultural ones (Bodo *et al.* 2016); storytelling enhances involvement and adds value to visitors' cognitive and affective experiences. Moreover, it enriches museum culture by promoting new interpretations. In a participatory and universal accessibility perspective, storytelling plays a unique and unmatched role, as a bridge between memories and imagination. Museums reveal to be invaluable laboratories for autobiographic, collective, intercultural, and transcultural stories.

Having established that storytelling is central to human experience with its various levels of individual and collective value, an overview of DS and Interactive Digital Storytelling (IDS), and how they have been used in the scope of CH and inclusion for wide varieties of audiences and projects is provided below.

From storytelling to digital and interactive storytelling

As digital interactive technologies have become part of the fabric of our everyday lives, they influence the way we tell and deliver stories. DS and IDS are interdisciplinary areas of research and application, which became popular during the last decades of the previous millennium. While DS is connected to the democratisation of digital tools, IDS has a more complex nature, where interaction and computing technologies play an important role.

Today, with the rise of inexpensive and high-quality digital tools, combined with easy-to-use web-based applications, the field of DS has evolved quickly, developing into more sophisticated forms, more interactive and with higher production values. Thanks to its descriptive potential, its versatility, and its applicability in any context – artistic, educational, social, and health – this methodology started to flourish and to be widely tested. DS is created to promote causes, entertain, educate, and inform audiences about different cultures. Nowadays interactive mobile networked technology allows users to autonomously produce, chart, and share their own stories in real-time.

While stories have been interactive well before the advent of digital technologies, the evolution of computing has transformed the art of storytelling and put the accent on the cooperative and agential potential of digital technologies. Moreover, IDS has been pushing for more democratic and inclusive production, consumption, and sharing of stories and cultural content in general. For ease of reporting, we group the IDS efforts into three main categories: story authoring platforms, projects that incorporate DS as a means for people to author and share their own stories and content; story viewing platforms, where DS is utilised as a means to view and experience stories and cultural content in novel ways; and the combination of story authoring and viewing platforms, where DS is a mean to both create *and* view stories, similar to what is known today as social media, which allow for more exchange and interactions among parties.

In the last 20 years, locative media has evolved from GPS tracing and locative games (Falk *et al.* 2001) to complex platforms for users to tell stories about places. In recent years, a plethora of story authoring and sharing tools have emerged, open source, easy to use and widely accessible. To illustrate this trend, we picked a few key examples among the many that have flourished. Northwestern University Knight Lab,[1] provides an open, collaborative environment for interdisciplinary exploration, where students and professionals learn together and from one another. They developed a series of easy-to-use storytelling tools, from map based to VR, timelines and data visualisations aids, "to help people tell better stories". Their tools are free and open source. Similarly, but for profit, ArcGIS storyMaps[2], propose tools and tutorials to create and combine stories with locations, events, and multimedia content, facilitating the illustration of spatial relationship.

Finally the izi.Travel[3] storytelling platform empowers users to create personalised location-based audio guides and make them available on smartphones and mobile devices.

As the rapid development and uptake of digital technologies democratised the storytelling craft, professional storytellers and artists were challenged and inspired by these technologies as well. At the turn of the new millennium, artists started to experiment with networked and multimedia stories (Nisi and Haahr 2006). With mobile technologies, physical locations become the place where history and memories can be celebrated, allowing physical places to function as their stage (Nisi *et al.* 2004, Bleecker and Knowlton 2006, De Waal and Knowlton 2008).

As technology evolved, authoring tools achieve means to search for and engage with stories in novel more complex manners; content creators and content viewers can cross-over and interact, as we can observe in popular social networks such as Instagram or Facebook. Offering an accessible storytelling framework, Floch and Jiang (2015) produced *Stedr,* a mobile application that allows users to share their experiences and heritage through stories of places. Working with cultural institutions and museums, Vrettakis *et al.* (2019) developed the *Narrlive Storyboard Editor* and the *Narralive Mobile Player,* a bespoke platform for the creation and promotion of localised stories and culture. In an educational project with primary schools, Lu *et al.* (2011) developed *ShadowStory*, a digital storytelling system for children to experience the local custom of Chinese shadow puppetry, promoting play, creativity, collaboration, and knowledge about this traditional form of performance. Digital stories are implemented by museum operators, mediators, curators, or visitors during or after the visits, to enrich exhibitions, ensure a more inclusive participation in the arts for all through the use of new technologies, enhance visitors' participation and reinforce relationships between museums and citizens. Much successful experimentation in art and science museums encourages exploring and improving the use of DS (Da Milano and Falchetti 2015).

In summary, as technologies evolve, our culture and heritage find new ways to appropriate them, pushing new modes of expression and archival, becoming more inclusive and accessible, as well as immersive and polyvocal. This excursus illuminates some of the efforts of researchers and creators of digital technologies at the service of storytelling and CH, paving the way for a sustaining interest of an even wider public to its fruition. Having presented in depth this methodology and its evolution in recent years, the final section illustrates the specific strategies through which DS has been employed to reach and engage the audiences of the MEMEX project through CH.

Digital storytelling for audience development

The MEMEX project starts from the idea that the use of DS and technology can generate positive changes in audiences, promoting cultural access and participation among socially fragile communities. MEMEX employs DS as a main strategy, as a manageable and effective tool to give voice to subjects at risk of marginalisation or exclusion, promoting creativity and personal expression, social and cultural empowerment, multiple skills and competences, and the valorisation of CH.

As introduced before, MEMEX tests different strategies to effectively engage communities at risk of social and cultural exclusion. This section focuses on the strategic approaches to AD that have proved to be more effective so far, and that are related to the topics of this book: capacity building, partnership, co-creation, use of digital, and data analysis. Since the project is ongoing, the following reflections are preliminary.

Capacity building refers to the need of training pilot partners – Interarts in Barcelona, Mapa das Ideias in Lisbon and Michael Culture and Dédale in Paris – their local stakeholders[4] and storytellers in the principles and use of DS and in their understanding of this methodology as a means to engage audiences. Pilot partners were provided with a document with resources and a 12-hour training addressing the topics of AD and DS from a theoretical and hands-on perspective, with a particular focus on sharing a common understanding of AD and its strategies, and of developing practical capacities to be able to guide and engage the pilot participants in the discovery and re-signification of CH through the creation of their own digital stories. Given the socially fragile circumstances of most of the participants, all the activities were mediated by the pilot partners and their local partners. The first step consisted of actively and attentively reading the expression of their needs and desires and working with them to enable them to fully own the DS methodology. Pilot partners were able to create safe spaces in which to engage the participants, through a work ethic based on empathy and respect. The analysis of the observations and interviews with pilot partners confirmed that, in general, participants showed a growing interest in participating in the workshops, creating and sharing their digital stories.

DS is strongly based on **co-creation** processes, giving MEMEX participants an active role not only in the enjoyment but also in the reinterpretation of CH. Moreover, the participants are the owners of their stories, meaning that the level of co-creation embedded in the final result is very high and strictly related to the level of engagement of the storytellers. In MEMEX, the DS implementation has been conceived as a tool and an opportunity to give voice to the participants, to promote personal expression and creativity, cultural and social empowerment, and promotion of skills and competencies. CH is the field within which their creativity, memories, emotions, beliefs, metaphors and social representations emerge and develop. Up to this point, and despite obstacles linked to the COVID-19 pandemic, which severely affected the implementation of the activities and the engagement of the participants, the conclusion of the first cycle of workshops and the production and preliminary analysis of the 20 digital stories created in the three pilots have proved that the vision and methodology of DS are effective in providing a safe space for the participants to share concerns, build relationships, generate dynamic debates and exchanges and promoting active and creative expression, participation, and engagement, when mediated by qualified teams. Through the process of creating their stories, participants have explored their memories, experiences, narrative skills and voices and expressed their diverse understanding of culture, re-interpreting the CH of each city through a personal lens. Moreover, the development of the MEMEX app has included user testing participatory phases, taking into account the feedback of partners and project participants, to improve its functionalities and tailor it to the potential users' needs.

In terms of **partnership**, DS is a collective process that, to be effective, requires co-operation between different stakeholders. In the case of MEMEX, strong partnerships have been established not only between the technological and social/cultural partners of the consortium, but also with external social/cultural stakeholders and the pilot participants. The three pilot partners have all worked – with different degrees of closeness – with different local stakeholders, especially during the phase of involving and engaging participants. Building productive partnerships is a crucial process that takes time and human resources, and MEMEX has been an opportunity for the pilot partners to build or progressively reinforce pre-existing alliances in the territory, that will hopefully continue beyond the scope of the project.

The use of **digital** in MEMEX is clear by now: the project experiments with digital tools in a thoughtful and strategic way. MEMEX develops an Augmented Reality (AR) App for smartphones based on the use of DS for the creation and visualisation of personal stories and experiences related to local tangible and intangible CH, digitally linked to geographical locations, giving voice and fostering active engagement and participation of non-expert users that are often excluded of cultural life. The methodology of DS has been successful in bringing participants closer to the fruition of a digital instrument. The pilots have been an opportunity to test and reflect on the role that digital tools can play in fostering access and participation in culture. Again, the participatory approach in the development of the MEMEX app has allowed defining the users' needs, requirements and potential challenges in the use of digital tools in permanent collaboration with the participants, in order to overcome potential limitations (such as the digital divide), improve its functionalities, and engage the communities through each phase.

Finally, the **collection and analysis of data** is a key strategy within the project; since the whole process of DS will be analysed through tools and indicators specifically created to measure the social impact of the pilot projects. In terms of user testing, both quantitative and qualitative methods have been employed to test and develop the app's usability and experience. At the social/cultural level, data analysis within MEMEX is developed through the social impact evaluation, aimed at measuring and validating the project results. Aligned with the goal of the project, the AD strategies, DS methodology, and social impact analysis are framed by the Theory of Change,[5] a comprehensive description and illustration of how and why a desired change is expected to happen in a particular context, in this case, how interconnected elements lead to accomplishing the MEMEX goal. It is a frame to lead organisations (the project's partners) through a logical sequence from desired impacts to required inputs. It helps define a causality chain that links each step to the other, focusing on what is needed to achieve those impacts (which value, for whom, and how it happens). This process leads to a logical path that links every single step to the other, helping to focus on what is needed (and eventually missing) to achieve the desired results. MEMEX employs a qualitative and phenomenographic approach, as it is the most suitable to capture changes in attitudes, preferences, concerns and motivations of the target communities and groups, in order to understand these audiences and then implement/improve AD strategies accordingly. The impact analysis evaluation is multidimensional, employing different instruments – questionnaires, interviews, observations and analysis of the stories produced by the participants – and analysing changes against 4 dimensions of analysis: cultural, social, spatial, and emotional, which has been key in assessing the results of the project at different levels.

MEMEX also employs two tools to assess the overall results/changes within the project: the MEMEX benchmarking tool and the Societal Readiness Level (SRL). Building on the MCP-Broker benchmarking tool,[6] the methodology, tools, and questionnaires were adapted to apply them to the selected groups of the pilot studies to see why the cultural offer is not responding to the needs of certain groups, therefore why there is no or limited access and/or participation to culture and, in particular, to the analysed CH. The MEMEX benchmarking tool was designed to analyse the perceptions, experiences, and needs of the respondents regarding CH and cultural participation. The instrument consists of three dimensions: meanings of CH, expression of CH, and cultural participation, each containing two to four indicators, measured in three levels: high, intermediate, and low. This process develops new procedures and novel analytical methodologies for understanding communities at risk of cultural exclusion. Its dimensions and indicators will continue to be refined and adapted, to provide a useful tool to measure and compare potential advancements in perceptions and experiences regarding cultural participation and CH in different projects and contexts.

The SRL, as defined by the Innovation Fund Denmark,[7] is a method to assess the level of societal adaptation of, for instance, a particular social project, a technology, a product, a process, an intervention, or an innovation (whether social or technical) to be integrated into society. If the societal readiness for a social or technical solution is expected to be low, suggestions for a realistic transition towards societal adaptation are required. SRL 1 is the lowest and SRL 9 is the highest level. The SRL analysis seeks to assess the solutions identified to maximise impact within MEMEX. The analysis focuses on the alignment of technology/broader societal hotspots (social, political, environmental, and economic demands and expectations). Being assessed every nine months shapes the roadmaps or actions to move towards increased societal readiness. Despite not being a widespread tool, the SRL model has proven useful in the context of MEMEX to analyse and reflect on the obtained results from a broader perspective and to make decisions to move forward. Table 2.1 summarises the SRL analysis of the MEMEX project (and the aspects already discussed in this contribution) up to the 23rd month of implementation of the project.

The preliminary analysis has shown that the actions implemented are in the direction of achieving a high SRL. It is important to note that this tool will be improved and refined at more advanced stages of the MEMEX project. According to the results of the social impact evaluation, it will be possible to review both the current and expected SRL and to eventually propose a customised SRL instrument that is applicable not only to MEMEX, but also for future projects of this kind, this is, initiatives that combine cultural, social, and technological elements to promote social cohesion and inclusion.

Conclusion

This chapter seeks to contribute to the reflection on the connections between cultural heritage, social inclusion and innovation, and digital technologies through the discussion of the MEMEX project. The discussion focused on the audience development approach employed in the implementation of the project, as a strategic and dynamic process where the public is placed at the centre; the use of the digital storytelling methodology as an effective tool to promote the creative valorisation of CH; and the first results of the MEMEX pilot projects in Barcelona, Lisbon, and Paris. Preliminary results suggest that DS as a strategy and CH as a field appear to be effective in generating safe spaces for the expression of experiences, the promotion of participation and dialogue and the development of skills, giving the opportunity to people from socially and culturally excluded backgrounds to express their vision around different forms of CH, emphasising the active role of communities in re-interpreting existing heritage as well as in co-creating plural meanings around it (Da Milano *et al.* 2021). It is still early to refer to the impact of MEMEX in terms of social cohesion and inclusion, as the project is in a phase of implementation. However, its development is promising in terms of diversification of audiences, in being a catalyst of creativity and inspiration, encouraging knowledge, understanding, awareness, interest, enjoyment and creativity and stimulating new forms of creative engagement with CH, and is an example of how digital technologies and trans-disciplinary and trans-sectorial approaches can contribute to audience

Table 2.1 MEMEX SRL preliminary analysis

Module	*Initial SRL*		*Expected SRL*		*Status*
Needs Analysis	SRL 2	A list of identified groups at risk of exclusion who have limited or no access or participation to cultural life in their communities. A set of existing tools to identify their needs and interests ready to be adapted to the project's context and variables.	SRL 3	A detailed matrix to match marginalised groups' needs and wishes with the cultural offer within their communities, by taking into account their stories, experiences, and perspectives.	The detailed matrix will be elaborated once the social impact analysis is completed.
Needs Analysis	SRL 3	Interface design given a single collection of requirements from users in the pilots.	SRL 5	Co-design approach involving the community boosting social cohesion and inclusion of the communities.	A co-design approach is part of the DS process that was carried out during the workshops, where participants co-create their own personal digital stories, boosting social cohesion and inclusion.
Development of the Project	SRL 4	Referring to a list of identified groups at risk of exclusion, a process of AD based on diverse strategies to tackle lack of access, participation, and representation of these groups to cultural activities.	SRL 5	A list of strategies and related objectives and indicators.	The main strategies employed are co-creation, capacity building, partnership, use of digital tools, and data analysis. The study on audience development. How to place audiences at the

(*Continued*)

Table 2.1 (Continued)

Module	*Initial SRL*		*Expected SRL*		*Status*
					centre of cultural organisations carried out by ECCOM in 2015 proposes different strategies for AD. The social objectives and indicators of the MEMEX project are based on this set of strategies.
Development of the Project	SRL 5	Referring to the list of strategies above mentioned, to identify a process of active engagement using the most appropriate ones with specific reference to outreach and active participation methodologies.	SRL 6	Connection between AD strategies and engagement processes based on outreach and active participation, based on related objectives and indicators.	The connection between AD strategies and engagement processes was achieved during the DS workshops, since they are based on active participation and engagement. The AD&DS training with partners and stakeholders represented an intermediate step towards achieving this level: through the creation of digital stories, they became actively involved in the DS methodology and its potential for narrating CH from a personal perspective.

Social Inclusion	SRL 2	A set of methodologies to increase marginalised groups' cultural participation and thus their social inclusion identified and ready to be tested.	SRL 4	A set of tested, refined, and validated methodologies that ensure participation and ownership of cultural heritage by marginalised groups.	The DS methodology, in its participative component and adequateness to ensure participation and ownership of CH by marginalised groups will be tested, refined, and validated through the workshops and social impact analysis.
Social Inclusion	SRL 4	A hypothesis of tool's features based on the observation and statistics on current skills and habits of use of digital tools.	SRL 6	A tool validated and actually used by a larger public than the participants directly involved in project activities.	The data-collection guidebook and AD&DS capacity building resources will be available to this end.

development and engagement of communities who do not usually have access to cultural experiences.

Notes

1 https://knightlab.northwestern.edu/
2 https://storymaps.arcgis.com/
3 https://izi.travel/en
4 In each pilot location, pilot partners have collaborated with different local stakeholders, as detailed later on. In Barcelona, local partners are the Centre de Cultura de Dones Francesca Bonnemaison-laBonne and Sindillar/Sindohar; in Lisbon the Instituto Marquês de Valle Flôr (IMVF), Academia de Produtores Culturais (APC), and Associação Lusofonia Cultura e Cidadania (ALCC); and in Paris Capacités, Rosa Parks Social Center, and Régie de Quartier.
5 https://www.theoryofchange.org/what-is-theory-of-change/
6 https://mcpbroker.eu/
7 https://innovationsfonden.dk/sites/default/files/2018-08/societal_readiness_levels_-_srl.pdf

References

Anttonen, R., *et al.*, 2016. *Managing art projects with societal impact study book for students, stakeholders and researchers.* Unigrafia.

Bleecker, J., and Knowlton, J., 2006. Locative media: a brief bibliography and taxonomy of GPS-enabled locative media. *Leonardo Electronic Almanac*, 14 (3), 1–17.

Bodo, S., Mascheroni, S., and Panigada, M.G., eds. 2016. *Un patrimonio di storie.* Milan: Mimesis.

Bruner, J., 1997. *The culture of education.* Cambridge: Harvard University Press.

Bruner, J., 2003. *Making stories.* Cambridge: Harvard University Press.

Carnwath, J.D., and Brown A.S., 2014. *Understanding the value and impacts of cultural experiences.* Arts Council England.

CHCFE Consortium, 2015. *Cultural heritage counts for Europe.* International Culture Center. Available from: http://blogs.encatc.org/culturalheritagecountsforeurope//wp-content/uploads/2015/06/CHCfE_FULL-REPORT_v2.pdf [Accessed 1 April 2022]

Council of Europe, 2008. *White paper on intercultural dialogue. "Living together as equals in dignity".* Available from: https://www.coe.int/t/dg4/intercultural/source/white%20paper_final_revised_en.pdf [Accessed 1 April 2022].

Council of the European Union, 2005. *Convention on the value of cultural heritage for society.* Available from: https://rm.coe.int/1680083746 [Accessed 1 April 2022].

Council of the European Union, 2018a. *Council Recommendation on key competences for lifelong learning.* Available from: https://eur-lex.europa.eu/legal-content/EN/TXT/PDF/?uri=CELEX:32018H0604(01)&from=EN [Accessed 1 April 2022].

Council of the European Union, 2018b. *Council conclusions on the Work Plan for Culture 2019–2022.* Available from: https://eur-lex.europa.eu/legal-content/EN/TXT/PDF/?uri=CELEX:52018XG1221(01) [Accessed 1 April 2022].

Da Milano, C., and Falchetti, E., eds., 2015. *Stories for museums, museums for stories.* Nepi: Vetrani Editore.

Da Milano, C., et al., 2021 Digital storytelling and lifelong learning education in informal contexts: the MEMEX project. In: M. Carmo, ed. *Education and new developments*. Lisbon: inScience Press, 37–61.

De Waal, M., and Knowlton, J., 2008. *The mobile city: a conference on locative media, urban culture and identity*. Rotterdam: Netherlands Architecture Institute.

Demetrio, D., 2012. *Educare è narrare*. Milan: Mimesis.

European Commission, 2010. *EUROPE 2020. A strategy for smart, sustainable and inclusive growth*. Available from: https://ec.europa.eu/eu2020/pdf/COMPLET%20EN%20BARROSO%20%20%20007%20-%20Europe%202020%20-%20EN%20version.pdf [Accessed 1 April 2022].

European Commission, 2014. *Towards an integrated approach to cultural heritage for Europe*. Available from: https://ec.europa.eu/assets/eac/culture/library/publications/2014-heritage-communication_en.pdf [Accessed 1 April 2022].

European Commission, 2017. *Study on audience development: how to place audiences at the centre of cultural organisations: final report*. Available from: https://data.europa.eu/doi/10.2766/711682 [Accessed 1 April 2022].

European Commission, 2018a. *European framework for action on cultural heritage*. Available from: https://op.europa.eu/en/publication-detail/-/publication/5a9c3144-80f1-11e9-9f05-01aa75ed71a1 [Accessed 1 April 2022].

European Commission, 2018b. *A new European agenda for culture*. Available from: https://eur-lex.europa.eu/legal-content/EN/TXT/?uri=COM:2018:267:FIN [Accessed 1 April 2022].

European Commission, 2019a. *Towards a sustainable Europe by 2030*. Available from: https://ec.europa.eu/info/sites/default/files/rp_sustainable_europe_30-01_en_web.pdf [Accessed 1 April 2022].

European Commission, 2019b. *EUROSTAT. Culture statistics*. Available from: https://ec.europa.eu/eurostat/documents/3217494/10177894/KS-01-19-712-EN-N.pdf/915f828b-daae-1cca-ba54-a87e90d6b68b [Accessed 1 April 2022].

European Union, 2017. Standard Eurobarometer 87 – Spring 2017. Available from: https://europa.eu/eurobarometer/surveys/detail/2142 [Accessed 1 April 2022].

European Union, 2019. *From social inclusion to social cohesion. The role of culture policy*. Available from: https://op.europa.eu/en/publication-detail/-/publication/e1b88304-f3b0-11e9-8c1f-01aa75ed71a1/language-en [Accessed 1 April 2022].

Falchetti, E., 2015. Dal pensiero narrativo allo storytelling digitale. In: C. Da Milano and E. Falchetti, eds. *Stories for museums, museums for stories*. Nepi: Vetrani Editore, 35–48.

Falchetti, E., Da Milano, C., and Guida, M.F., 2021. Heritage education and digital storytelling. Enriching students' soft skills, citizenship and participation in a RRI Perspective. In: P. Sandu, V. Tudisca, and A. Valente, eds. *Co-creating in schools through art and science*. Cham, Switzerland: Springer, 7–15.

Falchetti, E., and Guida, M.F., 2019. MUA – Musei accoglienti. Un modello di governance per l'intercultura, In: A. Dal Lago and E. Falchetti, eds. *I musei scientifici nell'anno europeo del patrimonio*. Museologia Scientifica Memorie, 20, 104–107.

Falk, J., Ljungstrand, P., and Björk, S., 2001. Pirates: proximity-triggered interaction in a multi-player game. In: *CHI EA '07: CHI '01 extended abstracts on human factors in computing systems*. New York: ACM Press, 119–120.

Floch, J., and Jiang, S., 2015. One place, many stories digital storytelling for cultural heritage discovery in the landscape. In: *2015 Digital Heritage*. IEEE, 503–510.

Graesser, A.C., and Ottati, V., 1995. Why stories? Some evidence, questions, and challenges. In: R.S. Wyer, ed. *Knowledge and memory: the real story*. Hillsdale: Lawrence Erlbaum Associates, 121–132.

Heritage Contact Zone, 2018. Toolkit. Available from: https://heritagecontactzone.com/toolkit/ [Accessed 1 April 2022].

ICOM and OECD, 2018. *Culture and local development: maximising the Impact*. Available from: https://icom.museum/wp-content/uploads/2019/08/ICOM-OECD-GUIDE_EN_FINAL.pdf [Accessed 1 April 2022].

ICOMOS, 2014. *The Florence declaration on heritage and landscape as human values*. Available from: https://www.icomos.org/images/DOCUMENTS/Secretariat/2015/GA_2014_results/GA2014_Symposium_FlorenceDeclaration_EN_final_20150318.pdf [Accessed 1 April 2022].

ICOMOS, 2021. *Heritage and the sustainable development goals: policy guidance for heritage and development actors*. Available from: https://www.icomos.org/images/DOCUMENTS/Secretariat/2021/SDG/ICOMOS_SDGs_Policy_Guidance_2021.pdf [Accessed 1 April 2022].

Lu, F., *et al.*, 2011. ShadowStory: creative and collaborative digital storytelling inspired by cultural heritage. In: *Proceedings of the2011 CHI Conference on Human Factors in Computing Systems*, May 2011. New York: ACM Press, 1919–1928.

Nisi, V., and Haahr, M., 2006. Weird view: interactive multilinear narratives and real-life community stories. *Crossings: eJournal of Art and Technology*, 4 (1), 1–13.

Nisi, V., *et al.*, 2004. Hopstory: an interactive, location-based narrative distributed in space and time. In: S. Göbel, *et al.*, eds. *Technologies for interactive digital storytelling and entertainment*. Berlin: Springer, 132–141.

Sabatini, F., 2019. Culture as fourth pillar of sustainable development: perspectives for integration, paradigms of action. *European Journal of Sustainable Development*, 8 (3), 31–40.

UNESCO, 1972. *Convention concerning the protection of the world cultural and natural heritage*. Available from: https://whc.unesco.org/archive/convention-en.pdf [Accessed 1 April 2022].

UNESCO, 2003. Convention for the safeguarding of the intangible cultural heritage. Available from: https://ich.unesco.org/en/convention [Accessed 1 April 2022].

United Cities and Local Governments, 2010. *Culture: fourth pillar of sustainable development*. Available from: https://www.agenda21culture.net/sites/default/files/files/documents/en/zz_culture4pillarsd_eng.pdf [Accessed 1 April 2022].

United Nations, 1948. *Universal declaration of human rights*. Available from: https://www.un.org/sites/un2.un.org/files/udhr.pdf [Accessed 1 April 2022].

Vrettakis, *et al.*, 2019. Narralive – Creating and experiencing mobile digital storytelling in cultural heritage. *Digital Applications in Archaeology and Cultural Heritage*, 15.

3 Digital pathways for enriched communities and futures: plantation heritage in São Tomé and Príncipe

Stefania Stellacci and Sara Eloy

Introduction

Today we are faced with the controversial question of how to critically rethink heritage sites that were shaped under centuries of European colonialism. However, practical results have been slow to follow from this debate.[1] It was once the case that European institutions showed a lack of interest in the topic, a tendency that José Mattoso attributes to the disintegration of the former European empires having fostered a strong disinterest in their cultural legacies (Mattoso *et al.* 2010). This attitude is hopefully now in the past, as testified by several initiatives[2] on the part of cultural institutions such as ICOMOS, UNESCO, and the Cultural Heritage Agency of the Netherlands (RCE). This issue should be addressed starting by bringing critical heritage studies, anthropology, architecture, human history, and digital humanities into dialogue, adapting their respective tools and methodologies to a holistic approach. Giving voice to unheard multi-ethnic communities, such as the living descendants of the workers from the colonised countries, some of them now Europeans, will make it possible to reverse Eurocentric dominant narratives, as discussed by a number of activists and heritage professionals (Logan and Reeves 2008, Smith and Akagawa 2008, Tlostanova and Mignolo 2012, Kølvraa and Knudsen 2020).

The issue is a thorny one, transcending cultural and geographical boundaries. The transnational scope of intervention arises from the dual parenthood of the shared heritage places, whose construction materials and techniques, habits, traditions, and memories belong to both colonised and coloniser. Indicating this dual parenthood, the term *shared cultural heritage* has been widely employed to recall the latent value embodied by material and immaterial assets related to colonial periods, beyond confined temporal and spatial realms. As defined by RCE:

> The Netherlands [and to large extent other European countries] shares a past with many nations and cultures around the world. These connections have left traces, commemorating the rich and complex history that

DOI: 10.4324/9781003277606-3

> we share. Think of buildings, archives, shipwrecks, museum collections and intangible heritage. These traces of a connected past are referred to as shared cultural heritage. (RCE 2021)

We are launched in an even larger dimension when we consider the forced labour that bloodies thousands of pages of colonial history, one in which we must view nationalist colonisations and economic monopoly related disputes as a world-spanning process. The *Atlantic World history*[3] arises from global trading relations between European, American, and African countries. The rise of the concept of Europe, as the locus of cultural interconnections and trade between colonisers (the Portuguese, Spanish, French, and Dutch especially), may be traced back to the transnational colonial markets made possible by the massive exploitation of land undertaken in their colonies from the 15th century onwards (Barros 2015).

As a case in point amid this complex picture, we analyse the plantation heritage sites in São Tomé and Príncipe (STP) known as *roças* (clearings).[4] Berthet (2012) associates the polysemic term of *roças* to *plantations*, the capitalist system for the production of monoculture for the international market and explains different interpretations provided by Tenreiro (1961) and Eyzaguirre (1986). The shape of architecture and the future planned for these plantations evoke the same unsolved questions around world shared heritage,[5] questions marked by *colonial aphasia* (recalling Stoler's concept applied to French colonial history (Stoler 2011, 2016), institutionalised histories, or current short-sighted tourism policies.

We begin by presenting a historical framework of the *roças*, followed by a brief discussion of the necessary heritage preservation actions. We then discuss the importance and complexity of adopting a decolonised perspective. In the last section, we examine challenges and concerns in potential applications of digital technologies to the *roças* as a way to uncover this shared past and inform preservation practices. We identify the potential offered to the target groups (the general community interested in cultural heritage and students of architecture) by the applications of e-learning tools within possible avenues of inquiry, in parallel with potential risks.

This study is situated in the broader framework of the critical rethinking of shared cultural heritage. It contributes to outlining the limits and challenges of the application of digital technologies towards social inclusion, approaching a decolonised perspective. We discuss the controversy that attends to the process of material and visual recollection of architectural colonial legacies, regardless of the type of human-device interaction and the modality of access, and consider how these difficulties should be incorporated in the design of the e-learning tools.

Architectural framework: plantation heritage in São Tomé and Príncipe

Brief description and literature review on architectural design of the roças

Among the numerous territories colonised by Portuguese settlers,[6] the small archipelago of São Tomé and Príncipe, located in the Gulf of Guinea along the West-African coastline, epitomised the western exploitation set up by European colonial empires in the bean belt, by leveraging extraordinary environmental conditions. This small insular territory, formed by the two major islands of São Tomé (836 km^2) and Príncipe (128 km^2), is known as *ilhas do meio do mundo* (*the islands in the middle of the world*), being located approximately at the intersection between Ecuador and Greenwich meridian.

The islands were seized and exploited under Portuguese colonial hegemony during two main waves of colonisation. Following the first phase in which the previously uninhabited islands were settled (1471–1472), the development of the sugarcane monoculture and the creolisation during the third Portuguese Empire (1825–1975) arose from intensive cocoa and coffee plantations and the tightening of colonial hierarchy and racial inequalities. The trade in commodities intensified to the point that these small insular areas became a key part of the global geostrategic map by the end of the 1890s.[7] São Tomé was the world's largest cocoa producer in 1910s and a main slave depot until the mid-17th century. In Portugal, Lagos and Lisbon were crucial ports in the Atlantic slave trade from 1526 to 1867, a global market involving an estimated 12.5 million enslaved Africans around the world. The human and symbolic geographies of these stunning islands are marked with over 200 *roças*, cultural legacies of the massive cash-crop production of the Portuguese second colonisation. *Roças* historically acted as large-scale structural and structuring entities in the cultural-socio-economic spheres. Being organised as multi-functional complexes, they include a hierarchical group of houses (grand administrator's mansion [*casa-senhorial*], housings for plantation workers and their families [*senzalas*]), huge production services (warehouses, greenhouses, bean-drying sheds), and supporting facilities (hospitals, schools). Regardless of their extreme variations, each settlement type was structured to optimise the production of intensive monocultures.

In approaching the history of São Tomé and Príncipe, Nascimento (2002), Seibert (2013), and Henriques (2019) tend to focus on the mutual relations between Portuguese and tropical cultures in an intermingling of forms, traditions, styles, and cultures, so that 'A memória colectiva recicla constantemente este tecido fundador'[8] (Henriques 2019). Distinct languages, functions, and roles characterise each social group living in *roças* across time. As their function has continued to be updated in the image of the settler-colonial power, *roças* represent the convergence and divergence of multiple levels of collective and individual memories, reflecting different types of cohabitation, ethnical divisions, and conflicts among *roçeiros* (plantation owners), farmers, workers,[9] and *filhos da terra* (sons of the land). To give an example of the coexistence of a plurality of views even among the workers in the same *roça*, Åkesson (2016) thoroughly contrasts the collective national memory of Cape Verdean national history with the personal history of an elderly Cape Verdean man, senhor Fernando, who worked in 1952 until 1960. 'A central theme in his narrative is how he acquired agency by being a good worker' (Åkesson 2016, p. 68).

Regarding their spatial layout, *roças* are divided into four types in the literature according to the territorial element around which the settlement was organised: avenue, farmyard, harbour, or city (*roça-avenida*, *roça-terreiro*, *roça-porto*, *roça-cidade*). The layout is organised following production-based logics, whose primary objective is the optimisation of the production resources. Machado da Silva (2018) stresses how the supposed approximation of the condition of the labour force to that of the European class was materialised at the level of volumetry, façade design, access/flow composition and spatial organisation the constructions. The spatial organisation of the workers' houses programme remains unchanged over time, as physical expression of the embedded unequal social system.

From an architectural point of view, the *roças* derive from European patterns adapted to the tropical environment by means of distinct construction systems: vernacular wooden structures (16th century), clay-filled timber framework systems (19th century), and concrete systems. Each system was an adaptation of Portuguese design patterns applied to building practices (labour force, raw materials) and cultural realms (workmanship, planning strategy), adapted to the local environmental constraints (topography, weather). These recall the fishermen's cabins, the *pombalino* system (the anti-seismic construction system used mainly after the 1755 earthquake in Lisbon), and the early concrete systems, respectively.

The overview of architectural configuration, zoning, and Europeanisation has so far been mostly written in the Portuguese language (Mantero 1910, Tenreiro 1961, Nascimento 2002, Fernandes 2005, Guedes 2021). Recent studies based on fieldwork and an extensive literature review have been carried out in the doctoral dissertations of Portuguese researchers.[10] These works offer a critical and insightful picture of architectural heritage that is stained with the crimes of prolonged exploitation. However, these works surprisingly inspire the desire to discover *roças* in the tropical forest for oneself, to get entangled in their history and lost memories.

What is needed? Integrated heritage preservation actions: critical analysis of polyvocal memories on the roças and rethinking on how to preserve them

What is apparent from the above-mentioned on-site surveys and in-depth analyses is the extraordinary beauty of these sites and their environmental context, as well as the variety of original layouts and their feasibility of converting their original uses, especially after STP's 1975 independence from Portugal.[11] These surveys also show that most of these settlements risk being abandoned to their fate, too numerous, grandiose, and expensive to maintain their preservation and reuse.

In recent decades, certain of the *roças* have shown extraordinary resilience and flexible use. In fact, these constructions have been converted into thematic museums, local businesses, refurbished luxury hotels, or popular squats, while a few settlements are still used for cacao harvesting or other agricultural activities. Other *roças*, endangered by neglect and shortage of funds, are now useless skeletons close to being lost to history. Almost swallowed by the equatorial forest, many buildings are on the verge of collapsing – roofless, with extensive damage and loss of the structural components and architectural features.

Besides low internationalisation, the studies disseminated so far offer little basis in a broader perspective for leveraging the cultural value embodied by these plantations and their related environmental transformations, especially for newcomers to these islands (tourists or new entrepreneurs). Multilevel narratives should be collected in order to understand the impact that past social segregation and large-scale exploitation have had on the contemporary multi-dimensional assets in STP, as well as on those in Portugal. Great effort should be directed towards presenting an integrated image as a tourist destination[12] in a way that shares and re-tells the complex history of this country.

The purposes and the logics behind contemporary interventions around these heritage plantations are multiple and challenging. The preservation of the *roças* may be pursued by different means, yet all of these must consider the management of human trauma.[13] Changes of ownership or use (e.g., when a *roça* is turned into a luxury hotel) inevitably suggest a critical statement about the involved stakeholders and their values.

The knowledge based on polyvocality and contextualised approach about those memories and views on past and present of the *roças* obtained from multiple stakeholders lay the basis for their critical value assessment and heritage actions. Along with other worldwide artefacts of controversial heritage,[14] the major challenge is to understand what and how can be proposed nowadays for this heritage today, trusting that "The architect will always dream of purifying this uncontrolled violence, channeling obedient bodies along predictable paths, and occasionally along ramps that provide striking vistas, ritualising the transgression of bodies in space" (Tschumi 1996, p. 123).

Decolonisation in practice

From Atlantic trade routes to decentring decolonisation discourse

For over 30 years now, researchers have traced long-distance geohistorical itineraries of Atlantic trade in slaves and commodities.[15]

In *Lugares de Memória da Escravatura e do tráfico negreiro,*[16] the format of which (in our view) recalls a tourist guide with a cover in blood-red, Isabel Castro Henriques (2019) examines four countries in the Atlantic and the Indian Ocean (Angola, Cabo Verde, Guinee-Bissau, Mozambique, and São Tomé and Príncipe) by interconnecting physical and symbolic footprints in territories of outstanding natural beauty and timeless enchantment. This cultural route and the relevant studies developed by Henriques are praiseworthy attempts to give shape to those "grey and empty" lessons of the History of Africa in Portugal in 1960s,[17] unveiling stratified interactions of half-hidden traces (in Portugal, especially in Lisbon) and other controversial legacies in former Portuguese colonised countries. Her analyses of deep-rooted impacts of Portuguese colonialism in the world seek to counteract Eurocentric Enlightenment perspectives and biased forms of heritagisation. To name an example, one of these unidirectional and institutionalised narratives was reaffirmed throughout the commemorative cycle organised by the *National Commission for the Commemoration of the Portuguese Discoveries* (in office from 1986 to 2002), whose influences can be grasped in the national education and cultural system, common mindsets, and international public debates.[18] This does not come as a surprise, since parallelisms to the presumed *exceptionality* of Portuguese colonisation (in *racial democracy* and the *civilised mission* promoted by Freyre (1964)[19] can be found also in other former coloniser countries, such as in Italy. In fact, the stereotypes of Italian colonisers in Somalia and Eritrea as *brava gente* (goodhearted people) still endures as commonplace in Italian popular thought.

With the firm belief that the meaning of place is the basis for developing a fair society and preserving the identities of its communities, new knowledge on critical cultural legacies should be gained using a set of specific methods for decolonising purposes. Cultural and epistemic approaches should be combined in the effort to dismantle hegemonic cultural concepts and "strengthen decolonisation scholarship" (Smith 2012). The need to articulate decolonised historical discourse vs *authorised heritage discourse* has recently arisen in social media campaigns. The debate on the decolonisation of museums, public space, and mindsets has only recently emerged in Portugal, where countless places showing remnants of these legacies can be found. Remarkable palaces in Lisbon (e.g., Palácio Vale Flor) testify to the massive profit companies and families were able to draw from the colonies, while other public squares (e.g., *Rossio*, *Campo das Cebolas*, and *Jardim do Império*) silently echo colonial exploitation.

Decolonised discourse must still be supported by hands-on activities that can reach everyone. Transnational, intercultural, and multiethnic communities should be the protagonists of a co-design process in rethinking the future of these cultural legacies and how these memories can be transmitted to the next generations. Calling on the audience to learn from past lessons in shaping the future of society, virtual environments and ubiquitous digital technologies expand the possibilities of future design scenarios. New challenges are not limited to the mere application of emerging technologies. The question is how to correctly and comprehensively integrate epistemological and technological methods from different disciplines to build counter-narratives around the three intertwined pillars of critical heritage studies: history, memory, and identity.

Challenges in decolonising the roças in STP: coexistence of multiple views and values

Delving into the specifics of architectural legacies and land transformations in formerly colonised countries, the process of critically reframing these histories with a forward-looking perspective will raise questions on both symbolic and practical levels. Admittedly, the built and landscape heritage can never be treated neutrally in view of the alteration, domestication, and instrumentalisation that this heritage has undergone over the centuries. More than any other heritage category, shared legacies are never a static product of the past, and the past itself will continue to be contested (Smith 2006, 2012).

Being able to take this vast and complex picture under consideration is an enormous challenge inherent in the necessary cultural overhaul. It means bringing together local and transnational communities, witnesses of colonial and post-colonial[20] issues. Policy-oriented organisations, entrepreneurs in agri-food systems and tourist sectors, civic associations, NGOs, and other critical stakeholders should together: (i) unfold narratives of colonial times and the post-independence era, unmasking historical biases and using a dialogic approach; (ii) identify impactful and sustainable design strategies for the reuse and valorisation of remarkable cultural legacies. Even in contemporary times, the former narratives (i) have been hampered by the predominance of one-way European debates or dominant Western European perceptions of heritage.[21] Regarding (ii), the process of solution-oriented design has been delayed by structural factors such as multi-dimensional difficulties to deal with colonial histories and the effect of colonisation upon the economy and the society (including ethnic divisions as argued in literature (Bertocchi and Canova 2002), resignation, lack of foresight and dependence from white-ruled systems, and low cohesion between intentions and actions. To hand down these polyvocal narratives and lessons drawn from the past, cross-country analysis and knowledge-sharing are urgently required.

Future digital paths can be shaped by leveraging the great visual and symbolic impact of cultural legacies in STP which link Africa to Europe and the Americas. This requires analysis of (i) the multiple narratives and conflicting emotions awakened by heritage plantations; (ii) the values to be promulgated in the digital age.

i *Multiple narratives and conflicting emotions awakened by heritage plantations:*

> (…) architecture has been instrumental in the installation and consolidation of settler-colonialism and the full spectrum of extractive, abusive, racist, capitalist, postimperial infrastructures of oppression. In the way that buildings are never just buildings, architecture is not a bubble.
>
> To address architecture is to engage with the multidimensional and material legacy of settler-colonialism, capitalism, and, as a direct result, racism. (Frankowski 2020, p. 4)
>
> In the face of pressing challenges, architecture would reject any form of apolitical approach to the post-digital collage as a purely aesthetical exercise, and would instead engage with the political content of images to generate collages with subversive potential. (Frankowski 2020, p. 30)

Taking a broad view, conflicting viewpoints and narratives should be considered for leveraging this heritage to a post-digital level, where *post-digital collage* falls within the *hegemonic concepts* (under the category of *hegemonic theory*) as defined in *A Manual of Anti-Racist Architecture Education* (Frankowski 2020). To pursue ecological justice, anti-colonialism, anti-imperialism, transformism, anti-ableism, and anti-racism, this manual/manifesto envisages forms around 13 themes: means of production, ideology and buildings, contextual artefacts, post-colonial landscapes, inclusive urbanism, models of collaboration, critical moving images, inclusive still images, critical text, critical and inclusive rhetoric, heterodox drawing (against the Eurocentric canon), collective world mapping, and reparations.

In a strikingly material way, shared heritage places epitomise not only hierarchical segregation, zoning, and human exploitation, but also economic imbalances, subjugation, and injustice, which sadly still influence the socio-economic milieu in the least developed countries (LDCs) as well as in Europe, as underlined by civic associations in London (*British Black Panther Movement*), Lisbon (*Djass*), to mention just a few. Van Roosmalen (2013) comments on how the value assessment of colonial architecture in Indonesia is similarly problematic:

> Architecture and town plans in themselves do not necessarily instil awareness and appreciation or lead to appropriation by a country's citizens or visitors. Appreciation and appropriation are even less common when the artefacts originate from a period of foreign domination, because they act as reminders of the period of foreign domination.

In STP, architecture practitioners, historians, landscape painters, and travellers might appreciate the aesthetic value, the grandeur, the eclecticism, the

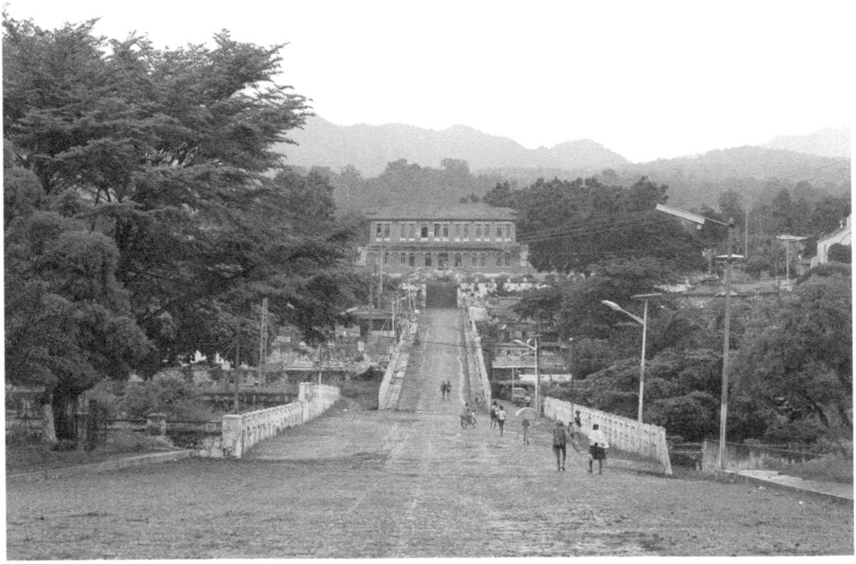

Figure 3.1 Roça Agostinho Neto in São Tomé (photograph by G. Borsoi, 2021).

authenticity in design, materials, constructions, morphological layout, and even the decadent beauty of the *roças* (Figure 3.1).

Newcomers to STP may be impressed by the relevance of the *roças* to the territory as well as the construction quality of some architectural components (e.g., wooden walkways, sinuous railings, and ogival windows) visible on-site as well as captured by photographers and bloggers.

On the other hand, a vast gamut of emotions, such as anguish, odium, embarrassment, surprise, and curiosity may arise, especially when noticing the differences in the living conditions between the *casa-senhorial* and the *senzalas*, as well as in realising the cruelty of the working conditions. In a process that demanded a huge number of workers, the cocoa beans had to be fermented, dried, cleaned, and packed – as visible in the great number of structures dedicated to the work (*armazéns* and *secadores*).

Beyond the evocative power experienced when viewing archival and current photographs,[22] one might have strong reactions when visiting artefact collections or exhibitions in memorial monuments or European ethnographic museums related to colonial histories.[23]

Leaving aside any nostalgic attitudes or aesthetic views and turning to more pragmatic concerns, it should be noted that the recovery, use, and maintenance of *roças* are also hampered by relevant physical constraints (e.g., size, type, location, surrounding conditions, and infrastructure connections), which can discourage investment especially by local agents and by diaspora ownerships.

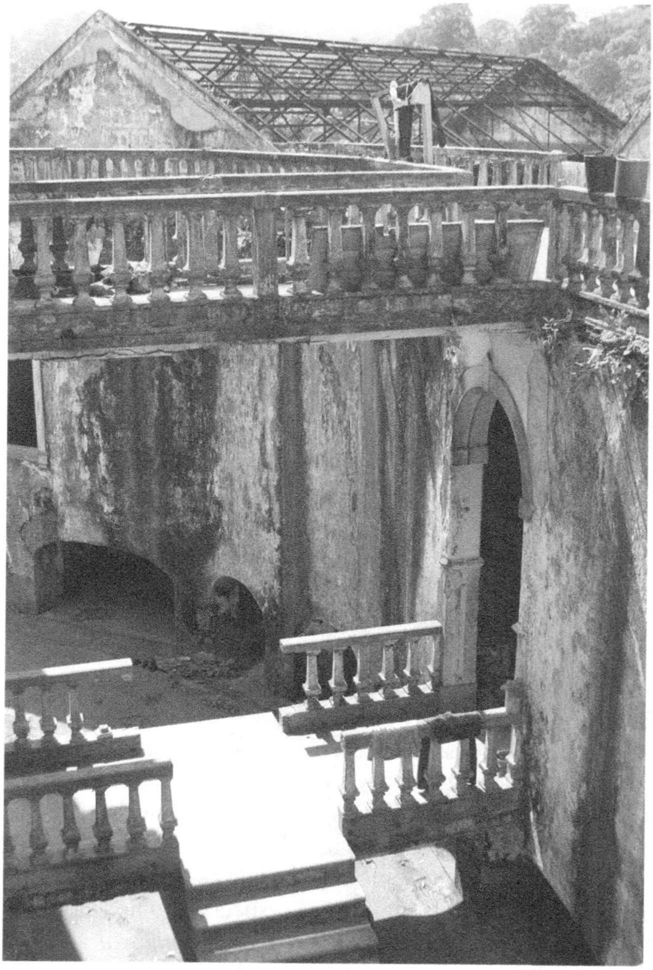

Figure 3.2 Hospital in Roça Água Izé in São Tomé (photograph by G. Borsoi 2021).

To one who might be reluctant to work with these controversial legacies for these or other reasons, we respond that the physical traces of many *roças* may soon disappear, overtaken by the regrowth of the tropical forest or lost to the fate of neglect (see Figures 3.2 and 3.3). The new generations who risk being deprived of this knowledge include Creoles (*forros*) – the descendants of African enslaved people and early white settlers – as well as Cape Verdean and Angolan inhabitants or any other communities historically attached to these places, including the Portuguese former settlers and their relatives (*retornados,* returnees).[24] In other cases, refurbishment as tourism accommodations (e.g.,Hotel Roça Sundy, in Príncipe) have similar undesired

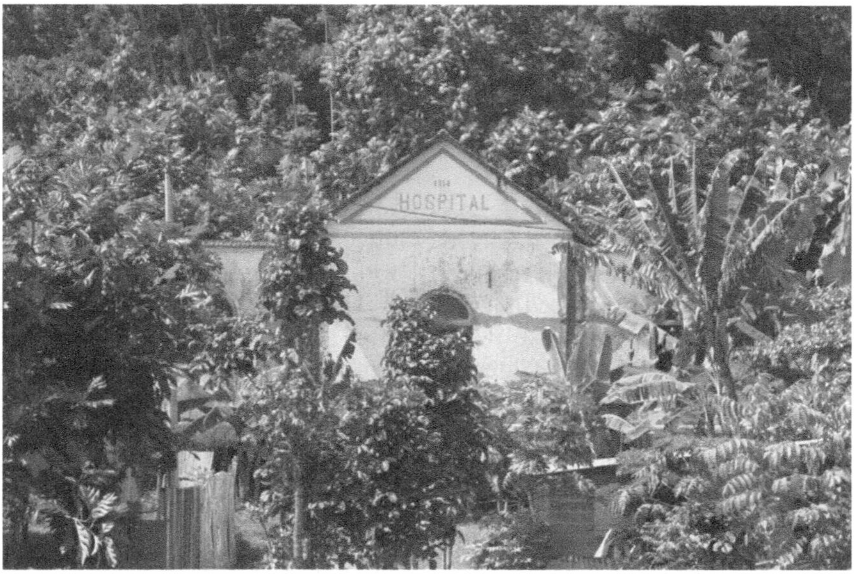

Figure 3.3 Old hospital in Roça Água Izé in São Tomé (photograph by G. Borsoi 2021).

effects, such as the reiteration of the pattern of racial relations. Yet these plantations and their memories represent an alternative history to that taught or seen in European public squares and spaces, in academic courses on history and geography, and in museum collections and expositions.

ii. *Values to be promulgated in the digital age:*
Heritage places serve as a threshold of collective memory of shared ideas that are constantly renewed with an opening in looking to the future. This process is supported and questioned by a myriad of individual memories, experiences and wishes, hence underscoring the idea of openness, diversity, historical heterogeneity and social interactions as sources of place meaning. (Gantois 2021)

The narratives to be imparted should encompass a value-sensitive design (VSD) approach – that is, they should be based on a set of values relevant to the critical stakeholders called to give witness to each history. By using a VSD approach, we can address challenges to human values at the intersection of multiple perspectives and respect the core ethical values of direct and indirect critical stakeholders. The set of values of critical stakeholders should be incorporated into the design of the architectural solutions (van den Hoven *et al.* 2015). In line with Schrijver's (2015) thought, we must keep in mind that roças, as architectural artefacts whose spatial layout was drawn for a specific purpose, incorporate values that have changed over time. Buildings and settlements are often designed and inhabited over long-term periods during which values can also change. Any interventions should reflect the multiple new values of the new inhabitants and people experiencing these heritage places today.

These multiple narratives cannot fail to omit historiographical (re)readings related to colonialism and the post-independence phase (1975 to present) to overcome the limitations of contextless architectural narrations. Delving into the reports of day-to-day life, each *roça* has its history in the *process of acculturation* undergone by both European employers and the African enslaved (or forced) workers.[25] Heritage contextualisation and transparency in history make it possible to show not just the plantation heritage but also its points of intersection with local cultural expression (e.g., art, dance, theatre), while the inclusiveness is considering in reshaping the future enriched from a historically aware perspective. This wider perspective should hope to escape falling back into a reductionist vision that elides the affirmation of African communities and their cultural resistance.

Potential digital technologies applied to shared cultural heritage

Multi-format representations

Digital technologies have proven their effectiveness for learning purposes in a variety of disciplines, notably in medicine and engineering, as well as in history, cultural anthropology, and architecture, including the Architecture and Engineering curricula (Eloy *et al.* 2016). Multi-technology simulation, such as augmented reality (AR) and virtual reality (VR), have been often used for infotainment and dissemination purposes within multiple cultural heritage domains. VR and AR have proven their effectiveness in e-learning contexts due to their capacity to immerse and engage.[26] AR superimposes virtual objects on the real world in order to immerse the user into new informed-enhanced realities, whereas VR delivers complete off-site simulations of the world through immersive computer simulation. AR guarantees non-intrusive interaction with the physical world, having been used to improve user engagement, foster inclusive social learning, and introduce new ludic ways of exploring cultural heritage. Serious games and gamification strategies are used to engage people in emotion-evoking activities, promoting relationships, and motivation (Khan *et al.* 2020). These tools improve social learning and lead to novel ludic approaches to cultural heritage exploration. Architecture and cultural heritage awareness games either offer an immersive experience for learning the values of cultural heritage sites or seek to persuade users into the real experience. Tan and Lim (2017) have developed an AR walkthrough tool for learning about tangible cultural heritage, while Vera and Sánchez (2016) use AR to enable users to create digital content about their surroundings. Basaraba (2018) presents a tool to co-construct cultural heritage-related experience through a web-based interactive digital narrative, while Vayanou *et al.* (2019) deliver a storytelling game in which promising performative cultural experiences are designed.

Core dichotomies in cultural heritage experiences with advanced technologies

For several years already, curators have used AR/VR tools to enrich cultural exhibitions worldwide by integrating data on physical artefacts or texts. However, a recent survey shows that few such examples can be found in Europe (UNESCO 2003, 2020, ICOM 2021). If they are to be deployed, these forward-thinking cultural services must adapt to some institutional rules (e.g., workplace organisation, customer management) as well as to venue and economic constraints. In the near future, the forced closures caused by the pandemic – as well as the economic slowdown – will induce all collections to strive to differentiate the cultural service they provide and to reach diverse audiences with web-based technologies.

The dissemination of shared cultural heritage using digital technologies is a complex task primarily due to the problematic value assessment of the type of heritage, as previously shown in STP. In analysing the permanent exposition in Lagos entitled *Núcleo Museológico Rota da Escravatura,*[27] Santos (2020) raises relevant questions which can be generalised within critical heritage studies around three core dichotomies: (i) playfulness of presentation vs the seriousness of the issue; (ii) the potential of integrating contents by means of digital technologies vs the intentional obscuring of micro-narratives or different perspectives of the same historical event; (iii) scientificity *vs* a more human approach.

Looking at this exposition in more detail, it uses advanced digital devices to display the remains of 158 enslaved Africans found in Vale da Gafaria. Multimedia contents in modern displays for electronic notebooks and AR glasses provide a wealth of information about printed maps and other exposed artefacts. Visitors can also use their smartphones to access AR apps if they are present at the museum. As explained by Santos, the enslaved Africans are represented by a group of black monoliths with electronic displays, while the entire exposition requires bodily interaction, which helps capture the interest, especially of children and groups. All its texts are translated into English since Lagos is a common international tourism destination.

Despite this gesture towards internationalisation, a whitewashed perspective remains embedded in the contents of the exhibition: "This museum-like space refers to the slave trade only as early globalization and multicultural dialogue" and

> Both forms of visual display and of written text turn these enslaved Africans, the first to have died on European soil, into invisible victims of

> the Portuguese state and its slave traders: they are visible only as depersonalized osteological pieces, rendered as scientific and archeological finds. (Santos 2020)

The above-mentioned core dichotomies should be carefully considered in the technological design process for cultural heritage experiences around the plantation heritage in STP. These pitfalls are as dangerous as those derived from the global digital divide, the duality between high tech vs low-tech-based technologies in the Global North and LDCs. In line with Kituyi's thought, Africans should "take part in the new digital world, not just as users and consumers, but also as producers, exporters and innovators, for creating and capturing more value on their path towards sustainable development" (UNCTAD 2019).

New insight into the past, present, and future of this shared heritage can thus also address the risk of digital space reiterating certain forms of social exclusion or even a new form of colonisation, understood as cultural or economical hegemony upon the community of a given country.

New frontiers of shared digital technologies in education about architecture and avenues of inquiry

Politically engaged research can be addressed in new shared digital infrastructures to overcome polarised perspectives through democratic processes in education, training policies, and governance. Given the fact that the education offered by architecture schools has tightened and materialised non-egalitarian systems: "[a]n Anti-Racist pedagogy across the world is only possible through decolonisation processes and reparations that address the colonial footprint of Architecture schools" (Frankowski 2020, p. 14).

We note that, by using advanced digital technologies, unprecedented pathways can be opened to provoke a great deal of new thinking about architectural and land planning, history, human geography, and cultural anthropology – this includes e-learning tools, walkthroughs, AR for real locations, or other multisensory artworks. Multiformat representations in different learning spaces can overcome the disjunction between the physical space and multiple (often silenced) narratives: the distance between material culture legacies and the meanings and values behind their form. Collective imaginaries can be shaped towards a global cultural overhaul, in which the reframing of material legacies can support systemic decolonisation.

Bearing in mind that younger generations (for instance students) tend to be at ease with interactive and multisensory content, the combination of digital technologies with co-learning processes has the potential to drive active and transformative learning, which may in turn influence architectural planning and design, as well as behavioural patterns such as staffing patterns, and a greater sense of acceptance, inclusion, identity, and security.

Context-based learning about controversial heritage or negative histories from across Europe is being developed under the *Historiana* initiative.[28] Teacher material (lesson introductions, lesson texts, lesson plans) and student material (worksheets) are provided for a number of historical themes and situated contexts. Students and critical stakeholders can share information, standpoints, beliefs, doubts, and ideas via free online access, discovering different perspectives on the places where they live. Among a large variety of selections of historical content, the website *Historiana* includes *Cultural Heritage: controversial buildings and their changing function*, a source collection that displays a range of monuments or memorials in Europe with a brief textual description and photo, part of the *Learning to Disagree* project. These are integrated with activities for classroom practice.[29]

Another important aspect is that a vast spectrum of digital tools can be designed using the architectural legacies of STP as a living source of learning, but these should remain complementary to any real on-site experience. Choosing a bottom-up approach across the new digital pathways will make it possible to design earning experiences that are inclusive, self-guided (or stand-alone interpretive), collaborative, and more democratic. This living source has the potential to bring together a large potential audience beyond Afro-descendants, including migrants from STP living in Europe. The user can view local and global sites, sharing this experience on social platforms, even without travelling to the actual site in person. Although the virtual experience can hardly replace the intensity and authenticity of an in-person experience, digital tools are inclusive and easily accessible. This aspect is particularly relevant in the post-COVID-19 world, since real experiences may be precluded by lockdown measures, as well as due to the cost of flights.

The impact of European colonisation upon human and environmental dimensions in colonised countries cannot be compartmentalised into separate domains of knowledge, packaged for each academic discipline. Nevertheless, with a focus on students of architecture and the community interested in cultural heritage, the approach to the *roças* and their surroundings can be addressed along multiple avenues of inquiry – especially geography, architecture, and social studies – integrating different databases, tools, and multi-format sources. This information can be combined to shape new textual and visual readings, inspiring students of architecture to innovate discourses and media outside of the institutionally perceived boundaries of architecture (Frankowski 2020, p. 44). Recent digital technologies, labelled as *interpretive technologies*, foresee several solutions that satisfy these requirements to guarantee a holistic approach and expand access beyond any geographic boundaries (Heritage Lottery Fund 2012).

Some priorities for the design of e-learning tools and their application in STP are outlined below:

1 *Incorporate information reflecting multiple perspectives:* It is important to bear in mind the dichotomies and conflicting perspectives that should be debated and shared. The cultural plurality of displaced people and agents involved in colonial and postcolonial societies should be expressed via close collaboration and debate throughout the whole critical design process. This process should also involve representatives of cultural institutions (including within academia), ICT (Information and communications technology) developers, critical stakeholders (communities of STP, Afro-Europeans, and *retornados*), activist groups, and civic associations. Beyond the application of methods for value-sensitive design, this requirement can be met using contemporary crowdsource technology that enables large communities to participate in the creation of common platforms for knowledge (e.g., Wikipedia).

2 *Enable diachronic and synchronic studies:* Several advanced tools, such as Machine Learning (ML), offer new opportunities to address diachronic and cross-sectorial analysis (Chen *et al.* 2021). Comprehensive analysis of digitised historical maps of STP can demonstrate the huge territorial alterations across different historical phases, monitoring their temporal evolution. Deforestation has been the most salient transformation of the landscape, having been pursued for planting crops, constructing the railways, and fuelwood consumption; wood is also largely employed for constructing local houses. Visual comparison and more detailed studies can be addressed in STP using digital documents of postcards, photos, and newspaper journals. This information can be retrieved from, e.g., historic presidential trips, and digital libraries portraying historical memories of STP for public access (even if metadata are in Portuguese): *Memórias de África e do Oriente*, developed by researchers from the University of Aveiro and the Center for Studies on Africa and Development (since 1997) to share documents from different archives (including those from *Arquivo Histórico de S. Tomé e Principe*), and *Casa Comum* organised within *Fundação Mário Soares e Maria Barroso* (since 2006). In *Casa Comum*, in addition to general and advanced search, the user can browse the documents using a classification tree and retrieve contextual elements to visualise the records and related meta-data organised into document series that, whenever possible, reflect the original order of their producer(s).

Additionally, GIS and Space Syntax analysis make it possible to explore the sociocultural dimension embedded in spatial systems over time and across different uses. The key advantage of these analyses is the ability to combinate tangible and intangible aspects of the physical space towards the identification of patterns of the use of space in different cultural periods (Palaiologou and Griffiths 2019).

The use of layers of virtual information via AV and VR or mixed-reality tools make it possible to depict changes in the characteristics and valuation of real environments over time. These tools should leverage multisensorial descriptors to facilitate the interaction between users and the complex realities in STP.

A crucial aspect towards a broader new perspective is taking stock of local emotions and insightful interpretations of existing cultural data, be these in physical contexts (in proximity to the heritage site) or in digital ones (archival collections or other repositories). Micro-narratives of descendants of who worked at, inhabited, and escaped from the *roças* could be made digitally available in resonance with heritage sites as if they were digital twins. We use the expression *digital twins* to indicate the virtual narration of memories to enrich the physical space, experienced simultaneously and commented on as the place is perceived by our sensory receptors.

3 *Be inclusive:* The type of information, its mode of representation (visual, textual, audio), the form of human-computer interaction, and the lexical choice[30] are all fundamental factors influencing the design process for inclusive e-learning activities as well as any digital cultural product, whether this is a web-learning tool, an app with AV/VR experience in a museum collection or cultural exhibition, a serious game, etc.

To develop inclusive tools, it is necessary to understand the varying levels of skill, background, interest, education, and abilities of each group of end-users and their ecosystem (Vosloo 2018). The power of visual language is not to be discounted. In STP as well as in other least developed countries, inclusiveness means providing translated content in multilingual platforms (e.g., Wikipedia), assuming an open science approach, making content also available on low-tech devices (e.g., google card box for VR instead of an expensive Head Mounted Display) and low speed Wi-Fi connections (e.g., avoiding the sharing of large amounts of data, using the cloud), so that diverse learning pathways are available for users of different ages, interests, and familiarity with technologies.

Concluding remarks

Digital transformation has not yet greatly influenced heritage preservation practices in the least developed countries. Heritage practice involves critically rethinking of the meaning of shared cultural heritage, arising from past European colonisation, and rethinking potential reuse by a large community with consideration of cross-sectorial politics. Problems related to the use of a set of advanced technologies, the involvement of different stakeholders, and the coexistence of conflicting values emphasise the importance of adopting a decolonising perspective.

Embodying both memories of violence and promises for future development, the *roças* in STP testify to conflicting and fluctuating values around both post-coloniality, with diverging prospects for their reuse. Although the exploitation of tropical commodities and racial inequalities remain persistent themes in the history of STP, these difficulties have not crushed the cheerful and welcoming spirit of these communities, in which the visitor is made to feel: "Afinal, chegamos a África, e sentimos que o que não nos corre nas veias, entranha-se na alma"[31] (ABVP 2020).

Critical reflections for effective actions are urgently required in STP, since the intergenerational transmission of colonial history is truly at threat. Moreover, most of the *roças* have been abandoned, inappropriately occupied, or turned into luxury hotels that echo racial segregation. The preservation and adaptive reuse of *roças* should encompass multi-dimensional approaches for unmasking and reacting to those overarching racial inequalities that have been fostered by Eurocentric policies.

Although there are no infallible recipes for intervention, and while certain contextual constraints may seem insurmountable, these cultural legacies have the potential to be conceived as living sources for learning, to give voice to untold yet irreplaceable narratives. Despite the real difficulties arising from the growth of the Global North/South divide, especially with the COVID-19 pandemic, and the need to face health/economic emergencies in STP, this architectural and environmental heritage harbours promise for a more inclusive and aware transnational society.

In the digital age, constructive action based on community-driven processes towards the re-thinking of cultural legacies and the improvement of learning spaces offers countless perspectives. In handing down lessons drawn from the past to new generations, these e-learning tools can raise awareness of the current state of uncontrolled development and careless usage, hopefully preventing the material loss of cultural legacies secured by the sacrifice of countless multi-ethnic workers and families.

Historical frameworks can be rethought using digital means in approaching marginalised ethnic groups whose roots are entangled in colonial histories. Their patterns of distribution and the public representations of their identity and culture worldwide reflect stereotypes, biases, and racial inequalities – a situation echoed by the historical narratives around plantation work in STP and Atlantic slave routes. Advanced digital technologies (e.g., AV and VR or mixed-reality tools, Machine Learning) have the potential to reconnect this part of history to contemporary European places, to provide engaging and non-stereotyped access to the heritage, and to inform more just, sustainable, and historically aware viewpoints. E-learning that is dedicated to providing an interactive diachronic overview of the architectural and planning dimension represents a promising new frontier, one that seeks to shed light on the past and on the (variable) cultural values presently embodied in physical space (both colonial heritage places and memorial markers). In fact, e-learning tools can counteract "collective amnesia" or the recurrence of internalised racism, while greater awareness can inform the tourist's choice of destination and their experience. Other exploratory pathways may address perceptions triggered by the built and natural environment in STP in a way that overcomes the rigid, backward-looking focus on colonial roots, by which people's views may become stereotyped or immobilised over time.

Notes

1 An example of the bureaucratic or operational slowness in Portugal is the proposal of *The Slavery Memorial* in Lisbon in 2008, submitted for approval under the Participatory Budget (a policymaking tool which allows citizens to participate in public budgeting decisions) then accepted in 2017 together with the interpretative centre on slavery and colonial history. Planned for installation in *Campo das Cebolas* and strongly promoted by the *Djass – Associação de Afrodescendentes*, these memorials have still not been executed. Public debates on this topic in Portugal are briefly addressed by Santos (2020).

2 For instance, https://www.icomos.org/en/77-articles-en-francais/72051-18-april-2019-theme-shared-cultures, https://en.unesco.org/shared-heritage, and https://dutchculture.nl/en/introduction-shared-cultural-heritage. See also, *Pressing Matter: Ownership, Value and the Question of Colonial Heritage in Museum* (2021–2025), promoted by The National Museum of World Cultures (NMVW) and the Vrije Universiteit, Amsterdam (VU). See also, https://decolonizing museums.com/

3 The term the *Atlantic World* was used between 1949 and 1973 especially by Western historians (Canny 2001).

4 Etymology: areas of brushwood (*mato*), small farming land (for the cultivation of *mandioca, milho, feijão*); rural area; field. The verb *roçar* means pull out, tear down the vegetation, cut, cut down bush or vegetation.

5 In critical heritage studies, those artefacts with inherent trauma, such as those from fascism in Italy (1920s–1930s) or from the communist regime in Eastern Europe (1950s–1980s), are labelled as *undesirable heritage* (Macdonald 2006), *difficult heritage* (Macdonald 2015), *negative heritage, dissonant* or *unwanted heritage*. More interestingly, Innocenti (2016) constructs the idea of *migration heritage*.

6 Being an expression of imperialism and adaptation of European design patterns and cross-cultural influences, the vast heritage assets were built under the Kingdom of Portugal over three periods (1415–1580, 1580–1822, 1822–1999). These include historic urban centres, military fortresses, hospital facilities, religious and civic monuments, public squares, and cultivation of the natural landscape (Mattoso 2010).

7 Sacks of cocoa (50-kilograms) were shipped to Lisbon and from there to Hamburg, Le Havre, New York, and London (Nascimento 2002, Macedo 2016).

8 "The collective memory constantly recycles this core tissue" (translated by the authors).

9 The workers in *roças* were recruited from Angola, Mozambique, and Cape Verde (Nascimento 2002, Seibert 2013).

10 These researchers base their works on previous inventories, some of which were carried out in the mid-20th century by Tenreiro (1961), among others. Machado da Silva (2018) provides in-depth architectural and historical analyses of *Água Izé*, *Boa Entrada*, and *Rio do Ouro*, while Ana Fernandes (2016) analyses the state of conservation, the typology, genesis, and layout of the settlements across time. Both provide in-depth analyses of selected case studies, suggestive photographic records, and 2d/3d survey representations.

11 In September 1975, all *roças* were nationalised. The land and the farmers were administered by the state of São Tomé during the process called *agrarian reform*.

Despite being presented as against any colonial-based system, the organisation of monoculture plantations inherited from colonial times was maintained into the 1980s, favouring just the cocoa production in detriment to other agricultural production (Berthet 2012).

12 See, e.g., https://visitsaotomeprincipe.st/en/destination/. Other similar tropical tourist attractions areas the Caribbean since the 1960s, discussed by Cameron and Gatewood (2008).

13 In intense monoculture plantations, even after the abolition of slavery, violence was an integral part of the management of indentured labor under a scientifically based colonial system. In São Tomé and Príncipe, enforced labour-recruiting policies endured after the 1875 abolition of slavery. "Those codes [Portuguese colonial labor laws in 1875, 1878, and 1880] adhered to the free labor market ideology, but in practice they legalized forced labor and colonial violence, in the form of 5-year working contracts that sustained former dependence relations" (Macedo 2016, p. 563).

14 See, e.g., Historiana (https://historiana.eu/historical-content/source-collections/cultural-heritage-controversial-buildings-and-their-changing-function), the Architecture of Violence by Eyal Weizman (https://www.aljazeera.com/program/rebel-architecture/2014/9/2/israel-the-architecture-of-violence), and Forensic Architecture (https://forensic-architecture.org/).

15 See, *UNESCO's Slave Route project: Resistance, Liberty, Heritage*. The Portuguese cultural assets bearing direct or indirect traces of the slave trade that are registered on the World Heritage List include the Central Zone of the Town of Angra do Heroismo in the Azores (1983) and the Historic Centre of Oporto (1996).

16 *Places of Memory of Slavery and the Slave Trade* as a part of the initiative promoted by the *Portuguese Committee of UNESCO's Slave Route Project* housed in the University of Lisbon, Centre for Studies on Africa and on Development (Henriques 2019).

17 "Em 1966 tive o meu primeiro contacto com África, depois de dois anos lectivos inscrita e frequentando o curso de História na Faculdade de Letras da Universidade de Lisboa, curso que me parecia cinzento e vazio [...]" ENG: "1966 I had my first contact with Africa, after two academic years enrolled and attending the History course at the Faculty of Literature of the University of Lisbon, a course that seemed gray and empty to me [...]" (translated by the authors) (Henriques 2019, p. 223). At international level, the colonial footprint of architecture schools is discussed in (Frankowski 2020, p. 14).

18 The question of how to concretely address this situation was raised at a March 2021 seminar in Lisbon, under the title *Descolonizar os museus ... isto na prática* (ENG: *Decolonize the museum ... this is in practice*) (authors' translation), where the debate focused on the decolonising practice in Portugal. Wayne Modest, director of Research Centre of Material Culture and subdirector of the Tropenmuseum in Amsterdam, discussed the semantic overhaul that will be implied by any such endeavour. Also taking part in this cultural event were Catarina Simão, Isabel Raposo Magalhães, Joacine Katar Moreira, Judite Primo, Luís Raposo, Manuel Santos, and Paulo Costa (video and audio available: https://gi-imperios.org/blog/pt/descolonizar-os-museus-isto-na-pratica-2/).

19 The "civilising mission" in Portuguese colonialism from 1870 to 1930 is discussed by Jerónimo (2015).

20 Osterhammel (2005) introduces the notion of *colonialism* that exists even in absence of a colony. It is a process of dominance or systemic capitalism occurring within a society. In this line of thought, the term *post-colonialism* is controversial since this process is still underway and ubiquitous.

21 Smith (2006) recalls how it comes to light during the *World Heritage Convention* (WHC) in 1972. See also Brumann and Gfeller (2021), Modest and de Koning (2016), and Logan and Reeves (2008).
22 http://casacomum.org/ and http://memoria-africa.ua.pt/
23 In Lisbon: *Padrão dos Descobrimentos Visões do Império* (2021, https://padraodosdescobrimentos.pt/evento/visoes-do-imperio/), *Retornar-Traços de Memória* (2015, https://galeriasmunicipais.pt/exposicoes/retornar-tracos-de-memoria/); Arquivo Histórico Ultramarino (2019), *Colonizing Africa: Relatórios das Obras Públicas em Angola e Moçambique (1875–1975)* (https://antt.dglab.gov.pt/exposicao-ahu-colonizando-africa-relatorios-das-obras-publicas-em-angola-e-mocambique-1875-1975/), *The worlds of (under)development: processes and legacies of the Portuguese colonial empire in a comparative perspective (1945–1975)* (2018–2022); Lagos City Council and Portuguese Committee of UNESCO's *Slave Route Project*, a slavery-themed exhibition (2016) (Santos 2020).
24 The group of workers from Angola and Cape Verde who arrived in the archipelago until the 1960s. Detailed analyses of relationships, hierarchies, and the co-existence of different ethnic groups are addressed by Nascimento (2002), and Seibert (2013), while critical questions related to Portuguese settlers and their families coming back in Portugal, so-called *retornados*, have been recently addressed by Peralta (2019).
25 "Not all Roças would be oppressive, nor would all human relations would be guided by strict racism or a strong personal subjection. However, in many cases there would not be much room for the manifestation of individual subjectivities and attitudes contrary to the dominant tone imposed by economic pressures and political circumstances" (Nascimento 2002, p. 401).
26 AR enables a synchronic interaction with reality in which both past and present information can be shared and experienced, as shown, e.g., in SeeArch (Raposo et al. 2017). In a similar way, VR enables the experience of a full or semi-simulated multisensory world in which a participatory, co-created experience can be offered.
27 Hosted in the *Mercados de Escravos* (slave market) building and inaugurated in 2016, this collection was conceived after the discovery of the enslaved Africans in one of the oldest of these burial sites in Europe.
28 Cohort-based activities are designed and shared on the *Historiana* platform (https://historiana.eu/), part of the *Europeana Creative* project. The development is financially supported by the European Union and the Evens Foundation, the historical content teams and EUROCLIO trainees.
29 https://historiana.eu/historical-content/source-collections/cultural-heritage-controversial-buildings-and-their-changing-function
30 Commercial rendering and other hegemonic forms are shown in *A Manual of Anti-Racist Architecture Education* (Frankowski 2020). Conceptual and semantic decolonisation practices are addressed in literature. Here, we just refer to the recent work of Wayne Modest (see endnote 19) https://www.tropenmuseum.nl/en/about-tropenmuseum/words-matter-publication.
31 "Finally, we arrived in Africa, and we feel that what doesn't run in our veins, enters our soul" (translated by the authors).

References

ABVP – Associação de Bloggers de Viagens Portugueses, 2020. *Viagens de Uma Vida 25 Bloggers de Viagem Portugueses*. Portugal: Idioteque.

Åkesson, L., 2016. Narrating São Tomé: Cape Verdean memories of contract labour in the portuguese empire [online]. *Etnografica*, 20 (1), 57–76.

Barros, A., ed., 2015. *Os Descobrimentos e as origens da convergência global = The Discoveries and the origins of global convergence.* Porto: Associação para a Divulgação da Língua Portuguesa.
Basaraba,N., 2018. Co-constructing cultural heritage through a web-based interactive digital narrative. In: R. Rouse, H. Koenitz, and M. Haahr, eds. Interactive Storytelling. ICIDS 2018. *Lecture Notes in Computer Science* (11318). Cham: Springer.
Berthet, M.A., 2012. Reflexões sobre as Roças em São Tomé e Príncipe. *Estudos Históricos (Rio de Janeiro)*, 25 (50), 331–351.
Bertocchi, G., and Canova, F., 2002. Did colonization matter for growth? *European Economic Review*, 46 (10), 1851–1871.
Brumann, C., and Gfeller, A. É., 2021. Cultural landscapes and the UNESCO world heritage list: perpetuating european dominance. *International Journal of Heritage Studies*, 28 (2), 1–16.
Cameron, C.M., and Gatewood, J.B., 2008. Beyond sun, sand and sea: the emergent tourism programme in the Turks and Caicos Islands. *Journal of Heritage Tourism*, 3 (1), 55–73.
Canny, N., 2001. Atlantic history: what and why? *European Review*, 9 (4), 399–441.
Chen, Y., Carlinet, E., Chazalon, J., Mallet, C., Duménieu, B., and Perret, J., 2021. Combining deep learning and mathematical morphology for historical map segmentation [online]. *Computer Vision and Pattern Recognition* Available from: https://arxiv.org/pdf/2101.02144v1.pdf [Accessed 7 August 2021].
Eloy, S., Dias, M.S., Lopes, P.F., and Vilar, E., 2016. Digital technologies in architecture and engineering: exploring an engaged interaction within curricula. In: D. Fonseca and E. Redondo, eds. *Handbook of research on applied e-learning in engineering and architecture education.* Hershey, PA: IGI Global, 368–402.
Eyzaguirre, P.B., 1986. Small farmers and estates in São Tomé, West Africa (Thesis PhD). Yale University.
Fernandes, A.L. da S., 2016. Entre Remediar e Solucionar: A estruturação e a participação como meios de gestão da escassez e ruptura do ciclo de pobreza. São Tomé e Príncipe como laboratório (Thesis PhD). Porto School of Architecture.
Fernandes, J.M., 2005. *Arquitectura e Urbanismo na África Portuguesa.* Lisbon: Caleidoscópio.
Frankowski, R., 2020. *A manual of anti-racist architecture education* [online]. Available from https://waithinktank.com/Anti-Racist-Education-Manual [Accessed 7 August 2021].
Freyre, G., 1964. *The masters and the slaves: a study in the development of Brazilian civilization.* New York: Alfred A.
Gantois, G., 2021. Built heritage as imagines agentes. *Collabra: Psychology*, 7 (1), 21194.
Guedes, M.C., 2021. *Arquitetura sustentável em São tomé e principe: manual de boas práticas.* Lisbon: IST Press.
Henriques, I.C., 2019. *Roteiro histórico de uma lisboa Africana, Séculos XV-XXI* [online]. Available from: https://www.acm.gov.pt/documents/10181/27754/Roteiro_historico_pt.pdf/05f9c291-fb3d-42c7-be73-fdc9f556b1a3 [Accessed 7 August 2021].
Heritage Lottery Fund, 2012. Using digital technology in heritage projects: good practice guidance [online]. Available from: https://www.heritagefund.org.uk/sites/default/files/media/guidance/using_digital_technology_good_practice_0.pdf [Accessed 7 August 2021].

ICOM, 2021. *Museums, museum professionals and COVID-19* [online]. Available from: https://icom.museum/wp-content/uploads/2021/07/Museums-and-Covid-19_third-ICOM-report.pdf [Accessed 7 August 2021].

Innocenti, P., 2016. Cultural networks and social inclusion of migrants in Europe: heritage, ICT, and participatory governance. *International Information & Library Review*, 48 (4), 274–286.

Jerónimo, M.B., 2015. *The 'Civilising Mission' of Portuguese colonialism, 1870–1930*. Basingstoke, England, United Kingdom: Palgrave Macmillan UK.

Khan, I., Melro, A., Carla, A., and Oliveira, L., 2020. Systematic review on gamification and cultural heritage dissemination. *Journal of Digital Media & Interaction*, 3 (8), 19–41.

Kølvraa, C., and Knudsen, T.B., eds., 2020. Decolonizing European colonial heritage in urban spaces. *Heritage & Society*, 13(1–2), 1–9.

Logan, W., and Reeves, K., eds., 2008. *Places of pain and shame dealing with 'Difficult Heritage'*. Routledge: London.

Macdonald, S., 2006. Undesirable heritage: Fascist material culture and historical consciousness in Nuremberg. *International Journal of Heritage Studies*, 12 (1), 9–28.

Macdonald, S., 2015. Is 'Difficult Heritage' still 'Difficult'? *Museum International*, 67(1–4), 6–22.

Macedo, M., 2016. Standard cocoa: transnational networks and technoscientific regimes in West African plantations. *Technology and Culture*, 57 (3), 557–585.

Machado da Silva, H.A.F., 2018. Roça de São Tomé e Príncipe. Génese, Processo e Lógicas Espaciais (Thesis PhD). Porto School of Architecture.

Mantero, F., 1910. *Mão d'obra em S. Thomé e Principe*. Lisbon: Typ. do Annuario Commercial.

Mattoso, J., 2010. *Património de origem portuguesa no mundo*. Lisbon: Fundação Calouste Gulbenkian.

Mattoso, J., Barata, T., and Fernandes, M.J., 2010. *Património de origem portuguesa no mundo – arquitectura e urbanismo. África, golfo pérsico e mar vermelho*. Lisbon: Fundação Calouste Gulbenkian.

Modest, W., and de Koning, A., 2016. Anxious politics in the European city: an introduction [online]. *Patterns of Prejudice*, 50 (2). Available from: https://www.tropenmuseum.nl/en/about-tropenmuseum/words-matter-publication [Accessed 7 August 2021].

Nascimento, A., 2002. *Poderes e quotidiano nas roças de S. Tomé e Príncipe: de Finais de oitocentos a meados de novecentos*. Lousã: Tipografia Lousanense.

Osterhammel, J., 2005. *Colonialism: a theoretical overview*. UA: Markus Wiener Publishers.

Palaiologou, G., and Griffiths, S., 2019. The uses of space syntax historical research for policy development in heritage urbanism. In: M.O. Šćitaroci, B.B.O. Šćitaroci, and A. Mrđa, eds. *Cultural urban heritage: development, learning and landscape strategies*. Cham, Switzerland: Springer, 19–34.

Peralta, E., 2019. The return from Africa: illegitimacy, concealment, and the non-memory of Portugal's imperial collapse. *Memory Studies*, 15 (1), 1–18.

Raposo, M., Eloy, S., and Dias, M.S., 2017. Revisiting the city augmented by digital technologies – SeeARch tool. In: R. Amoêda, S. Lira, and C. Pinheiro, eds. *REHAB – 3rd international conference on preservation, maintenance, and rehabilitation of historical buildings and structures*. Braga: Green Lines Institute for Sustainable Development, 637–646.

RCE - Cultural Heritage Agency, 2021. *What is shared cultural heritage?* Available from: https://english.cultureelerfgoed.nl/topics/shared-cultural-heritage/what-is-shared-cultural-heritage [Accessed 8 August 2021].

Santos, P.M., 2020. Bringing slavery into the light in postcolonial Portugal. *Museum Worlds: Advances in Research*, 8 (1), 46–67.

Schrijver, L., 2015. Design for values in architecture. In: J. van den Hoven, P.E. Vermaas, and I. van de Poel, eds. *Handbook of ethics, values, and technological design*. Dordrecht: Springer, 589–611.

Seibert, G., 2013. São Tomé and Príncipe: The first plantation economy in the tropics. In: R. Law, S. Schwarz, and S. Strickrodt, eds. *Commercial agriculture, the slave trade and slavery in Atlantic Africa*. Boydell & Brewer, 54–78.

Smith, L., 2006. *Uses of heritage*. London: Routledge.

Smith, L., and Akagawa, N., eds., 2008. *Intangible heritage*. 1st ed. London: Routledge.

Smith, L.T. 2012. *Decolonizing methodologies: research and indigenous peoples*. London: Zed Books, Lcd.

Stoler, A.L., 2011. Colonial aphasia: race and disabled histories in France. *Public Culture*, 23(1), 121–156.

Stoler, A.L., 2016. *Duress. Imperial durabilities in our times*. Durham and London: Duke University Press.

Tan, K.L., and Lim, C.K., 2017. Digital heritage gamification: an augmented-virtual walkthrough to learn and explore tangible cultural heritage. *Journal of Telecommunication, Electronic and Computer Engineering*, 9 (2), 125–129.

Tenreiro, F., 1961. *A Ilha de São tomé*. Lisbon: Ministério do Ultramar - Memórias da Junta de Investigações do Ultramar.

Tlostanova, M.V., and Mignolo, W., 2012. *Learning to unlearn: decolonial reflections from eurasia and the Americas*. Columbus, OH: Ohio State University Press.

Tschumi, B., 1996. *Architecture and disjunction*. 3rd ed. Cambridge MA: MIT P.

UNCTAD, 2019. *Digital economy report* [English] – value creation and capture: implications for developing countries [online]. Available from: https://unctad.org/webflyer/digital-economy-report-2019 [Accessed 7 August 2021].

UNESCO, 2003. *Convention for the safeguarding of the intangible cultural heritage* [online]. Available from: https://ich.unesco.org/en/convention [Accessed 7 August 2021].

UNESCO, 2020. *Museums around the world in the face of COVID-19*. Available from: https://unesdoc.unesco.org/ark:/48223/pf0000376729_eng [Accessed 7 August 2021].

van den Hoven, J.E. Vermaas, P., and van de Poel, I., eds., 2015. *Handbook of ethics, values, and technological design. Sources, theory, values and application domains*. Dordrecht: Springer.

van Roosmalen, P.K.M., 2013. Confronting built heritage: shifting perspectives on colonial architecture in Indonesia. *ABE Journal*, 3 (3), 1–26.

Vayanou, M., Ioannidis, Y., Loumos, G., Sidiropoulou, O., and Kargas, A., 2019. Designing performative, gamified cultural experiences for groups. In: Extended Abstracts of the 2019 CHI Conference on Human Factors in Computing Systems, New York, NY, USA: ACM, 1–6.

Vera, F., and Sánchez, J.A., 2016. A model for in-situ augmented reality content creation based on storytelling and gamification. In: Proceedings of the 6th Mexican Conference on Human-Computer Interaction. New York, NY, USA: ACM, 39–42.

Vosloo, S., 2018, *Guidelines. Designing inclusive digital solutions and developing digital skills. UNESCO.* [online]. Available from: http://bibliotecas.dglab.gov.pt/pt/Documents/GuidlinesServDigInclusivos.pdf [Accessed 7 August 2021].

4 The #iziTRAVELSicilia project: participatory digital storytelling for inclusive and co-creative processes regarding cultural heritage

Elisa Bonacini

Introduction

This chapter describes the co-creative and participatory digital approach carried out in Sicily through a specific case study named #iziTRAVELSicilia project, developed on the global platform izi.TRAVEL,[1] which involved local heritage communities in the democratic and inclusive process of co-production and dissemination of a digital cultural heritage (Bonacini 2017).

First, the chapter presents some examples and approaches of participatory culture digital storytelling and virtual platforms to underline the role they could have as regards participation and inclusion in digital cultural processes. The chapter describes the #iziTRAVELSicilia project, which, since May 2016, has explored digital participatory, crowdsourced, and inclusive strategies with the aim of enabling cultural institutions to co-create museum audio-guides for publication and city audio-tours within a large regional-scale process. This has been achieved thanks to the local involvement of public institutions, schools, universities, and individuals, in line with the principles of the *Convention on the Value of Cultural Heritage for Society*, known as the *Faro Convention* (2005). Local "heritage communities" were involved; as defined by the art. 2b "a heritage community consists of people who value specific aspects of cultural heritage which they wish, within the framework of public action, to sustain and transmit to future generations" (Zagato 2015).

The project soon transformed into a participatory process, involving more than 4,000 locals as "digital Ciceroni": they came from different Sicilian "heritage communities", ranging from students to scholars and museum curators. Since May 2016, about 350 audio-guides have been created.

In particular, many projects were carried out with pupils and students from schools and universities. At the primary and secondary school level, some pupils who had specific learning difficulties such as selective mutism and Down syndrome or cognitive disturbances were involved. In this chapter, specific guidelines and recommendations are available as well as methodological suggestions on how to use this free digital tool.

DOI: 10.4324/9781003277606-4

Participatory culture and digital storytelling: a literature review

According to the definition of cultural democracy (Evrard 1997), democratic participation in culture is based on three activities:

- Promoting the right to culture for everyone;
- Encouraging pro-active participation in local cultural life;
- Making cultural resources and contents related to heritage accessible to everyone.

Cultural engagement can be considered as part of *lifelong learning* and education, so encouraging the development of social, civil, and cultural awareness by enabling individuals to be more active citizens (List *et al.* 2017) and, according to the principles expressed by the Arts. 4a and 4b of the Faro Convention, have a more responsible attitude towards their heritage and its transmission to new generations (Zagato 2015). About 15 years have passed since Henry Jenkins coined the term *Participatory culture* (Jenkins 2006). Thanks to the growing diffusion of the web and digital communication tools including blogs, wikis, and social media, participatory culture and connected activities have grown in a global way, based on informal and conversational online communities, characterised by strong social connections, and focused on creating or participating in co-creating new content (Hellin-Hobbs 2010). New communities and a new social system have arisen, based on the participation and collaboration of users who share common interests and on the socio-cultural and emotional ramifications of producing, sharing and disseminating knowledge (Giaccardi 2012, Drotner and Schrøder 2014). Almost a decade has passed too since Nina Simon's milestone theorised on the *Participatory Museum* (2010) and on the role that new technologies and social media play, not only in the management of museums and in communication, but also in the relationship between museums, collections, and the public.

Thanks to global digital transformation, an era full of promises was inaugurated (prompting active citizenship, conscious consumption, widespread creativity, collective intelligence, and exchange of shared knowledge), which Jenkins defined *Participatory Age* and which, many years later, we can partly consider a fulfilled promise: participatory processes from civil society are now difficult to reverse. This bottom-up process has created a profound innovation in cultural communication, becoming bidirectional, dialogic, and participatory, aimed no longer at the public but at various categories of stakeholders who are increasingly interested not only in finding mere cultural information, but also in real stories and narratives (Kidd 2016, Black 2020). Within this framework, the *Faro Convention*, we have an innovative and democratic tool for facing cultural and social challenges, because it has definitively established that knowledge and use of heritage have the same value as all the other Human Rights and are part of the citizen's right to participate in cultural life (Zagato 2015, Pavan-Woolfe and Pinton 2019).

The *Faro Convention*'s great revolution concerns the introduction of the concept of *heritage community*, explained in the Introduction. In this way, cultural heritage and cultural participation define communities' identities and contribute to the social, cultural, and economic development of communities. People who are engaged in cultural activities are thus able to increase their own cultural and informational capacity and capital, which helps define their identity.

Therefore, heritage communities are called upon to cooperate in order to promote wide participation in the preservation and enhancement of the cultural heritage: it has already been proven that life quality, social cohesion and inclusion culture-based creativity, knowledge circulation and innovation, could all be improved by sharing cultural heritage, and so build up identity communities (Sandell and Nightingale 2012). Furthermore, scholars agree that, within the participatory model, culture-based creativity and crowdsourcing could be considered a strong example of a heritage communities building process. A specific participatory practice, from which the concept of co-creative User-Generated Content (UGC) emerges, is digital storytelling, considered "the modern way of telling stories, combining multimedia features" (Brouillard *et al.* 2015, p. 9), based on the use of digital tools.

Storytelling, in fact, has had widespread success in every field, transcending borders and different fields of application, to the point we can talk of a real storytelling revival and a narrative age (Salmon 2008). In the field of cultural communication, storytelling serves to attract users with stories that make cultural heritage attractive, creating an emotional approach and stimulating interest. It is no coincidence, therefore, that among the most innovative communication and interaction options between a cultural institution and its users there is digital storytelling, intended as a tool for democratising cultural content through specific languages (Lambert 2013, Handler Miller 2020), and a great trend in the cultural heritage domain, by facilitating the creation of UGC and participatory and crowdsourced approaches thanks to digital platforms and applications (Roued-Cunliffe and Copeland 2017, Hetland *et al.* 2020).

In general, digital storytelling can provide a direct impact on cultural institutions by enabling local museums and cultural sites to better develop communication and audience engagement, and by creating new cultural, social, and economic values. It has an indirect impact on visitors by creating new experiences with art collections and giving more engaging information, while creating a stronger sense of awareness and belonging for local communities. Scholars, in fact, recognise the value of cultural co-creation in promoting local heritage, and social integration and cohesion for local heritage communities (Bakhshi and Throsby 2012).

Thanks to personal evidence-based observations during six years of projects and to a transdisciplinary approach, the writer has had confirmation of the great potential of digital participatory storytelling, in line with other scholars' theories about this approach in community-building heritage processes (Ridge 2014, Keskin *et al.* 2016). This approach can give new life and a new meaning to culture and heritage thanks to developing a stronger sense of inclusion, and mutual synergies (Bonacini 2017), in line also with its increasing role in other specific contexts, such as long-term cultural audience development and audience engagement strategies (Bonacini *et al.* 2019), education (Bonacini 2021, Bonacini and Marangon 2021), and tourism (Bonacini and Giaccone 2019). People involved in participatory digital storytelling processes, and especially students, develop in the meantime a greater sense of responsibility, because they understand they are helping institutions whether they have strategies or not. In fact, many local institutions do not have strategies at all, for cultural involvement and digital enhancement.

Therefore, for museums and contemporary cultural institutions, digital storytelling is the perfect communication and participation technique to exploit their educational and inclusive vocation in an increasingly interactive, engaging, and co-creative way. However, it is still an emergent practice because it is closely linked to the evolution of new technologies, which continue to change not only forms and ways of cultural communication (Handler Miller 2020), but also the relationship between the public and culture itself (Keskin *et al.* 2016, Dunford and Jenkins 2017).

Storytelling as a didactic practice in approaching culture

In the field of educational and cultural mediation, storytelling is not just a technique for knowledge transmission, but an educational methodology based on the use of the narrative technique, exploited in its potential as a cognitive resource and social glue: stories have been considered the favourite tools for building community identity, thanks to the co-construction of social stories (Dunbar 2014), collective memories (Coman *et al.* 2009), or the preservation of a group and its culture in general (Wertsch 2002). The evolution of the museum's educational function in recent decades and the pedagogical rediscovery of the effectiveness of narratives in knowledge transmission have both favoured the transformation of storytelling turning it into an educational methodology, facilitating community identity building, by developing forms of life-long learning (Maraffi and Sacerdoti 2018) and learning by doing (Cuzzolin 2019).

One of the main challenges in the education field with new technologies is searching for new ways and places in which a new community dimension in the educational process could be created and digital storytelling is one of the most congenial learning tools for the new generations (Maraffi and Sacerdoti 2018). In contemporary teaching, technologies need to be considered a tool which enhances the knowledge experience, but without replacing it: *teaching by using technologies* and not teaching about technologies (Cuzzolin 2019). The use of digital technologies and new interactive forms of learning creates a positive appreciation of the learning process, facilitating innovative, flexible and unconventional forms of transmission, and knowledge re-processing and co-constructing (Benassi and Mosa 2019, Pizzato 2019), in particular concerning art, culture, and museums (Luigini and Panciroli 2018).

Over the last 15 years, participatory digital storytelling projects and methodologies have multiplied, developing real strategies for the direct involvement of users in works of artistic production. The process has thus become co-creative and pro-active, able to deeply affect the relationship with the public, favouring involvement, participation, two-way communication, and, finally, that sense of belonging to a community. In the meantime, the museum itself assumes a new role, from container of objects to holder of stories (Beale 2011) and finally to the "museum of connection" model, in which stories are the facilitators of digital and physical communication, which is participatory, co-creative, and bidirectional (Bonacini 2020).

Before introducing the benefits of a didactic cultural approach with digital storytelling, it is necessary to clarify the main functions of cultural storytelling. The functions identified in the political (Moroni 2017)[2] and management fields (Salmon 2008),[3] according to the writer can be amalgamated, so covering the marketing (Mathews and Wacker 2007),[4] evolutionary psychology (Gottschall 2013),[5] and cognitive definitions (Bietti *et al.* 2019).[6] Therefore, all the functions can be readapted in the eight functions of cultural storytelling (Bonacini 2020):

- *Community function*: it fosters the construction of a community sense;
- *Referential function*: it promotes the transmission of knowledge;
- *Empathic function*: it enhances emotion and involvement;
- *Mnestic function*: it creates the transmission of individual and collective memories' between generations;
- *Identity function*: it promotes identity construction;
- *Value function*: it transmits values;
- *"Springboard" function*: it helps people to understand what may happen in the future by reading what happened in the past;
- *Connective function*: it fosters the connection between institutions and heritage, individuals, and collectivities.

The first seven functions can be activated only when an emotional connection is created and this can only happen by abandoning the old methods of knowledge transmission, which are didactic and self-referentiality based. Then, by finding suitable language and arguments which arouse willingness to listen, the enjoyment of cultural content can begin. In this way, we can say that the connective function is the umbrella function, encompassing the others.

According to the *PoliCultura* digital storytelling platform for schools (Di Blas 2016), there are four kinds of benefits (depending on various factors including the initial situation of the class, the age of the students and the level of autonomy, the pedagogical approach and the objectives of the teacher, etc.), which arise from teaching with digital storytelling, which can be connected to the cited functions and be resumed as[7]:

- *Cognitive benefits*: better understanding of the subject matter, ability to grasp relationships, ability to synthesise, to understand connections and order between things and facts;
- *Relational benefits*: ability to work in a group, better relationship with peers and teachers, ability to negotiate and to apply specific model behaviours;
- *Motivational benefits*: great involvement in specific activities, greater involvement in school activities in general, in building an individual awareness within their own community, sense of belonging;
- *Benefits related to skills*: ability to use technologies to carry out educational tasks, ability to write texts for multimedia, ability to retouch audio and images, ability to search for information, images, materials on the net, ability to simplify and to clarify.

Digital storytelling platforms as a tool for participation and inclusion

Participatory platforms are gaining ground in social sectors like culture, sociology, education (Ciasullo *et al.* 2016) and tourism (Fernandez Vaz *et al.* 2018, Giaccone and Bonacini 2019). Accordingly, it is important to explore the potential of digital participatory storytelling platforms as tools to enhance local cultural heritage by engaging local heritage communities.

The role of storytelling platforms is significant but pushing people towards emotional and creative involvement in the co-creation and sharing of cultural content, knowledge, and narratives is even more significant, from a social and inclusive point of view. There are many digital tools and technologies capable of giving a voice to cultural heritage whether online, e.g., virtual museums, participatory and geo-social tagging digital storytelling projects, or in situ, e.g., multimedia exhibitions or customised mobile applications. There are some examples of participatory platforms, linked to crowdsourcing and, therefore, open to collaboration, with users sharing their stories. However, we must distinguish between two kinds of platforms: those that allow active user participation in the process of collecting stories or other digital content, i.e., have a content upload section or a content management system which allows this; and platforms that display content online which have been crowdsourced, collected without allowing users to upload themselves and which, therefore, are characterised by a strong curatorial aspect.

Some examples could be useful to compare how digital storytelling has been used in the past and how it is used today to encourage participation and inclusion, with the main goal of building identity processes. Participatory digital storytelling is used more for collecting and sharing memories or experiences of life than for providing inclusive access to a tangible cultural heritage. In most cases, since the great *Museu de Pessoa* Brazilian project[8] (1991), digital storytelling projects have been more akin to ethnographic documentation, dealing with collecting specific practices or memories, which become forms of digital documentation of intangible cultural heritage and forms of co-construction and sharing of collective stories. Their methodology, called *Social Memory Technology*, was based for years on three fundamental phases in the individual or collective storytelling construction: building, organising, and socialising through stories. The main benefits of the project immediately included dialogue and interaction. In 2006, the virtual museum coordinators were involved by Joe Lambert's group from the Centre for Digital Storytelling in San Francisco in the adoption of the Lambertian method of the *Story Circle* in its modalities of co-creation and collaborative co-production of video products, designing the *One Million Youth Life Stories project* together (2006–2008), so demonstrating how digital storytelling was able to affect the quality of life of young Brazilians, to the point of recognising, in the Virtual Museum, an organisation of public interest for civil society, and generating twin projects also elsewhere (Misorelli 2017).

Active since 2002, the *9–11 Digital Archive*[9] collects thousands of documents, photos, images, videos, and stories of Americans who want to help preserve the memory of the attacks on the World Trade Centre in New York, Virginia, and Pennsylvania. The Archive was soon included among the permanent digital collections of the Library of Congress and counts the Smithsonian Institute among its partners, thus guaranteeing the long-term digital maintenance of the platform, with its specific mnestic, identity, values, and educative purposes (Farinosi and Micalizzi 2016). The collections are diversified, ranging from digital projects carried out by individuals, to those by the Library of Congress and the Smithsonian institution. This project favoured the construction of collective sensemaking in relation to a story which became global, due to the strong emotional, social, and political impact that it may have had on a global scale.

One example of digital storytelling used for inclusion approaches to digital content is *The Pararchive Project*[10] (whose full name is *Pararchive: Open Access Community Storytelling and the Digital Archive*) funded by the UK Arts and Humanities Research Council (2013–2016). Through collaborative storytelling workshops and the reuse of available digital archives (such as the BBC, the British Library, the Europeana and the European digital library archives), the Pararchive project aims to make these digital resources available to specific community groups (minorities such as former miners, retired police officers, women's groups, local history groups, political activists etc.), to reuse and reinterpret their content, especially as regards historical facts and events, so that they can create their own "parallel" archive of stories, and thus challenge the official version, thanks to a new construction of identity and sensemaking. *Nantes Patrimonia*[11] is a great digital storytelling project, launched in May 2019 aimed at promoting local cultural heritage by involving heritage communities (and among them also minorities and people living in disadvantaged neighbourhoods), according to the principles of the Faro Convention. The most varied expressions of the tangible and intangible cultural heritage of the French city are collected; the platform is full of articles, galleries, and testimonies, and is open to the contributions of its citizens, who are called upon to join the initiative to promote their city by co-building their stories, providing testimonies or even just offering anecdotes. In Italy, a best practice for inclusion and interculturality in approaching cultural heritage is the *Patrimonio e Intercultura*[12] website of the ISMU Foundation (Initiatives and Studies on Multi-ethnicity in Milan), which aims to disseminate good practices implemented on a national scale by means of the co-narration of cultural heritage through forms of intercultural narration, through video storytelling, blogging, and podcasting content.

The #iziTRAVELSicilia participatory project

The #iziTRAVELSicilia project can be considered a socially and culturally sustainable heritage action where cultural institutions are able to create a culture of participation around their physical collections to co-create new digital content. Specifically, this chapter will now show how participatory methods and storytelling techniques have been used in Sicily (Italy) to co-create audio guides for museums and audios for city tours, by transforming people into digital storytellers (Bonacini 2017). In addition, in the next paragraph, the methodology adopted when teaching pupils with learning difficulties is described.

"Sicilia Beni Culturali" on izi.TRAVEL was an annual research project at the University of Catania underwritten by izi.TRAVEL itself in its first year, launched in May 2016 under a cooperative agreement between the Department of Cultural Heritage and Sicilian Identity and the University of Catania. Well-known soon as #iziTRAVELSicilia, as it was launched on social media, the project transformed into a real participatory process, existing since May 2017 without any additional external funding, and based almost entirely on the work of the writer, who voluntarily offered her expertise to train museum staff or students of all levels, through single local projects. The project's primary goal was to use izi.TRAVEL as a tool to improve digital content for cultural heritage promotion, so filling the well-documented (and tragic) gap of Sicilian cultural heritage communication online (Bonacini 2012). In fact, according to this previous analysis, which has not really evolved in the meantime (neither online nor via mobile applications), many Sicilian museums do not even have a website and, until the beginning of the project, almost no Sicilian museum had published their online collections. The second aim was to establish best practices for participating in and co-creating digital cultural content around museums and institutions by involving local people and by strengthening synergies between them and local institutions. Wider cultural participation, a sense of citizenship, and social cohesion developed by promoting new bottom-up relationships between people and their heritage, in line with the concept both of heritage communities highlighted by the Faro Convention and of the model of crowdsourced participation.

A large-scale regional project was launched in May 2016 which aimed to co-create cultural audio guides under a single regional-level coordinator, represented by the author. At the beginning of the project, seven guides existed. Convinced that the opportunity of the annual grant should be offered as widely as possible to the whole of Sicily, the writer involved all the heritage communities willing to join the project (and not only those under the control of the Regional Department of Cultural Heritage with its local regional museums and its Superintendencies, the first partner of the project): the Regional Department of Tourism with local tourist offices, municipalities, private museums, varied institutions, museum networks, dioceses and churches, associations, cultural and tour operators, primary and high schools with laboratories and workshops, the Universities of Catania and Palermo with university and post-university projects, and all those working on undergraduate, graduate, or doctoral theses.

Simply joining the project required enthusiasm, because of the lack of existing regional top-down strategies and tools for digital cultural dissemination: both the institutions and common people felt the need to do something about it and this is the real reason why this project was soon transformed into a spontaneous participatory process. On the one hand, local heritage communities and stakeholders thus contributed to strengthening the local identity and sense of belonging to a territory; on the other hand, the motivation to enhance a heritage was encouraged. A bottom-up, widely disseminated and participatory process guaranteed the common right to cultural heritage, as the Faro Convention requires. Together, the participants overcame the concept of heritage ownership (normally assumed when talking about regional heritage, civic heritage, diocesan heritage, private heritage, and so on), embracing instead the concept of a *common cultural heritage*. With support and coordination, a network of storytellers was created: more than 4,000 people were involved, becoming storytellers of their own heritage, from primary school to high school children and university students and to the museum curators and managers themselves.

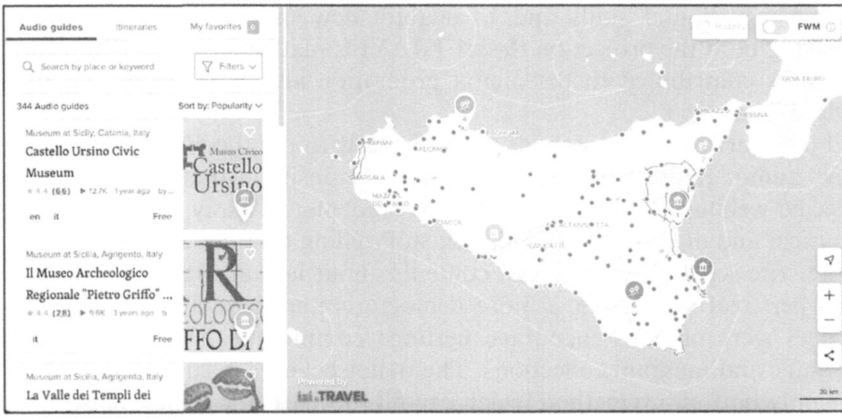

Figure 4.1 More than 340 published museums audio guides and audio tours in Sicily (courtesy by izi.TRAVEL).

As shown in Figure 4.1, after about 5 years, izi.TRAVEL audio guides in Sicily total more than 340, among them 139 sites and museums guides, 4 temporary exhibitions and 203 itineraries, out of 2,300 total audio guides available in Italian on the entire platform. As shown in Figure 4.2, Sicily accounts for roughly 2,500 tourist attractions (TA) of the 15,000 Italian projects on the platform (out of a total of more than 200,000). Numerous projects were carried out with primary and high schools. Projects with Sicilian high schools were included within the ministerial programme entitled *Alternanza Scuola Lavoro* (School-Work Alternation) and realised in collaboration with local authorities (municipalities,

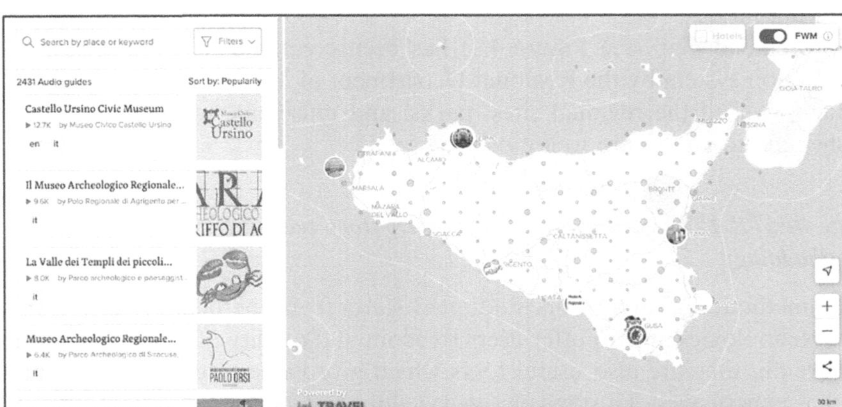

Figure 4.2 More than 2,400 tourist geolocated attractions (TA) freely available in the free walking mode (courtesy by izi.TRAVEL).

associations, museums, etc.). After training workshops, which aimed to create new digital skills and to acquire new narratives, and after explaining both the project on the izi.TRAVEL platform and its CMS, local students contributed to the digital promotion and enhancement of their cultural heritage.

First, participatory methods (teaching how to use the platform to create new audio guide projects, within specific onsite workshops or within specific webinars to trainees, including students, in many cases by mixing physical and digital works) and then storytelling techniques (teaching how to rewrite scientific and official contents about heritage in a more suasive and personal style, with a more democratic and accessible kind of language) were used to encourage heritage communities to promote local heritage and museum collections. The writer believes participation may be the only bottom-up method which can fill this lack of a digital presence in the communication of the Sicilian cultural heritage and that the use of storytelling techniques may be the only way to guarantee a real cognitive accessibility to this cultural content for all. In fact, the participants were encouraged to co-create and share cultural content and their knowledge or narratives through storytelling and creativity, providing original narratives, in an appealing style, with photos, videos and audio so as to make both the contents and the stories as attractive as possible. All authorities that published an audio guide certified all the content produced. People who contributed to the creation of audio guides are credited by name in the content summaries and on the platform. By actively participating in the project in a bottom-up way, they transformed themselves into hackable communities by having contributed to making their own cultural heritage and territories accessible: in fact, the digital content of each audio tour has been correctly located on Google maps, so providing online GPS access to hundreds of POIs, through the izi.TRAVEL app free walking mode.

A detailed map (see Figure 4.3) has been created as a cross-linking information system by the Regional Department of Tourism with Google My Map, with all the regional sites, parks, and museums, where all the published audio guides are well indicated.

The #iziTRAVELSicilia case: the participatory teaching methodology

The methodological approach adopted starts from the belief that not only are technologies able to offer users freedom and quality of information but, above all, they are also useful tools which give value to cultural and emotional experiences. Through the storytelling approach, they allow users to build their own "human experience" and understand their cultural heritage and the historical-social process that governed it. In all the produced audio guides, an effort was made to develop stories in a narrative way, by

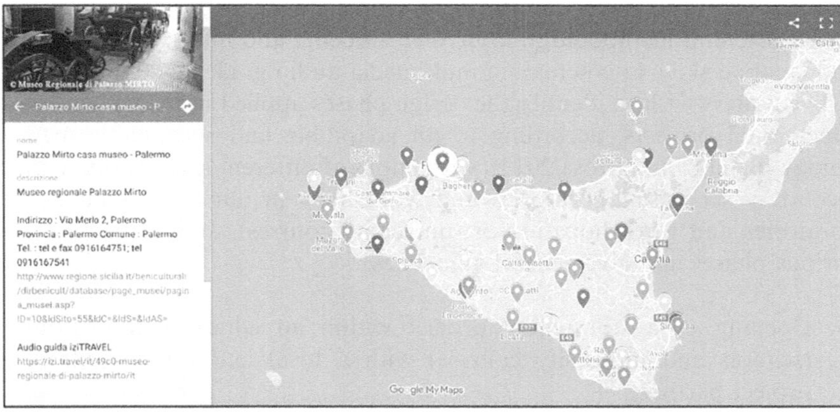

Figure 4.3 Sicilian Regional Museums and sites map.

expressing the scientific content simply and clearly. In any case, the validity, reliability, and authorship of the content have always had precedence over the story itself.

Thanks to this innovative teaching practice, a large number of audio guides have been produced and shared as the final result of the museum and heritage education projects which were carried out by regional schools, universities, and postgraduate laboratory projects, and on doctorates in collaboration with the Universities of Catania, Palermo, Macerata, and RomaTre. The protagonists of most of these projects were the students, the tutor teachers, the external cultural mediator, and the cultural institutions' partners. In some cases, the projects were carried out by teachers and students, without involving the mediator or specific partners.

In the specific case of the regional-scale project #iziTRAVELSicilia, a fundamental figure is the external cultural mediator (the writer) who takes on the role of the cultural creative designer (Pizzato 2019), an expert not only on this digital tool but also on participatory storytelling processes, which aim at achieving both educational goals and multimedia products.

After being approved, the audio guides were published on izi.TRAVEL, by the institutional profile partners (superintendencies, museums, museum networks, dioceses, municipalities, foundations, etc.), who are the real custodians of historical, artistic, archaeological, and naturalistic knowledge, or on the profiles of the institutions which developed the project (schools, local tourist entities, cultural and tourist local or regional associations). The approval of content by the partners has always been essential to ensure their authorship. The projects carried out with the students pursue the main objective of ensuring inclusive and equitable quality education and promoting lifelong learning opportunities for all, as indicated by the key actions of the UE 2030 Agenda (Maraffi and Sacerdoti 2018). The essential purpose of these educational projects, based on co-creative and participatory face-to-face and online class workshops (Benassi and Mosa 2019), was to develop a mixed teaching methodology to involve students and improve their digital and creative skills in co-creating multimedia audio guides.

The writers wish to identify the design phases applied in these co-creative educational projects, according to an adaptable and sustainable methodology (Benassi and Mosa 2019), with pupils of different levels (primary and secondary schools; laboratories and workshops in university courses; laboratories and workshops in post-university courses), and so indicate the various phases and give general guidelines:

1 Opening of a storytelling project within an educational institution (schools and university courses) with a local cultural institution as project partner;
2 Identification of the cultural heritage (a museum collection, a tradition, a selection of points of interest in a city) to be enhanced by the project;
3 Acquisition of scientific documentation given by the partner (brochures, catalogues, informative texts, didactic panels);
4 Co-creative planning of museum audio guides and audio tours;
5 Assignment of the students' tasks, according to the selected objects/places to be described;
6 Direct and guided experience of the places;
7 Digital documentation acquisition (photos, videos, etc.) through student's personal mobile devices (smartphones, tablets);
8 Creative re-elaboration of the scientific material provided and/or found by the students, on a digital writing software (Word, Open Word);
9 Revision of the descriptions by teachers and the external mediator;
10 Approval by the institutions partner of the project;
11 Uploading of textual, photo, and video contents on the izi.TRAVEL CMS platform and indication of credits;
12 Linking to other internal and external online resources on the CMS platform;
13 Voiceover of textual contents through mobile or pc applications (at school or at home);
14 Uploading of the voiceover on the CMS platform;
15 Final approval of the created audio guide;
16 Publication on the izi.TRAVEL platform and its application of the produced audio guide;
17 Dissemination through social media platforms and mobile applications (Messenger, WhatsApp etc.).

Each of those phases was based on the students' age, their learning abilities, the specific cultural projects, and the institutional collaborations, so as to activate informal learning environments, rooted in the collaboration and active interaction of all the participants. Once the topic to be narrated has been identified (collections, archaeological or historical itineraries, traditions, etc.), the institutional partner gives the scientific and/or informative material from which certified information can be obtained. The digital and creative skills acquired by the students varied according to their age and their learning capabilities (and in some cases their difficulties).

In general, pupils from primary (four to five children) and middle schools (two to three children) worked in groups to write down their stories to develop an aptitude for teamwork: during one or more guided tours of the places, they are invited to create their own photo documentation through their parents' devices (primary schools, where children were trained how to take pictures) or their own mobile devices (middle schools). Both were guided in the production of the content; they became familiar with writing platforms, with the production and selection of images, and with the connection between images and descriptions. They were able to create their own voiceovers of the texts (for primary schools, through the teachers', the mediator's, or the parents' home devices; for middle schools through their own devices). In some cases, a specific recording studio at school was used. During the content creation, students from middle school were trained to obtain information and deepen their knowledge through online searches. Finally, they participated in the uploading phase on the CMS platform, created by the teachers or the cultural mediator, until the final publication of their multimedia products; QR codes were created and printed, so as to be able to show them to their parents and friends.

In the case of students from high schools, they worked individually on their stories to develop their responsibility towards a collective and shared project; they were trained in online research and guided to correctly distinguish good and bad information online; in some cases, helped by teachers, they mounted videos in a documentary style. For these three main targeted groups, a previous well-established storytelling project was defined from the very beginning together with partner institutions. The difference between the previous groups and the university and post-university workshops lies in the freedom to create their own project, intended as a real "cultural project" made by a single student or little groups of two to three students (in some cases they created "theatrical" projects, with an original script, interpreting historical or mythical characters). They co-designed the organisation of the audio guides, producing their content for the audio guides in a more individual and less choral way, dividing the creative and productive tasks among themselves to individually develop their aptitude for teamwork and skills in the field of cultural and tourist planning; they were invited to discover places by themselves and to produce their photos and video documentation.

In the case of high school pupils and university students, they were both invited to analyse and re-elaborate the official scientific content in a more creative and narrative style; once the textual content had been corrected and validated, they directly uploaded them online during the classroom workshops or at home, by registering their credentials (personal email and password) on the izi.TRAVEL CMS platform; they were trained to create the correct credits for images downloaded from the web and to search and upload their own videos or videos specifically identified on YouTube; they were trained to transform the normal written text into a hypertextual one, by linking to other interesting online resources; they personally published their multimedia products; they were invited to share them on their social media profiles and on WhatsApp.

After the re-elaboration process of scientific and/or didactic content provided by the cultural institutions, the publication of new content in friendly, narrative language was authorised only after a final verification and revision by the institutions themselves. The story, therefore, maintains a balance between scientific knowledge on the one hand and the democratisation of knowledge and ad hoc languages on the other; this simplification did not lead to the trivialisation of terminology and scientific content.

While the audio guides produced within school projects are in any case choral products of an entire class or interclass, in which learning times, methods and difficulties were respected and for which, however, the credits relating to the contribution of each student are always indicated (under every page of the text, including voiceover authorship), the audio guides published within university and post-university workshops and laboratories are, instead, multimedia products of the students' talents; so far, their authorship is always recognised in the summary of the audio guides. There were no differences in the cases of workshops where students with cognitive or other problems participated. For group work, students with difficulties were placed in groups where there were other students they were already on good terms with to facilitate collaborative work; these schoolmates thus helped and supported their classmates with disabilities, under the observation and coordination of adults. The students with disabilities participated in the drafting of the texts as well as in the creation of the photos and, when they themselves asked for it, they recorded the text, so feeling part of the common project. For the tasks students worked individually on, the student with disabilities was supported while researching, drafting, and rewriting the texts, as well as during other operations, up to the production of the voiceover and the loading of the content produced on the platform and its final publication.

The works produced have always been perceived, by all the students at any level, as "choral projects" in which one participated as a team and as individuals; the schools, the partners and those who worked on the projects disseminated them on their own channels and/or through the display of special posters, just as the students did, with enthusiasm. Where the projects ended with public presentations, parents were also involved, so recognising the great value of what their children produced. In the cases of older students, their works could be followed also on Telegram or WhatsApp groups if they needed support or any clarification on how to carry out the project, produce or verify the voiceovers, or share content within the group. In many cases, the students preferred to make the voiceovers at home (sending them to WhatsApp for verification and validation), rather than during the laboratory (as they had to find an acoustically non-invasive environment for recording). In many cases, students themselves asked to redo the voiceover, understanding the need for a qualitatively optimal product, thus revealing they had acquired an individual responsibility towards a collective product.

The #iziTRAVELSicilia case: examples of an inclusive approach and benefits

The first project to be mentioned, for its high educational level and its inclusiveness, is that of the audio guides produced by the pupils of the "Lombardo Radice – Pappalardo" Institute of Castelvetrano (Trapani), as part of an educational project carried out in collaboration with the Archaeological Park of Selinunte and Cave di Cusa. Pupils from third, fourth, and fifth classes of primary school produced the audio guide *The Temples and the Metopes – Children's Guide,*[13] while all the classes of the middle school created the two audio tours *The little Selinuntini recount (the ancient Selinunte)*[14] and *The little stonemasons recount the Cave of Cusa.*[15] At the end of each text or point of interest, the guides are equipped with quizzes to test the user's acquired learning. 66 classes were involved, for a total of about 900 children coordinated and assisted by over 50 teachers, all trained by the central coordinator with a specific workshop on storytelling techniques and the use of the izi.TRAVEL platform and the CMS. The three audio guides consist of a total of 66 sheets, with 66 different voices, a different child for each class. The voice of a little girl should be mentioned, as it exemplifies inclusiveness: despite suffering from selective mutism, she still wanted to participate, recording at home (instead of in the school's recording studio, as the others did). Introducing themselves as children of ancient Selinunte, the children of Castelvetrano told their peers about the cultural heritage of their city and the nearby quarries of Cusa, in simple language and through the technique of narrative storytelling.

A real case of a long-term strategy used on participatory and inclusive projects on izi.TRAVEL is the audio guide of the *Ursino Castle Civic Museum*[16] in Catania, where the museum staff, from 2016, coordinated hundreds of students as "digital Ciceroni" for more than three years; these students implemented the audio guides of the museum and its collections in Italian and English. This is a perfect example of how the activities of a museum have quickly adapted according to a strategic plan of communication and enhancement of the collections. The izi.TRAVEL museum audio guide is offered at the entrance of the Castle as the official digital audio guide. It has more than 100 texts online, translated into English. The project has continued until now and many other texts will be created (Bonacini *et al.* 2019).

Numerous classes of students have alternated over the years in the project, building portions of the story of the audio guide. Among them, there have been some cases of students who revealed some learning difficulties, often also when reading the texts aloud. It was decided not to leave anyone behind, allowing each student to participate in the creative project according to their potential. The emotional drive to be part of a community project, together with their peers, was the motivation for these students to test themselves, trying to improve where they went wrong. All the pupils involved in the project, without any difference, recount their common cultural heritage with the same dignity and the same seriousness that the "role" of a digital storyteller entails. Pupils with learning problems or disabilities were helped, by the tutor, by the teachers or by their classmates, in the re-elaboration of the contents entrusted to them, and all were able to produce what was requested. The same motivation was found in a couple of cases when pupils suffered from Down Syndrome: the motivational drive to create, like the others, a product in which they all felt like protagonists was the real incentive that allowed them to produce a qualitatively appreciable job.

These specific inclusive cases, the whole #iziTRAVELSicilia project, and the considerations regarding the eight functions of storytelling indicate that the benefits that these functions can have in teaching and especially within participatory storytelling projects, can be summed up as:

- Cognitive benefits derive from the *referential* (since this function favours the transmission of knowledge, developing narrative skills of a descriptive type), *mnestic* (since this function develops on the one hand narrative skills in the transmission of individual and collective memories, favouring memory), *"springboard"* (since this function develops the sense of awareness of the meaning of historical events) and *connective* (since this function develops the sense of belonging to a community that is also identified in its own material cultural heritage and intangible);
- Relational benefits derive from the *community* (since this function develops the sense of belonging to a community – that of students and teachers – with the same planning), *identity* (since this function favours the development of the sense of belonging to a community which wants to promote its own identity) and *values* (since this function favours the development of the sense of belonging to a community with the same values) functions;
- The motivational benefits derive from the *empathic* function (which, on the one hand, arouses emotionality and promotes involvement, on the other helps to develop evocative narrative skills);
- The benefits related to skills do not derive from a specific function of storytelling in general but are directly connected to those forms of digital storytelling, produced with new technologies.

izi.TRAVEL: a participatory tool for digital storytelling

Founded in Holland in 2011 and launched as a start-up in 2013, with reference to the platform content diffusion (9M monthly usage; 110M yearly usage) and the high number of published audio guides (+15.000), today izi.TRAVEL is one of the leading digital storytelling platforms, with global, multilingual, open, bottom-up and free main features. The cost-free app, installed 5.1 million times, is available on the Apple App, Google Play, and Windows Phone stores, with destinations in more than 60 languages and in more than 120 countries.

Founded to help heritage and tourist institutions bring their stories to life, it represents a flexible, intuitive, and friendly digital key tool not only for visits on the spot and for itinerary planning, but also for institutions, associations and individuals, since it offers them the opportunity to upload and manage self-generated content: texts, photos, videos, audios, or sound recordings through its web-based Content Management System. Based on the principles of participatory culture, through the democratisation of cultural content and languages, creativity and storytelling, thanks to being cost-free – both for the content producer and for the user, izi.TRAVEL is also a digital key tool: it offers institutions the opportunity to upload and manage self-generated content to enhance on-site visits or to facilitate itinerary planning. In this way, it plays a great key role in democratisation and the promotion of culture and territories, allowing people to discover culture and tourist places via the web platform and via the izi.TRAVEL general app, available from the main app stores.

Among the most innovative elements, the izi.TRAVEL platform and app allow destinations to be discovered in multiple ways: the user can discover destinations during pre-fruition and post-fruition phases, on-site, on the web and via the app, by GPS activation, by geolocating on Google Maps, by scanning QR codes, and so reach a destination, discover new information about places, and select all audio guides or points of interest mapped on Google.

This way, people can discover cultural sites and stories in the right location using their smartphones. By downloading audio guides in advance, they can be used in offline mode. Audio guides and audio tours can offer people four types of media content: audio, text, video, and photographs. In the mobile app, a free walking mode is automatically activated by GPS and people can walk around and listen to the stories while doing so. Content can be bookmarked and synchronised on a specific section of the app. From the "Scan QR" section, users can directly enjoy the content. The app is directly connected with the major social networks, and users can share content on Facebook, Twitter, or via email or leave rating feedback and comments.

As regards the content provider, izi.TRAVEL offers CPs the opportunity to easily create a multimedia audio guide through its CMS.

Video tutorials are available, both on the izi.TRAVEL blog[17] or on the specific izi.TRAVEL Academy channel[18] and on its official YouTube channel.[19] With a single CP's profile they can produce and manage an unlimited number of audio guides, by self-creating and publishing audio guides equipped with text, audio content, photo galleries, and videos (linked to YouTube or directly uploaded as digital content). Texts can be linked to other web sources, so transforming a multimedia audio guide into a hypertextual one. Intellectual and data property rights remain with the content provider. Users themselves can be CPs, by using a specific function of the mobile app to directly create and geolocate a single story as a "tourist attraction", by uploading text, photos and audio recordings, without any access to the CMS. Finally, izi.TRAVEL has just published a free map available to use through widgets, for other websites and applications.[20]

Conclusion

The #iziTRAVELSicilia framework resulted in significant output achieved within Sicilian heritage communities, especially through heritage education programmes, and can now be considered a best practice for local promotion on a free and global digital storytelling platform. Individuals, ranging from school children to museum directors, co-created cultural content, highlighting the importance that community-based initiatives have in enhancing local culture and attractions through user involvement and knowledge sharing.

Thanks to this project, which can be considered highly experimental and highly participatory and inclusive, Sicily has become the only region in the world to experience a large-scale coordinated, participatory, democratic, and horizontal content creation process, which has been recognised by the Culture Commission of UE and the Faro Italia Association.

According to izi.TRAVEL staff members, no other example exists like #iziTRAVELSicilia, in terms of the number of people who participated, the results, the overall coordination, crowdsourcing, and co-creation of content, and storytelling techniques, presented by the locals. It provided a replicable model of collaborative and co-creative partnership giving the public, cultural, and tourist institutions and local heritage communities the opportunity to relate to each other, so obtaining a greater democratic, horizontal, participative, and inclusive action.

As regards the role of heritage communities, the #iziTRAVELSicilia project could be considered as a socially, culturally, and intelligently sustainable heritage action, having investigated how cultural institutions have been able to create a culture of bottom-up participation around their digital content, collections, information, and services, putting into practice the principles of the Faro Convention itself. By disseminating hundreds of audio guides and digital content, #iziTRAVELSicilia tried to bring the user closer to Sicilian art, archaeology, nature, and traditions, by simplifying language and making Sicilian culture more approachable; through evocative narration, it also tried to subvert the distance between those who have specific knowledge and those who have not and who are therefore excluded from understanding and describing art and culture. A great number of Sicilian students were the protagonists in this experiment: the narratives they created promote their own heritage, so transforming izi.TRAVEL itself into a formidable instrument of inclusivity, creating a sense of community while cultivating participation in an active cultural citizenship. People joined the project thus realising both the "right" to be part of common cultural heritage and the "responsibility" in contributing to the digital and creative promotion of their territory to support the development of knowledge and tourism, thus demonstrating how creative involvement is the key today to create sustainable and long-term cultural processes.

Focusing on the use of digital storytelling as a didactic tool, the experiential and direct approach and the collaborative learning processes adopted, as assessed by scholars (Dewey 2008, Gonzáles-Gonzáles *et al.* 2016), let students fully feel themselves to be co-authors and co-protagonists of multimedia products. Focusing on the exploration of the successful experience of #iziTRAVELSicilia in general, participatory culture demonstrated it meets the need of institutions in promoting collaboration and participation of users and communities of interests around museum collections and heritage management, with the aim to co-create memories, so revealing how culture sustainability and awareness can be enhanced, by promoting value co-creation and participative cultural and tourism experiences (Sfandla and Björk 2013, Rihova *et al.* 2015).

The #iziTRAVELSicilia project can be definitively considered a process which has already transformed the Sicilian cultural context: together, Sicilian people and institutions are already bridging their digital cultural gap with digital online and mobile technologies and they are also realising what kind of benefits can be related to the cultural heritage promotion they produced, such as the spread of dissemination of knowledge about local cultural heritage and their contribution to filling the digital gap of many Sicilian museums, whose collections are now online.

This pilot project could encourage schools, universities, cultural and tourist institutions, academic people or people involved in museum management and didactic projects, to digitally enhance their heritage through new digital participatory and inclusive approaches, by using this innovative tool for stimulating emotional and creative involvement of people in the co-creation of digital cultural contents. Finally, it could be recognised as a good practice of new collaborative and inclusive city-making practices through cultural content and values co-creation, by engaging people in heritage communities, able to promote their cultural landscape and create a holistic digital city framework.

Notes

1 https://izi.travel/it.
2 Community, referential, empathic, mnestic, and identity functions.
3 Value and springboard functions.
4 Understanding the origins; defining the individual and group identity; communicating tradition and delineating taboo; simplifying and providing perspective; illustrating the natural order of the things; concisely communicating complex history; communicating moral and ethical positions and the transference and preservation of values; illustrating relationships to, and with, authority; describing appropriate responses to life or model behaviours; defining reward and detail the paths to salvation and damnation.
5 According to the author, we can recognise these functions well described across the volume: ethic, emphatic, community, cohesive, transmissive of memories, identity, value, and springboard functions.
6 The adaptive function recognised by the authors covers functions very similar to the just cited ones, between which the collaborative, the social cohesion, the transmission of knowledge and skills, the clarification of intergroup relationships and the sensemaking function (by which the other functions of storytelling are realised) must be cited.
7 https://www.policultura.it/impatto-didattico/.
8 https://museudapessoa.org.
9 https://911digitalarchive.org/.
10 https://pararchive.com.
11 https://patrimonia.nantes.fr/home.html.
12 http://patrimonioeintercultura.ismu.org.
13 https://www.izi.travel/it/7dc4-i-templi-e-le-metope-guida-per-bambini/it.
14 https://www.izi.travel/it/02eb-i-piccoli-selinuntini-raccontano/it.
15 https://www.izi.travel/it/e39e-i-piccoli-scalpellini-raccontano-le-cave-di-cusa/it.
16 https://www.izi.travel/it/8282-museo-civico-castello-ursino/it.
17 https://izi.travel/en/blog.
18 https://academy.izi.travel/.
19 https://www.youtube.com/channel/UCvidztWMbxuJ3hArkZIaIhg.
20 https://map.tmatic.travel/en/tour.

References

Bakhshi, H., and Throsby, D., 2012. New technologies in cultural institutions: theory, evidence and policy implications. *International Journal of Cultural Policy*, 18 (2), 205–222.

Beale, J., ed., 2011. *Museum at play: games, interaction and learning*. London: MuseumEtc.

Benassi, A., and Mosa, E., 2019. Accompagnare la scuola nei processi di innovazione. Spazi, tempi e strumenti per una nuova didattica. In: F.A. Pizzato, ed. *Una nuova frontiera della didattica. Metodi, tecnologie, esperienze italiane*. Roma: Carocci, 45–70.

Bietti, L.M., Tilston, O., and Bangerter, A., 2019. Remembering with others: conversational dynamics and mnemonic outcomes. In: L.M. Bietti and C. Stone, eds. *Topics in Cognitive Science*, 11 (4), special issue, 710–732.

Black, G., ed., 2020. *Museums and the challenge of change: old institutions in a new world*. London: Routledge.

Bonacini, E., 2012. La visibilit@ sul web del patrimonio culturale siciliano. *Criticità e prospettive attraverso un survey on-line*. Catania: Maimone.
Bonacini, E., 2017. #iziTRAVELSicilia, a participatory storytelling project/process: bottom-up involvement of smart heritage communities. *International Journal of Interactive Communication Systems and Technologies*, 7 (2), 24–52.
Bonacini, E., 2020. *I Musei e le forme dello storytelling digitale*. Roma: Aracne.
Bonacini, E., 2021. Storytelling digitale in ambito culturale e il suo ruolo in ambito educativo. *Culture Digitali*, n. 0, June 2021, online journal.
Bonacini, E., and Giaccone, S. 2019. Digital participatory tools for territorial promotion: the #iziTRAVELSicilia case study. In: V. Cantino, F. Culasso, G. Racca, eds., *Smart tourism*. Milan: McGraw Hill Education, 417–436.
Bonacini, E., and Marangon, G., 2021. Lo storytelling digitale partecipato come strumento didattico di divulgazione culturale. *Cuadernos de Filología Italiana*, 28, 73–93.
Bonacini, E., Noto, V., Camarda, S., and Santagati, C., 2019. Digital storytelling and long-term participatory strategies for a new hackable museum-making model: the #iziTRAVELSicilia and the Ursino Castle Civic Museum case. *DigitCult*, 4 (2), 1–14.
Brouillard, J., Loucopoulos, C., and Dierickx, B. 2015. Digital storytelling and cultural heritage. *AthenaPlus WP5 creative applications for the reuse of cultural resources*. Milano: Officine Grafiche Tiburtine.
Ciasullo, M.V., Gaeta, A., Gaeta, M., and Monetta, G., 2016. New modalities for enhancing cultural heritage experience. The enabling role of digital technologies. *Sinergie Italian Journal of Management*, 34 (99), 119–138.
Coman, A., Brown, A.D., Koppel, J., and Hirst, W., 2009. Collective memory from a psychological perspective. *International Journal of Politics, Culture and Society*, 22, 125–141.
Cuzzolin, M., 2019. La scuola davanti alla rivoluzione digitale. In: F.A. Pizzato, ed. *Una nuova frontiera della didattica. Metodi, tecnologie, esperienze italiane*. Roma: Carocci, 33–43.
DeWey, J., 2008. Logica sperimentale. *Teoria naturalistica della conoscenza e del pensiero*. Macerata: Quodliber.
Di Blas, N., 2016. *Storytelling digitale a scuola*. Santarcangelo di Romagna: Maggioli.
Drotner, K., and Schrøder, C., 2014. *Museum communication and social media: the connected museum*. London: Routledge.
Dunbar, R. (2014). How conversations around campfires came to be. Proceedings of the National Academy of Sciences, 111 (39), 14013–14014. https://doi.org/10.1073/pnas.1416382111
Dunford, M., and Jenkins, T., 2017. Digital storytelling. *Form and content*. London: Palgrave MacMillan.
Evrard, Y., 1997. Democratizing culture or cultural democracy? *Journal of Arts Management*, 27 (3), 167–176.
Farinosi, M., and Micalizzi, A., 2016. Geolocating the past: online memories after an earthquake. In: A. Hajek, C. Lohmeier, and C. Pentzold, eds. *Memory in a mediated world. Remembrance and reconstruction*. New York: Palgrave Macmillan, 90–110.
Fernandez Vaz, R.I., Fernandez, P.O., and Rocha Veiga, A.C., 2018. Interactive technologies in museums: how digital installations and media are enhancing the

visitors' experience. In: J.M.F. Rodriguez, C.M.Q. Ramos, P.J.S. Cardoso, and C. Henriques, eds. *Handbook of research on technological developments for cultural heritage and eTourism applications*. Hershey: IGI, 30–53.

Giaccardi, E., 2012. *Heritage and social media: understanding heritage in a participatory culture*. London: Routledge.

Giaccone, S., and Bonacini, E., 2019. New technologies in SMART tourism development: the #iziTRAVELSicilia experience. *Tourism Analysis*, 24, 341–354.

Gonzáles-Gonzáles, C.S., Collazos, C.A., Guerrero, L.A., and Moreno, L., 2016. Game-based learning environments: designing the collaborative learning processes. *Acta Scientiae*, 18 (4), 12–28.

Gottschall, J., 2013. *The storytelling animal: how stories make us human*. Boston: Mariner Books.

Handler Miller, C., 2020. Digital storytelling. *A creator's guide to interactive entertainment*. Boca Raton: CRC Press.

Hellin-Hobbs, Y., 2010. *The constructivist museum and the web*. Poster session presented at *EVA London 2010*.

Hetland, P., Pierroux, P., and Esborg, L., eds., 2020. *A history of participation in museums and archives: traversing citizen science and citizen humanities*. London: Routledge.

Jenkins, H., 2006. *Convergence culture: where old and new media collide*. New York: University Press.

Keskin, H., Ali, E.A., Cemal, Z., and Hayat, A., 2016. Tales of cities: city branding through storytelling. *Journal of Global Strategic Management*, 10(1), 31–41.

Kidd, J., 2016. *Museums in the new mediascape: transmedia, participation, ethics*. London: Routledge.

Lambert, J., 2013. *Digital storytelling: capturing lives, creating communities*. New York: Routledge.

List, R.A., Kononykhina, O., and Leong Cohen, J., 2017. *Cultural participation and inclusive society*. Strasbourg: Council of Europe.

Luigini, A., and Panciroli, C., 2018. *Ambienti digitali per l'educazione all'arte e al patrimonio*. Milano: FrancoAngeli.

Maraffi, S., and Sacerdoti, F., 2018. *La didattica innovativa: digital gaming e storytelling*. Limena: Libreria Universitaria.

Mathews, R., and Wacker, W., 2007. *What's your story? Storytelling to move markets, audiences, people, and brands*. New Jersey: FT Press.

Misorelli, C., 2017. *One million life stories*. In: Dunford Jenkins, ed. London, United Kingdom: Palgrave Macmillan, 35–39.

Moroni, C., 2017. Le storie della politica. *Perché lo storytelling politico può funzionare*. Milano: FrancoAngeli.

Pavan-Woolfe, L., and Pinton, S., 2019. *Il valore del patrimonio culturale per la società e la comunità. La convenzione del consiglio d'Europa tra teoria e prassi*. Padova: Linea Edizioni.

Pizzato, F.A., 2019. Introduzione: didattica, ultima frontiera. In: F.A. Pizzato, ed. *Una nuova frontiera della didattica. Metodi, tecnologie, esperienze italiane*. Roma: Carocci, 13–22.

Ridge, M., ed., 2014. *Crowdsourcing our cultural heritage*. Farnham: Ashgate.

Rihova, I., Buhalis, D., Moital, M., and Gouthro, M., 2015. Conceptualizing customer-to-customer value co-creation in tourism. *International Journal of Tourism Research*, 17 (4), 356–363.

Roued-Cunliffe, H., and Copeland, A., 2017. *Participatory heritage*. London: Facet.

Salmon, C., 2008. *Storytelling. La fabbrica delle storie*. Roma: Fazi Editore.

Sandell, R., and Nightingale, E., eds., 2012. *Museums, equality, and social justice*. London: Routledge.

Sfandla, C., and Björk, P., 2013. Tourism experience network: co-creation of experiences in interactive processes. *International Journal of Tourism Research*, 15 (5), 495–506.

Simon, N., 2010. *The participatory museum*. Santa Cruz.

Wertsch, J.V., 2002. *Voices of collective remembering*. Cambridge: University Press.

Zagato, L., 2015. The notion of "Heritage Community" in the council of Europe's faro convention. Its impact on the European legal framework. In: N. Adell, R.F. Bendix, C., Bortolotto and M., Tauschek Between Imagined Communities of Practice. Gottingen Studies in Cultural Property, Vol 8, Gottingen University Press (umlaut over the O in Gottingen).

5 CultureLabs: Recipes for social innovation

Eirini Kaldeli, Danilo Giglitto, Eleanor Lockley, and Luigina Ciolfi

Introduction

Over the past few decades, the field of cultural heritage has been characterised by two major transformations that have reshaped the ways in which cultural heritage organisations think and function, as well as the ways in which their role is perceived by society. Firstly, Cultural Heritage (CH) is no longer seen solely as an educational outlet, but as a form of social, civic, and cultural representation and empowerment. Museums have questioned their expert-centric approaches (Simon 2010) to seek a more active participation from local communities (Crooke 2008, Black 2010), with a growing focus on "outsiders" and marginalised communities (Galani *et al.* 2020, Simon 2016, Innocenti 2016). In this context, social innovation has gained momentum in the cultural field as a practice that can help CH institutions connect to civic society and grassroots initiatives with the aim to meet a variety of social needs and resulting in new means of organisation and cooperation (Eid 2019a).

Secondly, heritage institutions have undergone an unprecedented level of digital transformation. Digital technologies have been used to enhance the preservation of CH collections, to increase their accessibility and visibility, and to engage in new forms of interaction with various audiences, for example through interactive exhibitions, storytelling, and crowdsourcing campaigns (Hornecker and Ciolfi 2019, Kenderdine 2016, Kaldeli *et al.* 2021). Additionally, museums and other heritage institutions are increasingly taking advantage of social media platforms as a means to increase their publicity and broaden their reach beyond their traditional audiences. The pivot to digital platforms and channels has become normative during the COVID-19 pandemic, as a means to sustain the connection between museums and the public in a time when the opportunities for face-to-face interactions were heavily hampered (Kidd 2020).

These two transformations have had multifold ideological, organisational, and operational implications on the discourse around cultural heritage and, in many cases, they have taken place hand in hand. Digital technologies influence the way in which forms of participation around heritage occur and

DOI: 10.4324/9781003277606-5

contribute towards the shift from authoritative and expert approaches to more democratic and inclusive exchanges with communities. Research in the fields of cultural heritage technologies, digital heritage, human-computer interaction (HCI), and participatory and co-design explored ways to deploy digital tools and technologies to support participatory engagement and the results of sustained efforts to generate innovation value through co-design (Avram *et al.* 2020). Participatory approaches have been applied to the design of cultural heritage technologies for some time, particularly to engage certain demographics of visitors in the process and refine museum interpretation strategies (Taxén 2004, Roussou *et al.* 2007, Smith and Iversen 2014), while more recently we are witnessing more systematic work towards the wider representation of voices and values in heritage settings (Arrigoni and Galani 2019, Claisse *et al.* 2020), such as through the explicit focus on the critical heritage concept of polivocality (Whitehead *et al.* 2021). The participatory engagement of communities at risk of exclusion, such as migrants and refugees, in relation to digitally enhanced exhibitions is even more recent (Galani *et al.* 2020).

However, despite the promising use of digital technologies for enhancing accessibility, engagement, and interactive experiences with museum collections, the potential of digital practice as a means to advance the social role of CH organizations still remains untapped. How digital technologies can contribute to social purposes in the CH sector is a question that recently attracted interest from both researchers and practitioners (Parry 2018, Eid 2019b). The need for a deeper contemplation of the co-contextual relationship between social innovation and digital practices comes along with a need to understand the several barriers that CH professionals and other involved stakeholders encounter in their effort for more inclusive and socially purposeful participatory practices in the cultural sector (Lynch 2011). Digital tools and technologies may hold particular promise, but also present challenges and demands (Kidd 2018, Clarke 2016, Ciolfi *et al.* 2017). Overall, the lack of adequate evidence about the views and concerns of stakeholders in the cultural sector and their collaborators from civic society limits the offering of appropriate digital solutions that may facilitate participatory practices for social innovation.

The CultureLabs approach

Situating itself in this multidisciplinary context at the intersection of heritage the digital, and the social, the Horizon 2020 CultureLabs project[1] explored participatory approaches that may create bridges between CH institutions and under-represented or marginalised communities, focusing particularly on approaches that can promote the social inclusion of migrant and refugee communities. The project sought to support actors who wish to pursue such initiatives, paying particular heed to the role of digital technology as an enabler and mediator of social innovation in and via CH. In this vein, the following questions emerged: what kind of digital tools can serve the actual needs of practitioners in the field working in different real-world settings that call for technological solutions that go beyond customary or fancy applications for the management of digital CH and its interactions with museum audiences? And how can more inclusive and participatory approaches be ultimately weaved into CH institutions' digital practices and build meaningful social impact?

In its course to gain a better grasp of these questions, the CultureLabs project started by conducting mixed-method empirical and desk research to collect and reflect on the perspectives, challenges, and expectations of institutional and community actors who do the frontline work in projects with a focus on social inclusion and community empowerment in the field of cultural heritage and beyond. Taking into consideration the identified needs, CultureLabs has developed an online platform[2] that aims to streamline and facilitate the organisation of participatory projects. The platform makes openly available and searchable a rich pool of resources, including policies, co-creation tools, impact assessment methodologies, digital tools, reports of past participatory projects, as well as novel ideas and approaches that can facilitate social innovation through culture. These resources, which we call "ingredients", can be combined in various ways to form a "recipe" that describes the defining elements and the process of carrying out a participatory project. The proposed methodologies and digital infrastructure have been applied and evaluated in practice in the framework of four participatory pilot projects, which involved different actors and migrant communities. In the next sections, we provide an overview of the work that has been carried out in the course of the CultureLabs project, explaining how the needs analysis informed the development of the online platform and concluding with the results of the on-the-field evaluation and the lessons learnt.

Researching intersecting fields

In the context of CultureLabs, we set about researching at the intersection of cultural heritage and social innovation through three interrelated research activities carried out across Europe. The first study investigated the role of technologies in bridging the gap between cultural heritage and communities and, in doing so, produced the functional requirements of the platform (Giglitto *et al.* 2019). The second set of research identified the needs of institutional stakeholders directly or indirectly involved in cultural approaches and/or in the promotion of social integration of disadvantaged groups, particularly migrants (Cesaroni *et al.* 2019). The third part of the research identified the needs and expectations of migrant community members who are active or interested in participatory projects at the intersection of the cultural and social work sectors (Giglitto *et al.* 2021). Besides the intrinsic value of exploring perspectives that are crucially important for advancing the discourses around participation, cultural heritage, social innovation, and digital technology, part of the findings thus produced also informed the design and development of the CultureLabs platform. The findings of the three research activities are presented respectively in the following subsections, while further details about how certain needs were translated into functional requirements for the CultureLabs platform can be found later in the chapter.

Requirements for digital technologies

The selection of user requirements with respect to desirable technological solutions that can be useful in the context of social innovation projects was a multifaceted process involving both the members of the CultureLabs consortium and identified external stakeholders. The external stakeholders were cultural professionals (n = 32) involved in the GLAM sector or in arts- and heritage-related fields such as heritage education or research, and community facilitators (n = 34), namely professionals who deal with the welfare of migrant and/or refugee communities. The research was based on a mixed-methods approach that gathered the perspectives of these actors through surveys and in-depth interviews.

The findings of this research provided helpful insights into the wider discourse around the types of digital technologies deployed for cultural heritage and social innovation. According to the perspectives of cultural professionals, digital technologies can have the potential to help them overcome two of the main sets of engagement-related barriers they face: the barriers to participation and the difficulty of learning from each other in the GLAM sector. The barriers to participation mostly manifest in two ways. Firstly, the intrinsic challenge to engage marginalised communities who may lack the time, interest or confidence to attend cultural venues. Closely related is the question of "why should community members care?", which remains fundamentally unanswered as cultural professionals often struggle to provide convincing arguments about why community members should partake in cultural activities. Some of these barriers can be tackled through a proper configuration of digitally-mediated communication tools. Such tools should be explicitly designed to foster synchronous and asynchronous communication around the participants, rather than relying on existing "generalist" social media platforms. The second set of challenges perceived by cultural professionals relates to the intrinsic difficulty of learning from other professionals from the same sector and the scarcity of genuine information about best practices and guidelines on how to approach specific communities. One of the aims of the CultureLabs platform was to respond to the necessity of bringing relevant information together, enabling users to contribute with information on their own practices and lessons learnt, as well as collaborating by contributing to the same recipe template.

Two sets of challenges that somewhat resonate with the ones above were identified by the community facilitators. The first challenge relates to the "cultural distance" that could negatively affect the extent of the engagement of certain disadvantaged communities in participatory activities. To alleviate this, digital technologies should hold three main characteristics: being familiar among participants, presenting culturally accessible content, and embedding the idea of safety. Similarly to the perspectives of cultural professionals, the second challenge relates to the difficulty in both getting a sense of the state-of-the-art of their sector and in determining which best practices they could draw inspiration from. Again, an online platform such as CultureLabs – namely, a digital environment that hosts a list of potential collaborators, existing practices, tools/methodologies, and, more importantly, information on immigration law and policy from a variety of countries – is acknowledged as the right way to facilitate the sharing of best practices and the exchange of ideas between stakeholders.

Identifying needs at the intersection of cultural heritage, institutions, and civic society

The CultureLabs consortium carried out mixed-methods research aimed at gathering information, and lessons learnt from institutional stakeholders directly or indirectly involved in cultural approaches and/or promoting social integration of disadvantaged groups, particularly migrant and refugee groups, in order to understand what they may need to facilitate cultural heritage-oriented participatory and inclusive initiatives.

Ninety surveys were administered to stakeholders working at the intersection of cultural heritage and social innovation. The survey's goal was to gather insights about the barriers these actors face in the implementation of participatory approaches and the measures adopted to overcome them. Semi-structured interviews (n = 17) expanded upon the survey data, and were carried out through an opportunistic sample of the survey respondents.

The findings provided relevant insights in relation to the configuration of approaches for participatory projects, the main barriers faced, and the level of impact achieved. Several data-driven recommendations have also been produced. A first crucial aspect – relevant for shedding light on the facilitating role that digital tools can play – is a perceived lack of digital options that may facilitate the creation, planning, and implementation of cultural heritage participatory projects. Specifically, the research participants identified tools that enhance information, data, and knowledge exchange (n = 28), tools for collecting feedback from participants (n = 25), and online exhibition builders (n = 24) as currently scarce and, therefore, most desired. Relatedly, the research participants also highlighted a lack of digitally-mediated tools for effectively gathering rich feedback from targeted communities, with current options enabling only more superficial surveying capacities.

Another set of identified complex challenges relates to linguistic barriers, which can have a negative impact on participatory projects by inhibiting migrants' access to opportunities. As a result, staff members must be trained to confidently interact with groups with a variety of linguistic competencies, and this may have not been planned for. There may also be a need to acknowledge the different dynamics of groups depending on various language skills since those with more proficiency can serve as gatekeepers and be heavily relied upon by the community. Careful consideration should be given to understanding these dynamics and promoting these types of relationships.

Although the surveyed participatory work was carried out to various degrees of success, challenges and barriers are always around the corner. It is perhaps not surprising that one of the most compelling barriers is related to a fundamental lack of a deep understanding of migrants' cultural and social norms, characteristics, and needs. To ensure quality and fair participation while reducing the risk of unilateralism, a proper assessment of these aspects should be a pre-requisite to any attempt at engagement.

Communities' needs

Finally, the CultureLabs consortium carried out mixed-methods research exploring the needs and expectations of migrant and refugee communities in several European countries in relation to communicating and sharing their cultural heritage practices as well as of cultural and civic institutions that plan to support this.

One hundred and one surveys were administered to people working with/for or belonging to migrant and refugee communities in several hosting countries, mostly Italy and Germany, while the countries of origin of respondents covered four continents. The survey consisted of closed-ended questions and was structured into eight thematic areas related to a balanced mix of independent and dependent variables for the generation of correlations and clusters. The thematic areas included: background information; employment status; socioeconomic status; residency or migration status; individual preferences, attitudes, and activities; intercultural awareness; extent of interest and preparedness to become actively involved in cultural activities; and access to and use of digital tools. Twenty-seven semi-structured interviews were also conducted.

The findings were aggregated per type of respondents: cultural institutions; non-governmental organisations (NGO) and civil society organisations (CSO); and migrant and refugee communities. Establishing the needs of a community starts with the need to understand a community's motivation for participation. The perspectives of cultural professionals suggested that it is intrinsically difficult to provide grounds for participation. This difficulty manifests itself in a great deal of uncertainty in terms of understanding and fostering the motivation and willingness of migrants and refugees to engage in cultural activities. Besides, cultural professionals generally experience very few opportunities to collaborate across sectors.

This lack of collaborative opportunities is worsened by the fact that, in the context of participatory projects with marginalised communities, they would benefit from the support of professionals dealing with the welfare of such groups. The impact of this scarcity of collaborative opportunities is exacerbated by cultural professionals' lack of specific intercultural competence and training at hand in approaching migrants and refugees, especially in small museums and institutions.

NGOs' operators offer a different, yet complementary, perspective. It is deemed that migrants' associations are rarely included and often only at the recruitment stage. Furthermore, the sector sees a few tendencies that should be avoided. For instance, certain culturally- and professionally-based practices that may not be shared with the participants are often utilised. This pairs with another tendency to racialise ethnic differences, risking the reproduction of cultural stereotypes even within participatory projects. Instead, the focus should be on holistic approaches that provide support to individuals and communities as a whole rather than targeting the participants' ICH background, age, gender, and/or language.

The migrants and refugees partaking in the research revealed the expectation that cultural institutions should be open to intercultural outputs and to managing diversity as part of their policies. However, their interest in cultural activities is usually subordinated to having addressed more urgent needs such as acquiring a certain level of language proficiency and securing a job. Having said that, their motivations can be fostered through the possibility of contributing to cultural representation. This is particularly true when there is a negative discourse around their country of origin that they could counteract. They also expressed the desire for approaches that raise heritage awareness among the youngsters and young adults in their communities.

Overall, this research showed how promoting and supporting the safeguarding of migrants' and refugees' cultural heritage is important not only to strengthen community ties but also to provide ground for meaningful dialogue and intercultural understanding with native and settled people.

Understanding needs and translating them into requirements for the CultureLabs platform

The perspectives from the participants and resulting findings from the research shed new light on the complex relationship between migrant communities and CH institutions and reflect on effective ways in which digital technology can be used to facilitate best practices in this respect. The insights have been used to directly inform and guide the design of the CultureLabs platform both in terms of desirable functionalities and of the content made available through it. In fact, the feedback we collected helped us better understand some recurring shortcomings in the process of organising participatory projects and also the type of materials and tools that stakeholders mostly lack access to.

A recurrent theme that underpinned stakeholders' responses was the need for access to the knowledge and experience gained from previous participatory projects. A sentiment widely shared by both cultural heritage professionals and community facilitators was that the legacy of participatory projects often comes down to positive reports about successful final results, while there is often a lack of awareness and self-reflection about what happened on the ground. Often, the information that can be found about past projects is limited to the presentation of catchy outcomes, embellished to impress the funding body or the audience. What is usually missing is the *how*, the inside information and the whole process that was followed, including the methodologies and tools that were used in each stage, the challenges that were encountered, and the "unsuccesses" as one of the interviewees put it. This type of valuable information is scarcely documented, systematised, and maintained, making it difficult to pass on and build on the knowledge accumulated through a project, even within the framework of a single organisation, especially when the people involved move on. Approaches and ICT solutions that can reinforce the replicability and adaptability of good practices, so that past successful projects can be customised to serve different settings and actors, are therefore particularly valuable.

Furthermore, respondents pointed to a wide and diverse variety of resource types and digital tools that would be useful in a social innovation setting depending on the focus of their work. Having an assortment of assets and digital technologies easily accessible in a centralised platform was considered to be particularly beneficial, especially given the difficulty of discovering the appropriate best practices from which to draw upon. In terms of resources, stakeholders expressed the need for policies and recommendations, co-creation and evaluation methodologies, reusable CH material, capacity building resources for the acquisition of intercultural skills as well as very practical exploitable resources such as printable tools, questionnaires, etc. The range of requirements for digital tools was equally broad, spanning from tools that facilitate decision-making and feedback collection, to the offering of collaborative functionalities and safe communication means that support different languages. A series of various tools that facilitate the management and creative reuse of digital CH, such as virtual exhibition editors and storytelling tools, were also mentioned.

The analysis of needs gave rise to a series of questions for the offered technological solutions to respond to. How can the high-level and heterogeneous needs of diverse stakeholders be translated into functional requirements for the technological platform? How can a centralised platform serve such diverse needs while working towards the common goal of social innovation? How can elements from successful participatory projects in cultural heritage (and beyond) be structured in a way that makes them reusable and useful for other projects, organisations, or community groups?

An iterative and user-centred approach was followed in order to drill down and translate the results of the need analysis into functional requirements for the CultureLabs platform. Partners and consortium-external stakeholders representing the end beneficiaries (museums, NGOs, local government foundations, etc.) stood at the centre throughout the design cycle and gave their feedback at all stages from conception to implementation. Prototypes and intermediate versions of the platform were iteratively evaluated by potential end-users and new requirements that cropped up from pilot projects were taken into consideration to revise the development process accordingly.

This continuous process of analysing user requirements and mapping them to functional requirements for the platform posed several challenges, calling for appropriate middle-ground solutions and design choices. Given the multiplicity and diversity of the collected requirements and of the circumstances encountered by different actors (e.g., different objectives, target audiences, means, existing practices, etc.), it became evident that it is not feasible to serve all user needs via functionalities exposed by the platform itself, either directly as integral parts of it or in the form of plugins. To overcome this limitation, requirements were prioritised in terms of their popularity, technical feasibility, and centrality with respect to the main CultureLabs vision. The requirements assessed to be particularly important as well as feasible were translated to concrete functional requirements for the technical infrastructure. For the remaining user requirements, the decision was made to aggregate, document, and make information about external digital tools available and searchable as "ingredients" in the platform's repository, thus, enabling users to discover relevant resources and make informed decisions about what is fit for their own purposes.

Another important dimension that called for careful and balanced decisions concerned the appropriate approach to systematising the knowledge of participatory projects in the form of "recipes". What types of data should the platform serve to the user, that is, what pieces of information should a recipe and an ingredient consist of? On the one hand, we are looking for a comprehensive template that guides users to capture all essential information that can be of interest for future initiatives, from the target groups considered and the steps that were followed to the hurdles and the means used to overcome them. On the other hand, the documentation of detailed recipe descriptions requires considerable time and effort from the user. Therefore, appropriate design decisions had to be made to ensure the creation of high-quality recipe descriptions, while at the same time keeping the documentation process simple enough to encourage users of the platform to add new material.

The CultureLabs platform

As a result of the continuous collaboration between stakeholders representing end-users, human–computer interaction experts, and the technical teams and an iterative methodology of feedback collection, evaluation sessions, revisions, and extensions, the main functionalities and respective technological components of the CultureLabs platform were derived. The overall goal of this process was to design a platform that can serve the actual needs of diverse stakeholders while working towards the common goal of social innovation. In the following, we first outline the main services offered by the CultureLabs platform, then go on to provide an overview of the main data structures it uses, namely the recipe and ingredients templates, and, finally, we briefly describe its technological infrastructure.

Main functionalities offered by the CultureLabs platform

Services for systematisation

Through appropriate data models and user interfaces, users are guided to document their participatory projects as recipes by capturing the "behind the scenes" knowledge and uploading relevant accompanying resources – as ingredients – that can be useful for the replication of similar initiatives in the future. The template served by the platform supports the consolidation of the experience gained from previous projects, the progressive documentation of ongoing projects as they develop from their first steps to completion, as well as the structuring of ideas about future projects. When a recipe creation process is completed, users are encouraged to make the information public so that others can benefit from that knowledge. This systematic documentation process – covering mainly past projects identified as good practices but also ongoing projects as well as some novel ideas for future projects – has resulted in creating a rich open repository of diverse recipes and ingredients. Currently, there are more than 200 ingredients of various types, from policy recommendations and co-creation methods to digital tools and training material, which can be found on the platform as well as more than 40 fully-fledged recipes which platform visitors can access and draw inspiration from. Moreover, the platform supports dedicated functionalities for uploading information about organisations from different sectors (cultural heritage, educational, civic society, government sectors, etc.) that collaborate in participatory projects or can potentially support them by offering resources, facilities, and know-how.

Search and navigation services

Through its open, well-documented, and searchable repository, the CultureLabs platform facilitates access to inspirational material and good practices that are usually otherwise dispersed and cumbersome to find. The platform provides advanced search capabilities which allow users to discover items (recipes, ingredients, and organisations) that match their requirements. The search methods combine keyword-based search with filters-facets, allowing users to narrow down search results by applying multiple filters based on terminology relevant to the domain of social innovation, considering different target group types, fields of focus, resource formats, etc. This way, users are able to explore the items made available through the platform's repository by applying multiple search criteria in different combinations, for example, for past projects led by particular organisations (e.g., a museum) and targeting groups with certain characteristics (e.g., female migrants). The user can navigate through the various resources residing in the CultureLabs repository via different presentation views and retrieve more information about items of interest.

Collaboration services

The platform offers a set of added-value services that facilitate knowledge exchange and collaborative work between different actors across sectors. By taking advantage of the user groups and rights management system supported by the platform, a user can share the recipes they create with other individual users or user groups and grant them different levels of access rights which entail different degrees of collaboration. For instance, a recipe creator can grant edit access to their colleagues (see Figure 5.2), so that they can assist them with the recipe specification and give away read permissions to external collaborators and community members in order to receive feedback in the form of private comments while preventing them from making direct changes. The platform also allows interested stakeholders to discover potential partners and supporters through a searchable registry of organisations such as funding agents, community facilitators, or providers of facilities, services, and expertise.

Adaptability and reusability services

Offering the possibility to reuse elements of existing good practices and customise them so as to serve different settings and actors is considered crucial for reinforcing the replicability of good practices in light of the unsuitability of 'one-size-fits-all' solutions. The platform enables users to create clones of existing recipes that they find useful and reconfigure them depending on their needs. Users can reuse and combine elements from different recipes uploaded by others, make changes, and complement them with their own material in order to build a new participatory project.

Recipes and ingredients for social innovation in cultural heritage

One crucial aspect of the CultureLabs platform is a systematised and streamlined process for the development of recipes for social innovation. To this end, it has been crucial to defining coherent, comprehensible, and flexible enough structures for representing recipes and ingredients, so as to reinforce their uptake by other interested stakeholders and their adjustability to different circumstances. The template was created taking into consideration the types of information identified as the most important by project partners representing end users as well as participants taking part in the multiple evaluation sessions of the project. The aim was to then come up with a data model that provides a comprehensive overview of all aspects that are useful to know about a participatory project and, at the same time, is also generic enough to facilitate its reuse/replicability. Since recipes are intended to serve as *templates* for participatory projects, implementation-specific aspects such as timelines were not included as part of the description. The template creation process had to find a middle-ground solution between ensuring high-quality recipe- and ingredient descriptions, which require considerable effort and time from the user while keeping the documentation process simple enough to encourage users of the platform to add new resources.

A r*ecipe* is a structure meant to describe how to carry out a participatory project. A recipe is characterised by a set of descriptive attributes including aspects such as "Title", "Description", "Collaborators", "Target groups", indicative "Duration", and "Cost". It also comprises a sequence of *steps* describing the activities-tasks of a project, a set of *challenges* together with possible ways to overcome them, and some *tips* referring to useful pieces of practical advice. A recipe is associated with a set of *ingredients*, which are individual data structures representing resources that may be useful for the organisation of a participatory project. Ingredients may refer to files uploaded by users and stored in the CultureLabs database (e.g., textual documents, images, etc.) or links to external resources (e.g., digital tools or project websites, etc). In both cases, an ingredient is accompanied by rich a metadata structure that documents at a glance its most important aspects. Ingredients cover a very broad spectrum of topics that have been identified as relevant during the user requirements analysis; they may refer to policies about migration or about CH, co-creation methodologies and tools, digital tools, training material, CH objects, impact assessment tools, etc. It should be underlined that the same ingredient is very often used in more than one recipe (Figure 5.1).

Platform architecture overview

The CultureLabs platform is composed of three main layers: the database layer, the service layer, and the user interaction layer. The database layer is in charge of the storage and low-level management of all basic resources and concepts (e.g., users, recipes, permissions, etc.). It handles all store, update, and query requests from the service layer above, from updating the passwords of users to changing attributes of recipes. The data storage is a hybrid design that uses a relational database as the primary storage of all data, with the addition of an indexing engine that efficiently indexes words and phrases, thus supporting optimised full-text search. The indexing and query

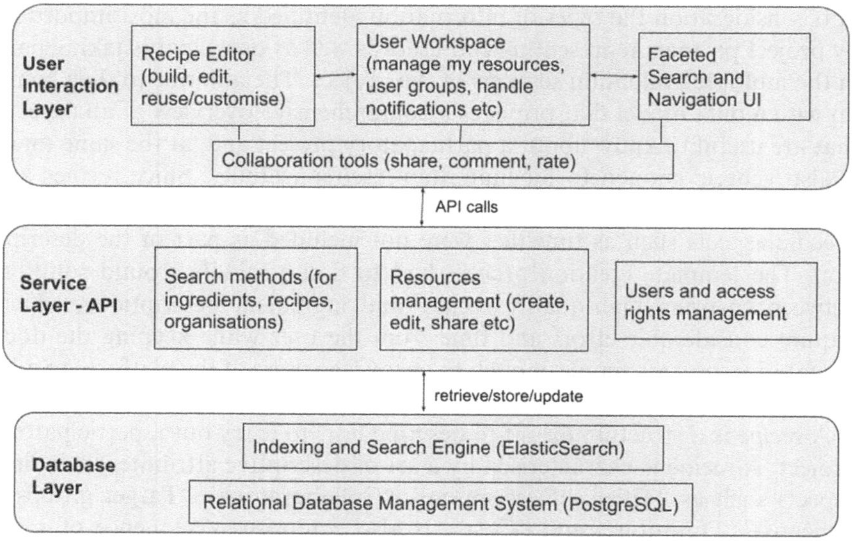

Figure 5.1 Overview of the CultureLabs technical architecture.

engine supports the advanced search capabilities exposed by the higher levels, by processing, optimising, and combining the lower-level requests for rendering the relevant information from the datastore, in compliance with data types, lock management, etc.

The service layer implements the Application Processing Interface (API) exposes in a uniform way the capabilities offered by the platform and acts as an intermediate layer via which the User Interaction layer interacts with the database layer. The API is defined using the Representational State Transfer (REST) architectural style and prescribes a number of methods for retrieving and adding resources to the database, editing metadata, user rights management, and access control (granting permissions, managing user groups and roles, etc.), and for performing advanced search. It should be underlined that the API is not only meant to serve the platform's user interaction layer but can also be reused by third-party applications in different contexts and thus promote the broader exploitation of the CultureLabs assets in an interoperable way.

The User Interaction (UI) layer builds on the lower-level layers in order to deliver the supported services to the end user in a functional, intuitive, and appealing manner. The UI exposes a User Workspace that allows the user to access, organise, and manage assets . It offers a dashboard that allows the user to navigate through the recipes and ingredients created by them as well as the ones with which they are collaborating. It also enables the user to view and manage the user groups they belong to. The most important component the User Workspace interacts with is the Recipe Editor, which enables users

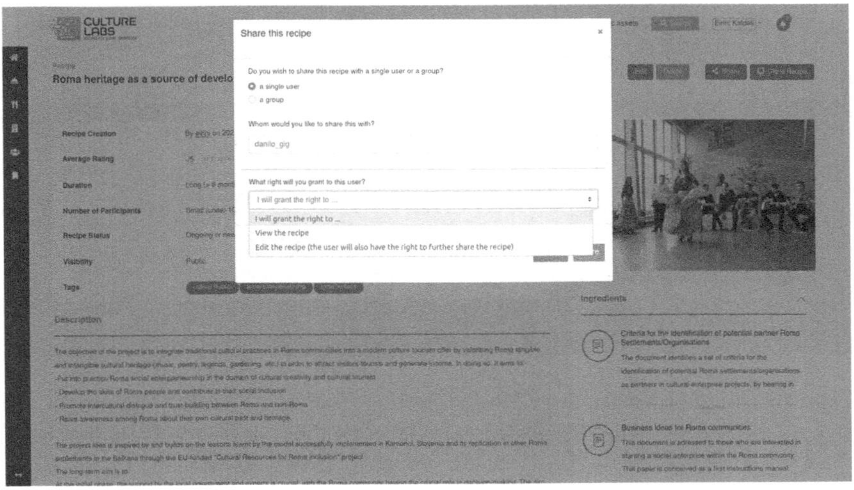

Figure 5.2 Screenshot of sharing a recipe with another user.

to create new recipes following the template outlined in above as well as to create clones of existing ones and customise them. The Search and Navigation component enables the user to discover various types of resources-ingredients, recipes, and organisations through the advanced search functionalities described above. Finally, a set of added-value collaboration functionalities allows users to share their recipes with other users (see Figure 5.2), co-work on a common recipe under development, exchange private feedback, as well as to publicly rate and comment on available recipes.

Uptake of the platform in pilot participatory projects and user evaluation

In the framework of the CultureLabs project, four participatory projects have been implemented as pilot actions in Finland, Italy, and the United Kingdom, with the aim to demonstrate how cultural heritage can become a vehicle for building stronger communities and for promoting intercultural understanding and social inclusion. The pilot projects involved different actors such as museums, non-governmental organisations, artists, migrant associations, local governments, and schools, and employed various means of creative interactions with cultural heritage – from webcomics and photographic storytelling to mixed media canvases and costume exhibitions – to engage with different migrant and refugee groups in their localities.

The pilot participatory project called "More in Common"[3] was organised by the People's History Museum in Manchester, UK, with the aim of

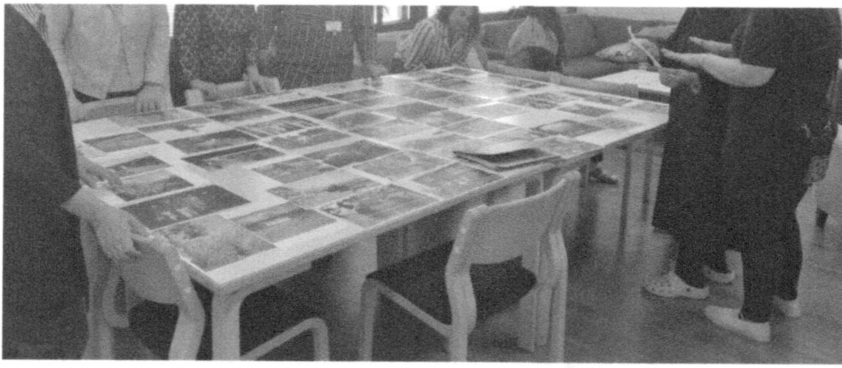

Figure 5.3 Migrant women inspecting a selection from Museovirasto's photographic collection. Photograph taken in the context of the "Zoom In on Heritage" pilot project.

creating opportunities for people with diverse backgrounds living in the Greater Manchester area to meet, discuss, and explore what they have 'in common'. The culmination of the pilot project was a physical exhibition that took place in the summer of 2021 to mark the fifth anniversary of the MP Jo Cox's murder by a far-right terrorist. "Zoom In on Heritage"[4] took place in Helsinki, Finland, and was led by Museovirasto, the Finnish Heritage Agency. It involved members of the Russian-speaking minority and a group of women migrants (see Figure 5.3). The participants brought new perspectives to the museum's photographic collections, were engaged through storytelling, and co-created a series of virtual and physical exhibitions that enriched the photographs of the museum's Picture Collections with their own photographs, interpretations, and thoughts. The project "Building Culture through Arts"[5] was organised in Ancona, Italy, by the social co-operative Cooperativa Sociale Marche Onlus. This pilot brought together migrants and locals living in a multi-ethnic low-income neighbourhood. Participants used theatre-based techniques to overcome language barriers and explored several artistic forms, such as collages and animations based on paper-based drawings, to express their different cultural identities, experiences, and thoughts. Finally, "So Distant, Incredibly Close"[6] led by the regional government foundation Fondazione Sistema Toscana, took place in Pisa. It involved sub-Saharan migrants and women with several migration backgrounds living in the area surrounding Pisa through guided tours in four different museums with exhibitions on Italian history, science, technology, and nature. With the assistance of arts students, the participants' thoughts and experiences were translated into webcomics proposing alternative narratives about the museums' collections.

The pilot participatory projects served as a means to evaluate in practice how the resources and the services offered by the CultureLabs platform could benefit institutional stakeholders and migrant communities as well as serve different social innovation-related ambitions. The platform was used to organise and facilitate in a digital environment the different stages of the pilot projects: from the ideation phase, as a means to structure and refine preliminary ideas, to the implementation phases of the various activities by supporting an efficient digitally-mediated collaborative process between the pilot leaders, their partner organisations, and the targeted community partners. The CultureLabs platform proved particularly useful for mitigating the challenges brought about by the coronavirus pandemic, which broke out in the midst of the pilot projects, by allowing involved actors to take full advantage of state-of-the-art digital tools and functionalities. Most importantly, the use of the CultureLabs platform ensured that the multi-level experience gained by the pilot projects can be built upon. The process followed by the pilot projects as well as the various material they used and produced have been documented in the form of openly accessible recipes and ingredients for other interested parties to take inspiration from and reuse.

Evaluation in the framework of the pilots and beyond

The CultureLabs platform has been extensively evaluated in terms of its usability and the content it offers. Building on existing work and best practices on usability evaluation (Sharp *et al.* 2017, Damala et al. 2019), our evaluation process was organised around two rounds. The first round was based on the use of online surveys filled in by targeted stakeholders representing potential users of the platform, including cultural professionals and community facilitators, as well as cooperative evaluation with identified design and human-computer interaction experts. The second evaluation round was organised within the framework of the four pilot projects and involved pilot collaborators and community participants. In this respect, the second round of platform evaluation saw the deployment of a rather diversified approach, different for each pilot, to allow for some flexibility to suit different study contexts, institutional practices, participants' and collaborators' preferences, and levels of digital literacy. Considering both rounds of the evaluation, 52 participants have been involved through a series of mixed-methods techniques that included focus groups, usability surveys, semi-structured interviews, open-ended questionnaires, and cooperative evaluation.

The collected feedback has been invaluable towards informing the design and development of the CultureLabs platform as well as proving helpful insights into the various ways in which it can support the creation and management of participatory projects employing cultural heritage to promote social innovation. Overall, the usefulness of the platform was broadly acknowledged in terms of, among others, fostering collaboration, systematising knowledge about participatory work, enhancing online visibility, and gaining access to inspirational and helpful material.

One of the main sources of added value of the platform is linked to the possibility of connecting with other institutions, which addresses the intrinsic difficulty of many professionals to collaborate with each other, especially inter-sectorally (Giglitto *et al.* 2019). More generally, the benefit of connecting organisations and the possibility of collaborating on common projects was strongly perceived as valuable, especially in consideration of the scarcity of other similar platforms around offering this type of service. Participants particularly appreciated the fact that the CultureLabs platform provided useful mechanisms to co-create projects with participants and mediators, especially in light of generating ideas quickly in time-sensitive settings. Overall, CultureLabs' methodologies and tools enabled the partnered organisations to continuously reflect upon the adopted approaches so as to revise pilots as they progressed. It was also stressed that the CultureLabs platform is especially useful for projects that do not have the capacity to create a website to increase their web presence.

Additional value also stems from the possibility of browsing other successful projects that may serve as sources of inspiration for others, in a "hindsight library" fashion. Again, this may mitigate the impact of a shared complaint in the sector revolving around a perceived lack of easy access to genuine information on other people's work (Giglitto *et al.* 2019). Intrinsic value was attributed to the breadth of social innovation topics that are promoted by the platform. Some of the social issues that are widely addressed by the recipes hosted in the CultureLabs platform such as social inclusion and intercultural understanding are often overlooked by mainstream media, therefore, the platform could potentially become a point of reference to generate systematic, valuable, and concrete ideas for cultural integration processes. As one of the participants put it, the CultureLabs repository "demonstrated how useful open and in-depth knowledge and experience sharing is for developing new and improved approaches [...]". The platform was acknowledged by another participant as "a very useful tool for learning about other projects, getting new ideas and for seeing what others have done before". To enhance this capability even further, the platform would need to further enrich its content to become a point of reference for European culture-based approaches promoting social inclusion, in light of having more practitioners motivated to publish their projects on it.

The feedback collected throughout the evaluation also highlighted the transferability potential offered by the CultureLabs' infrastructure for future work. Added value was identified in the logical organisation, display, and structure in which recipes are written and devised. The resources made available through the platform were seen as a way to generate new ideas and best practices, while the platform as a whole was perceived as a place where to "systematise future cultural projects" and "document and share them with the world", as was put by one of the collaborating organisations. In this respect, it was also stressed that the CultureLabs platform is especially useful for projects that do not have the capacity to create a website to increase their web presence.

The platform was also recognised with respect to its perceived contribution to organisations' capacity, especially in terms of new useful lessons learnt, skills acquired, and network expansion. One of the collaborating organisations believed that "important knowledge has been gained about methodologies that can be replicated", while the experiences from the pilot projects in combination with the access to the material made available through the online platform have strengthened the understanding of participatory actions, the resources needed, and the value of participatory approaches. In this regard, many participants felt that the CultureLabs platform and the participatory approaches it advocates can represent the first step towards a wider and more systematic deployment of social innovation approaches, and thus bring a longer-term impact on organisational practices in the CH sector and beyond.

The feedback collected during the evaluation sessions also pointed to certain limitations of the current version of the CultureLabs platform and to directions for future work and further improvement of the platform's functionalities and content provision. Some participants posited that the entire process of creating a recipe could be too long for people who are time-poor (for instance, part-time staff). At the same time, participants particularly appreciated well-documented recipes with comprehensive descriptions of steps, challenges, and ingredients, which are exactly the elements that require the most effort to add. As a response to this comment, an attempt has been made to restructure the recipe creation process so that it can become more lightweight or more detailed depending on the inclination or circumstances of the user. Moreover, some participants suggested that the support for simultaneous co-editing on a common recipe and for tracking changes would significantly enhance the collaborative capabilities of the platform.

Besides the evaluation of the specific digital services and possibilities offered by the platform, the platform and the overall collaborative, needs-driven, and self-reflective methodology it operationalises were also assessed in terms of the change it brought to the practices of the involved organisations. Changes were discussed in terms of how organisational missions, priorities, mindsets, practices, and ways of working were influenced by the organisations' participation in the CultureLabs project. In this respect, the platform played a crucial role in integrating and widening participatory engagement approaches within the existing organisational practices. The platform was considered particularly helpful for understanding the practicalities relating to participatory projects, especially for ensuring that different perspectives are included in decision-making processes. Its contribution to the organisations' digital strategy was particularly appreciated. As one of the respondents mentioned, "the pilot projects' digital element was one of the first times [we] have a strong built-in element like this in its design and it definitely contributed to [our] aspirations to expand our digital offer". Of note is the impact of CultureLabs on organisational strategies, which in some cases took the form of guidelines or updates to the organisations' business plan. A member of staff from the organisations involved in the pilot projects said that CultureLabs has given them an opportunity "to work closely with people to share their stories and lives with a wider audience, and we're now working to a new business plan which is very much focused on impact-led engagement with a focus on inclusion and access across everything we do".

Conclusions

Building on perspectives from heritage studies and human-computer interaction, in this chapter we set out to report the contributions of the CultureLabs project to bridging technology, CH institutions, and civic society to widen participation in cultural heritage. We discuss aspects related to participation, inclusion, and the promise of the digital: themes that are nascent and likely to become more prominent as the social dimension of museums are increasingly being recognized and encouraged in the sector. By adopting a socio-technical lens and trying to encompass both the researcher's and the practitioner's perspectives, we explore the role digital technologies can play in shaping the dynamics between CH institutions and communities and how this process can lead to new models of collaboration and interaction around heritage and culture. In doing so, we report on the findings of original empirical research and the design and use of an innovative digital platform which aims to systematise and facilitate the organisation of social innovation projects in the field.

CultureLabs' contributions reported in this chapter can be broadly understood along three main dimensions, which offer complementary insights into socially innovative approaches in the cultural sector. Firstly, we have provided empirical evidence and novel insights towards understanding the existing landscape of participatory initiatives in and via CH, by turning to the viewpoints of CH practitioners as well as their community partners who do the front-line work. The findings of this in-depth qualitative research have helped us untangle the practical and conceptual challenges associated with cultural, resources, and knowledge barriers and allow us to take a renewed look at how digital technologies can promote participation in the cultural heritage sector.

Our second contribution revolves around service innovation and concerns the development of an innovative digital platform that aims to operationalise the societal value of cultural heritage through a knowledge base and a set of functionalities for systematising and facilitating the organization of projects. What distinguishes the CultureLabs platform is that it brings into effect a holistic and collaborative approach to the governance of cultural heritage, which goes beyond the traditional orbit of digital technologies around purposes of preservation, presentation, and user engagement. The platform provides in an integrated way digital tools and services supporting the whole process of designing and implementing social innovation projects around culture, through knowledge sharing and ideas exchange, streamlining of activities, and co-working between different actors. The normalisation of digital approaches during the pandemic places further importance on the work conducted through the CultureLabs project and the legacy that it leaves.

Finally, our third contribution concerns the lessons we have learnt by examining and evaluating the practical use of the CultureLabs platform and the methods it foregrounds in the context of four case studies involving diverse institutional stakeholders, migrant communities, and cultural activities. The insights we have gathered reflect on the transformative processes such practices can bring about at the individual and institutional levels and point us to challenges and opportunities that can be beneficial for informing the action of future practitioners. This analysis has led to the production of a set of policy recommendations[7] for the more effective implementation of participatory approaches at the intersection of cultural heritage, civil society, and migrant communities. Put together, the contributions of CultureLabs make the case for a cultural heritage that critically embraces digital technologies as a means for social innovations, whose implications and impact can transcend the boundaries of the CH sector and diffuse to local and global communities as well as society at large.

Acknowledgements

The work presented herein has been supported by funding from the European Union's Horizon 2020 research and innovation programme under grant agreement No 770158. The sole responsibility of this publication lies with the authors. The European Union is not responsible for any use that may be made of the information contained therein.

Notes

1 More information about the CultureLabs project can be found at this link: https://culture-labs.eu/
2 The CultureLabs platform can be found at this link: https://recipes.culture-labs.eu/
3 More information about "More in Common" can be found at this link: https://www.youtube.com/watch?v = kQZxNZzqq-A
4 More information about "Zoom In on Heritage" can be found at this link: https://kohtaamispaikkanakuvat.fi/en/pictures-as-a-meeting-place/
5 More information about "Bridging Culture through Arts" can be found at this link: https://www.youtube.com/watch?v = uQNw95ii-KY
6 More information about "So Distant, Incredibly Close" can be found at this link: https://www.sma.unipi.it/culturelabs-comics/

7 The CultureLabs' policy paper can be found at this link: https://culture-labs.eu/wp-content/uploads/2021/05/CultureLabs_Policy_Paper.pdf

References

Avram, G., Ciolfi, L., and Maye, L., 2020. Creating tangible interactions with cultural heritage: lessons learned from a large scale, long term co-design project. *CoDesign*, 16 (3), 251–266.

Arrigoni, G., and Galani, A., 2019. Digitally enhanced polyvocality and reflective spaces. In: A. Galani, R. Mason, and G. Arrigoni, eds. *European heritage, dialogue and digital practices*. London: Routledge, 37–61.

Black, G., 2010. Embedding civil engagement in museums. *Museum Management and Curatorship*, 25 (2), 129–146.

Cesaroni, F., Triccoli, F., and Boraso, R., 2019. *D2.1: Institutional stakeholders needs and services analysis report*. CultureLabs.

Ciolfi, L., *et al.*, 2017. *Cultural heritage communities: technologies and challenges*. London: Routledge.

Claisse, C., *et. al.*, 2020. Crafting critical heritage discourses into interactive exhibition design. In: Proceedings of the *2020 CHI Conference on Human Factors in Computing Systems*, April 2020. New York: ACM Press, 1–13.

Clarke, R., and Lewis, R., 2016. Re-configuring inclusion, decolonising practice: digital participation and learning in black women's community-led heritage. *Journal of Adult and Continuing Education,* 22 (2), 134–151.

Crooke, E., 2008. *Museums and community: ideas, issues and challenges*. London: Routledge.

Damala, A., Ruthven, I., and Hornecker, E., 2019. The MUSETECH model: a comprehensive evaluation framework for museum technology. *Journal on Computing and Cultural Heritage*, 12 (1), 1–22.

Eid, H., 2019a. Digital social innovation and the evolving role of digital in museums. In: *Museums and the Web 2019 Conference*, 2–6 April 2019 Boston.

Eid, H., 2019b. Museum innovation and social entrepreneurship. *A new model for a challenging era*. New York: Routledge.

Galani, A., *et al.*, 2020. Designing for intersubjectivity and dialogicality in museum interactive installations about migration. *Digital Creativity*, 31 (4), 302–319.

Giglitto, D., *et al.*, 2019. Bridging cultural heritage and communities through digital technologies: Understanding perspectives and challenges. In: Proceedings of the *9th International Conference on Communities & Technologies – Transforming Communities*. New York: ACM Press, 81–91.

Giglitto, D., Ciolfi, L., and Bosswick, W., 2021. Building a bridge: opportunities and challenges for intangible cultural heritage at the intersection of institutions, civic society, and migrant communities. *International Journal of Heritage Studies*, 28 (1), 74–91.

Hornecker, E., and Ciolfi, L., 2019. *Human-computer interactions in museums*. Morgan & Claypool.

Innocenti, P., 2016. Cultural networks and social inclusion of migrants in Europe: heritage, ICT, and participatory governance. *International Information & Library Review*, 48 (4), 274–286.

Kaldeli, E., *et al.*, 2021. CrowdHeritage: crowdsourcing for improving the quality of cultural heritage metadata. *Information*, 12 (2), 64.

Kenderdine, S., 2016. Embodiment, entanglement, and immersion in digital cultural heritage. In: S. Schreibman, R. Siemens, and J. Unsworth, eds. *A new companion to digital humanities*. Chichester: Wiley, 22–41.

Kidd, J., 2018. Public heritage and the promise of the digital. In: A. Labrador, M.and N. Asher Silberman, eds. *The Oxford handbook of public heritage theory and practice*. Oxford: Oxford University Press.

Kidd, J. 2020. Social media and participation: The selfie as a curious cultural artefact. *In*: G. Black, ed. *Museums and the challenge of change: Old institutions in a new world*. Routledge.

Lynch, B., 2011. *Whose Cake is it anyway? A collaborative investigation into engagement and participation in 12 museums and galleries in the UK*. Paul Hamlyn Foundation. Available from: https://www.phf.org.uk/wp-content/uploads/2014/10/Whose-cake-is-it-anyway.pdf [Accessed 18 Mar 2022].

Parry, R., 2018. Socially purposeful digital skills. In: Let's get real 6: connecting digital practice with social purpose. Report from the sixth Culture24 Action Research Project, 3435. Available from: https://www.culture24.org.uk/lets-get-real-6/ [Accessed 18 Mar 2022].

Roussou, M., Kavalieratou, E., and Doulgeridis, M., 2007. Children designers in the museum: applying participatory design for the development of an art education program. In: Proceedings of the *6th International Conference on Interaction Design and Children*. New York: ACM Press.

Sharp, H., Rogers, Y., and Preece, J., 2017. Interaction design. *Beyond human-computer interaction*. John Wiley & Sons.

Simon, N., 2010. *The participatory museum*. Santa Cruz, CA: Museum 2.0.

Simon, N., 2016. *The art of relevance*. Santa Cruz, CA: Museum 2.0.

Smith, R.C., and Iversen, O.I., 2014. Participatory heritage innovation: designing dialogic sites of engagement. *Digital Creativity*, 25 (3), 255–268.

Taxén, G., 2004. Introducing participatory design in museums. In: Proceedings of the *8th Participatory Design Conference: Artful Integration: Interweaving Media, Materials and Practices – Volume 1*. New York: ACM Press.

Whitehead, C., Schofield, T., and Bozoğlu, G., 2021. *Plural heritages and community co-production: designing, walking and remembering*. London: Routledge.

6 Civic museums, social need, and inclusive digital practices

Lara Perry

The work of civic museums

Both the US and the UK have a rich legacy of civic museums, institutions that formed in parallel with national museums but with a rationale to develop identity and belonging for a town or urbanised area for the individuals who dwell within it (Hill 2013). In the last 30 years of continuously reducing investment in public services, and particularly the public services that are associated with the infrastructures funded by civic bodies that are known in the UK as "Local Authorities", UK's civic museums (as well as other elements of civic government) have faced the need to revisit their engagement with audiences. Relationships with their local communities have been intensified by the increasing dependency of museums on visitors for their financial sustainability, and conversely, of communities becoming increasingly dependent on museums for access to civic space and public services. While reliance on funding coming from audiences is more familiar to US institutions which have relied heavily on philanthropy for much longer, the shift to community-led in addition to patron engagement has been a change for the sector: even before the public health crisis of COVID-19, rising social inequality in the US and the UK has identified new community needs in addition to the recognised museum function of supporting education, research, and leisure pursuits.

Promoting mental health and community "well-being" has become a new focus for museums in the wake of economic, climate, and social crises that have underscored the potential and actual importance of local or civic museums in sustaining the social fabric (Morse and Munro 2018). This new focus for museum work presents a variety of challenges, including changes in museum practice and processes that are required to facilitate different functions; the effects on staff of refocusing their roles; the change in resources required to address health and well-being; and the question of how such activity can be evaluated and understood. Community engagement activities designed to promote health and well-being are often dependent on premises-based physical and social interactions (Todd *et al.* 2017). The emphasis on physical touch and interaction with objects and other visitors

DOI: 10.4324/9781003277606-6

is understood to make the most of the traditional museum functions of object collection and the social element of museum visiting. For older adults and for young people, the well-being benefits associated with cultural participation and social interaction are seen as the key drivers of this new form of museum service (All-Party Parliamentary Group on Arts, Health and Wellbeing 2017). The emphasis on physical contact leaves the potential for using digital communications less fully explored than it could be.

Digital content and delivery have been heralded since the early 2000s as a means of making museums more democratic by facilitating direct engagement between audiences and institutions via web 2.0 mechanisms such as social media-based engagement and crowdsourcing, as well as making collections and the knowledge about them more accessible to visitors. The pattern of investment by museums in digital communications primarily for marketing and collections access is well-established and continued even during the COVID-19 pandemic closures (Samaroudi *et al.* 2020). But it has often been observed that digital communications have simply provided new platforms for interactions that replicate the existing physically based modes of engagement (e.g., Proctor 2013). As Taylor and Gibson observe (2017), even the most democratizing initiatives in digitising heritage access are prone to replicate the "authorized" values of heritage and its institutions, and to adopt the values of universality or "community" which do not always serve the groups that are most in need of inclusion. Digital surrogates for museum artefacts, and associated metadata, are incredibly effectively communicated by means of digital engagement, and the construction of a "virtual" museum increases accessibility to the collection beyond physical and geographical constraints. But it also maintains the focus on the collection and/or exhibitions of artefacts as the source of the meaning and value of the museum, a focus which does not represent the full potential of a museum's engagement with its community (Proctor 2021).

The value of digital activities to civic museums' promotion of well-being, and their social value to their communities, can be better captured by shifting the focus from the impact on the "well-being" of individuals or groups of visitors to the question of the values that inform the relationship between user and organisation. Milligan and Wiles (2010) argue that "care landscapes" are complex relationships that are formed by emotional and social proximity and not simply physical proximity. This suggests that the potential for using digital interactions to bridge the barriers to social inclusion and cohesion has significance beyond current typical uses. Civic museums, which often serve geographically local audiences and have only rare opportunities of developing other constituent audiences for their organisation, are most likely to need to develop tools oriented for working in more diverse ways with the individual and social needs of the community. In a project which proposed that augmenting or enhancing such spaces with digital interventions might be a mode by which audience inclusion could be promoted, we devised a number of strategies that used digital communications with the aim of improving accessibility and inclusion for audiences who face different kinds of physical, social and emotional, or financial barriers to participation in civic museums. These were not conceived of as standalone projects but ones that augmented the premises-based offer of the different organisations, although as a result of the COVID-19 pandemic these activities were converted to wholly remotely delivered programmes. We considered different ways that social inclusion could be advanced through digital tools and focused our plans on three different dimensions of the work.

One question that we explored was how to diversify the types of digital technologies used by civic museums in order to increase and extend engagement. Researchers who do cultural work with marginalised communities from Newcastle to Peru have emphasised that adapting communications to suit local practices is key: Clarke and Lewis (2016) found that the marginalised women in the English North-East with whom their project sought to engage were quick to share their activities via commonly used social networking platforms, and "argued that technology was in fact helping them to connect with others" and to share the project with their communities (p. 146). In some cases, cultural organisations will be accessing highly developed digital communications skills, as suggested by Innocenti (2016) and Nedelcu and Soysüren (2020) in relation to refugee communities; but even where digital technologies are not widely used, digital tools can be successfully used by "centering the human relationships that are easily sacrificed at the altar of technological innovation" (Brown and Tucker 2018, p. 58). These kinds of insights guided our choices of tools and mechanisms.

Secondly, we considered how diversifying the available modes of engagement by enhancing sensory accessibility or creating alternative content would increase positive responses to digital provision. In these aspects, we were drawing both on familiar models of adapting materials to mitigate sensory impairments such as low vision or those related to mobility issues that are important planks in inclusive practice. But beyond the question of accessing information, we were interested in how engagement might be promoted by developing content based on the promotion of mental and emotional health that is foregrounded in the well-being approach to the cultural provision that is emphasised in current UK civic arts policy. In terms of foregrounding this priority as an element of digital practice, we considered new work, which is exploring, for example, the engagement that can be accessed by appealing to different senses: in her work, Jenny Kidd (2019) has argued that diversifying sensory engagement can enhance empathy and audience satisfaction with digital activities. We therefore sought to consider different sensory inputs and the potential, particularly of audio recording as a means to promote audience engagement.

Finally, our project aimed to explore more directly how social bonds between organisations and their local communities could be strengthened and sustained through digital engagement. As artist Simone Leigh (2016) has written in respect of her project the Free People's Medical Clinic, "giving care is based on trust and relationships" (p. 86). All the institutional participants in our project consider that their work is heavily based on respectful engagement and inclusion of diverse audiences and often foregrounds participatory programming. In our project, we considered how digital projects could be integrated into longer-term initiatives at the same time that they supported temporally focused projects.

The programme of work

Between the spring of 2020 and of 2021, the organisations which formed the project partnership developed and implemented a variety of projects that tested the viability and usefulness of different uses of digital engagement in their specific local context. The partners included three cultural organisations which were selected to represent different approaches to civic or locally oriented programming. They included the Peale in Baltimore, MD, USA (lead partners were the Director Nancy Proctor and curator of the Redefine/ABLE exhibition, Audra Buck-Coleman); the De La Warr Pavilion, an art exhibition and performance space located in the small coastal town of Bexhill on Sea in England (lead partners were Rosie Cooper, Director of Exhibitions and Ashley McCormick, Head of Learning and Participation); and the Royal Pavilion and Museums in Brighton and Hove, also on the south coast of England (lead partner was Kevin Bacon, their Digital Manager). These organisations share similar purposes in terms of serving a local constituency, but also have in common that they are based in historic buildings that are the primary site on which their programming is delivered. For these and similar organisations, the physical site was, and continues to be, a major asset with which we sought to enhance engagement through digital engagement tools. The programme of work was disrupted by the onset of COVID-19 and the earliest episodes of lockdown, which required the work to shift to wholly digital mediations of, around and near the physical sites.

The most resource-intensive and dramatic undertaking was developed by the Peale Museum in relation to their planned exhibition, Redefine/ABLE. This exhibition had been developed to mark 30 years of Universal Design Principles that underpin disabled access in the United States, but also to draw attention to how ableism continues to be "designed in" to social and physical spaces. Students from the University of Maryland had worked together with disabled consultants to design an exhibition that celebrated the achievements of Universal design while also challenging audiences to reflect on whether the principles of universal access had been assured through its implementation. The exhibition had been carefully planned to make the most effective use of the Peale's temporary building that would be one of the exhibition's key display sites (one of a similar scale and age to its permanent home) including restricting the exhibition to the ground floor in order to ensure physical accessibility. A number of displays were designed to heighten awareness of the impact of sensory impairments through the use of mechanisms that fostered audience engagement with aural and spatial as well as visual information. The original plan was to provide tablets and other digital tools within the exhibition space to allow visitors to improve the accessibility of the exhibition by adjusting the presentation of the interpretive material and elements of the displays, but the Peale suspended its use of physical premises during the spring of 2020, halting the installation.

The Peale devised an innovative alternative to a physical exhibition which was to move the exhibition and the whole museum into the virtual world platform Second Life, and to develop complementary content on a project-based website and linked social media sites. Second Life is a web-based virtual environment that mimics three-dimensional space in how users, in the form of avatars, navigate the site's content. Avatars interact with the environment in ways that replicate physical movement through space (complete with collisions). The Second Life world consists of "islands" that are developed according to particular themes and uses, including the creation of virtual versions of actual physical sites that can be visited by Second Life's users. In the summer of 2020, the Virtual Peale with its version of the Redefine/ABLE exhibition opened. The site provided a three-dimensional navigable version of the historic Peale building with an enhanced entrance hallway that displayed images of the building over its 200 years of history; a virtual display of the materials designed for the Redefine/ABLE exhibition; and an outdoor garden in which live events were held. Second Life is available via the web with an ordinary computer and does not require any specialist equipment such as a VR headset to navigate. Over the course of the first six weeks of the exhibition, the virtual Peale received more visitors than had been anticipated at the originally planned physical sites.

Slightly later in the summer of 2020, the Royal Pavilion and Museums in Brighton and Hove launched one of their inclusive digital engagement activities, titled "The Mindful Garden". This was a web-based audioguide to a well-used outdoor site that is at the heart of the Royal Pavilion and Museum's city centre estate, in which visitor services were significantly reduced even in a short interim period between nationally mandated COVID-19 lockdowns. While the historic buildings that frame the site are the focus of the museum operations, the garden is characterised by well-tended plantings and lawns that experience heavy usage by visitors picnicking and enjoying an outdoor café in Summer, attracting a constituency of users that is not determined by deliberate interest in cultural heritage. The mindful garden tour was accessed via the internet on the users' own devices and in eight different segments provided of audio content that related to different elements in the garden, including specific natural and built features as well as the physical experience of the space as a whole. The content was written and recorded by a novelist and dramatist, Craig Jordan-Baker, and it invited the listener to engage with the sensory experiences of the garden including sound, perception of colour, scent and emotional responses that might be associated with some elements of the site. This represented a significant step change from the interpretive content normally developed by the Royal Pavilion and Musuems Brighton, which strongly associates the physical environment with the history of the building and the historical figure who was most important in developing its distinctive character. The Mindful Garden content did not set expectations around knowledge of or interest in the typical historical interpretation of the site, but focused on the visitor's sensory and emotional relationship to the garden. The technology of a web-accessible tour that was accessed through the users' own devices, and the data efficiency of audio content that did not need to be downloaded, maximised the potential for casual and more deliberate visitors to interact. The user data indicated that while uptake in numbers of users was modest, the "dwell-time" that this provision did attract from individual listeners was generous, signalling the potential for engaging users through different technical solutions and content of interpretive material.

The programme of work which was undertaken by the De La Warr Pavilion also required a significant but meaningful adaptation in response to the COVID-19 pandemic. Originally planned as a weekend of convergence that would see programming contributed by local community organisations as well as the curatorial team, the intention was to foster closer ties with community organisations – and by extension, the community itself – through partnership working. That aim remained the focus of their programme but was significantly redefined from supporting more diverse engagement with physical workshops through digital to providing the platform by which the "community" would constitute itself through convergence in live events. Like many organisations, the De La Warr Pavilion developed a remotely accessible programme using standard proprietary video calling/broadcasting platforms which ran in the spring of 2021 (a period of stay-at-home mandates in the UK), and whose content was developed in partnership with local artists and activists. These focused on solidarity building in the local community with marginalised social groups who had been active in promoting accessibility, equality, and community cohesion during the previous ten months of stay-at-home mandates. The focus of the events included migrant rights, state racism, community-led urban design, and the implications of social interdependence between many different social groups. Two elements were complemented with activities using more bespoke digital content, one of which was introduced as part of an artist workshop and one of which was provided as an adapted version of the web-based tool for developing collaborative content that is used at the Peale.

All of these programmes of work were evaluated by the host organisations, using different mechanisms and the findings can be discussed broadly under three different themes: optimising technology choices for greater accessibility by a range of audiences; the benefits of supporting inclusive content in enhancing accessibility; and the organisational implications of expanding digital provision as a mechanism for driving inclusivity in locally focused cultural heritage institutions. One of the challenges that all the organisations faced in delivering wholly, versus partially, remotely accessible programs was that evaluation of audience reach and experience was challenging: qualitative data was difficult to access due to the transactional and sometimes completely anonymous character of engagement with remotely delivered events, and quantitative data that was collected was limited in volume and did not allow for a straightforward comparison to other datasets. More important to this project has been the experience of those closest to the organising and delivery of the programming, as an index not only of the impact of changing practices but also the potential to create long-term and sustainable approaches to inclusivity through patterns of working with external partners. The following discussions are based on the reports provided by the participating organisations, and conversations between the project lead for each institution as the programme unfolded. What we learned about the evaluation of these projects and how that relates to specific aims around inclusion and diversity are discussed as part of the implications for organisations seeking to expand their digital inclusivity.

Optimising technology choices

Each of the three organisations explored the use of a technology that was new to them in the course of the programme. Their existing use of digital technologies varied quite considerably in that the De La Warr Pavilion had effectively no experience of audience engagement via digital tools beyond marketing and communications; the Peale had an existing audience participation tool in the form of an iOS app (for Apple device users) that facilitates users both to access the Peale's collection of Baltimore stories, and to contribute their own content; and the Royal Pavilion and Museums Brighton had a significant existing digital programme based mainly in a large website that gives provides a wide range of content including access to a collections database. The RPM also has used various mobile tools including a guided audiotour using a traditional museum-provided handheld device. Each of the projects undertaken by the project partners involved the organisation taking a step into new formats of digital engagement that pushed the boundaries of what they were accustomed to working with. The condition of the lockdowns meant that the user data from before and after the introduction of the new platforms does not give a reliable indication of whether there was a growth in audiences resulting from digital, and specifically whether the audiences expanded to include new users who previously had found the physical and digital inaccessible, but there is certainly evidence of changes in audiences for the partner organisations through digital tools.

Both the Peale and the De La Warr Pavilion noted that one effect of extending the institutions' digital offer was to extend the audience for the organisation beyond those who had easy physical access to the institution. Whether the barriers to physical participation were financial, mobility based, or related to decisions about time and travel, the development of a programme that was remotely accessible extended the audience for the programme. Events hosted on proprietary video calling and broadcasting platforms such as Zoom and YouTube included participants from both local and remote locations; this at least partly relates to the specialised topics for the programming that may have been produced to address local issues but which attracted those who took a specialist interest in the content. The use of affordances including American Sign Language, visual captioning, and transcription to enhance video broadcasts hosted by the Peale seems to have encouraged audiences of disabled people to participate in live events and the potential reach of web-hosted video recordings that are available indefinitely is another extension to the accessibility of the content. Events at the De La Warr Pavilion had from three to six times the "rewatch" audiences as the events attracted "live" attendance.

The greatest step towards a digitally enabled visit was undertaken by the Peale as it moved into Second Life and the creation of a wholly virtual environment that provided a digital proxy for the existing physical establishment. Museums have been experimenting with "virtual" experiences on different scales for a number of years, and the blended use of 3D modelling and virtual reality technologies is one of the futures that is envisioned for museums by ICT specialists (see for example Margetis et al., 2021). The production of a virtual reality online museum was an incredibly resource-intensive undertaking that was inspired by the radical impact of COVID-19 on physical operations; and one of its significant impacts was to alter the audience for the museum and its exhibition. The evaluation written by Naliyah Kaya states that "Second Life visitors who completed surveys were more likely to identify as having a disability (37.5%) than visitors of all other components of the Redefine/ABLE exhibit (11.1%) who completed surveys, it would seem to indicate that the Second Life virtual museum exhibit was a success in terms of not only attracting a large number of attendees but also in terms of reaching more visitors with disabilities". Because the Second Life platform has specialised support and resources for disabled users (some of which are created by the non-profit organisation Virtual Ability) this platform may offer an exceptional opportunity to engage with disabled users; whereas the programming partners at the De La Warr Pavilion expressed some concerns about the accessibility of online formats for their audiences in terms of digital poverty, digital skills, and digital fatigue.

The Royal Pavilion and Museums did not have access to such location data for the audience for its audiotour but reported that, from 1 April to 30 June, the overall website traffic was down by 45% as no one needed to access pre-visit information. This is interpreted by the Royal Pavilion and Museums Brighton to suggest that about half of their website users come for information that is not related to a physical visit. Kevin Bacon, their Digital Director, writes: "this is a big change from 2014 when research indicated that very few of our website users were interested in anything but pre-visit information, which informed the site-centric information architecture of the current website". The evolving digital engagement in the population at large, as well as the pandemic situation, suggests that visitors are much more likely than five years ago to substitute a physical visit with a digitally enabled visit. These changes have also affected The Royal Pavilion and Museum Brighton's Mindful Garden audiotour of the Pavilion Gardens coincided with their pilot of a "bring your own device" version of the audioguide for the Royal Pavilion Museum building. The uptake of this offer was sufficiently encouraging for the organisation to firmly place developing digital content for access with users' own devices at the heart of the organisation's strategic plan for future digital development. In replacing a device-provided service, this move improves accessibility because there is no need for an individual user to acquire, learn to use, and adjust the settings on an institution-provided device, and there is sufficient alignment between the Royal Pavilion and Museums Brighton's audience base and the users of digitally enabled mobile phones to be able to rely on the user already having an appropriate device to use.

What demonstrated less success in expanding audience engagement was extending the content of the specific programmes into the platforms provided by proprietary social media or apps that had been designed to support adjacent projects. The only project which deliberately mobilised social media as a platform for sharing content was Redefine/ABLE, which reused elements of the physical exhibition design as assets to be shared on social media platforms including Twitter, Instagram, and TikTok, using new accounts specifically related to the exhibition. The data available for this element did not suggest that this was a particularly effective mode of dissemination or expanding audiences. The other digital platform that our project experimented with is a "bring in, take out" audio file sharing programme, which is used at the Peale under the title of "BeHere" as an IoS (Apple user) app and an online version which has been introduced to enable remote access by other types of mobile devices. The addition of a web-based service to the Peale's existing IoS app service has had an impact on usage (54% of 4,515 listens accessed the content via a web-based, Android, or similar device). These are significant outcomes for a programme whose emergency initiatives did not have dedicated marketing budgets and did not benefit from significant opportunities to interact with the potential users on site. The lesson learned is that digital tools need an institutional investment in their promotion and that digital offers related to temporary exhibitions or activities benefit from being linked with overall institutional provision.

The benefits of inclusive content

One of the most consistent findings of the different aspects of the programme was the importance of developing inclusive content that signals to audiences that their specific needs are considered and addressed by the institution. This was evident across the projects but particularly in relation to the Mindful Garden (with respect to audiences whose needs and desires are oriented more towards improving well-being and generalised mental health), and in the evidence gathered in relation to the sensory and mobility needs that were addressed in the content of the Redefine/ABLE exhibition. Interestingly, one of the elements of audience feedback that was offered in relation to Redefine/ABLE was that the more explicit content related to invisible disabilities such as mental health would have been welcomed, which reflects some changing perceptions and values around the social conditions that are considered to require particular affordances.

The Redefine/ABLE exhibition provides the richest data on the question of the impact of content because the process through which the exhibition was developed and evaluated recruited the most extensive qualitative feedback from a variety of stakeholders. Both audiences and contributors to the exhibition reported positive outcomes from their engagement. Disabled visitors and consultants on the programme valued the way the exhibition centred the experiences of disabled people in its design, respecting and communicating their experiences in new and thoughtful ways. Non-disabled visitors and the student designers who contributed to the exhibition design process also gave positive feedback on the impact of the exhibition content on their thinking about disability and ableism. Some of the most interesting qualitative feedback on this point was returned in relation to the Second Life exhibition, in response to which disabled respondents were extremely candid. Their feedback included detailed notes about where technical elements of the display hindered accessibility (e.g., where speech bubbles obscured other visual content) but also the importance of rendering the virtual space with accessibility affordances that would be functional if offered in physical space such as wheelchair ramps. These comments underline the importance of accessibility as part of the museum imaginary, and not just as part of its physical site.

The nature of the content of the Royal Pavilion and Museum's Mindful Garden audiotour has similarly been central to the perception of the success of the project and the planning of future developments in the Museum. Described by the Digital Director Kevin Bacon as a "radical proof of concept" for a change in an approach to content development for the Museum, the Mindful Garden tour decentres fact-based learning and encourages active reflection on the user's environment. This approach employs the principles of "mindfulness" which is a practice that has evolved through various global spiritual traditions over centuries and in the last 50 years has been adopted in Western medicalised psychology as a mechanism for promoting good mental health. The audiotour did not receive a huge uptake in terms of volume compared to the Museum's other web-based offers (counted in tens rather than thousands of users), but it does attract extended engagement from the visitors who access it (dwell time averages 23 minutes, which suggests some repeated listening). The results of the Mindful Garden tour have been considered by the RPM in relation to other evidence of the Museum's web audience preference for content during the pandemic (for example, a higher interest in jigsaw puzzles than content aimed at supporting school curricula) as well as the initial success of a mobile app that engages visitors in visually investigating objects in the museum through prompted questions that relate to storytelling. Together, these projects offered what is considered decisive evidence that the character of the content that is offered by the museum and the nature of the engagement that it attracts from audiences needs to be reconsidered as a central part of the Museum's online strategy.

The content that developed in the De La Warr Pavilion's projects to develop programming in partnership with activist groups addressing community cohesion provided little evidence of audience response to content except in terms of quantitative data, so it is more difficult to draw any conclusions about the appeal of the content for the intended audiences. The community partners remarked on how rare it was in their experience for cultural organisations to prioritise community-led agendas over institutional "missions"; and their perception that the more effective steps were taken by giving over the capacity to commission content or programming rather than by inviting the groups to make use resources that had already been developed. Their view was that altering the focus of the programme from the De La Warr's core activities of exhibitions, musical performance, and cinema could extend the organisation's audience to individuals whose experience of those activities has been one of the barriers to participation, but the data collected did not allow us to evaluate this proposition.

Organisational implications

The importance of museums in promoting health and well-being is often promoted in relation to the outcomes for the individual user (Thomson and Chatterjee 2015). In our study we acquired limited but useful intelligence as to the impact of our different initiatives on individuals or user groups defined by a certain social characteristic; but possibly more importantly we have also framed our programme as a means to study the pattern and nature of the organisational changes that need to be developed in order to embed inclusivity in the digital programming offered by locally oriented institutions.

Feminist and other evaluations of curatorial or museum projects that seek to foster community engagement have often described the lack of sustainability of these initiatives because of their over-reliance on the emotional and social labour of curatorial staff (V. Horne *et al.* 2016). The investigation of the sustainability of digital developments for well-being in civic historic museums is as paramount to developing good practice as is the question of their efficacy for individual visitors. One of the most consistent and emphatic outcomes of each of the component projects was the importance of external engagement to the effective consideration and integration of inclusive practice. This took place through a number of mechanisms in the project: consulting external advisors who represent the user community identified for inclusion; inviting professionals with skill sets beyond those normally found in museum staff to support the development of content as well as implementation; and finally, engaging in partnership working with selected external collaborators including letting them set the agenda for content, and ideally, in the selection and development of the mechanisms for digital engagement. None of these observations was specifically focused on particular aspects of digital technology, but highlighted the extent to which digital activities benefit from dialogic and decentralising processes that characterise inclusive practice in museum work more generally.

The benefits of considering inclusive practice as an organisational, rather than a technical, activity were particularly signalled in the project at the Peale. In the context of thinking about accessibility for disabled audiences, the Peale's move to replace the physical exhibition with a digital one brought several elements to the foreground for the organisers in terms of thinking about accessibility. Chief among these was the levelling out process that was experienced by the team as they migrated into a digital space in which needed additional support in terms of training, learning, and practice for them to navigate successfully. The humbling experience of being demoted from experts to neophytes as they learned to navigate a new space offered the team insights into the conditions of disabled people who are effectively deskilled by the requirements of physical spaces that are not adapted to their use. This experience promoted amongst staff a more generous attitude to the provision of affordances in the accompanying programming, which in turn fostered participation. The impact of involving disabled people in the initial design process echoed throughout the delivery stages of the project.

The question of consistency in terms of institutional personnel and community participants is a crucial one. The structure of the different projects allows for a comparison between the ways that different organisations approached the question of external engagement in the production of museum content. While the report from the De La Warr Pavilion highlights the extent to which the project development process was fractured by interrupted work patterns for the DLWP staff during the pandemic and its associated programmes of "furlough", more sustained working partnerships characterised the project at the Peale and the Royal Pavilion and Museums Brighton. At the Peale, input from disabled people was structurally incorporated into the design, delivery, and evaluation processes. This input did not rely on the consistency of individual participants but on the continuity of working with particular interest groups as a programme is developed, executed, and the learning from it is advanced into new projects. At the Royal Pavilion and Museums Brighton, the oversight of a number of different projects by one individual in a named role (Digital Manager) is what has allowed for the alignment of external input with organisational ambitions. The capacity to translate the expertise and insights of external experts is clearly integral to the success of these programmes and committing resources to enable and sustain those partnerships is clearly essential.

The requirement to invest resources in these partnerships highlights one of the significant risk areas of partnership working inclusively with marginalised communities, which is that it is likely to offer challenges to the established priorities of the organisation. These challenges come in terms of allocation of resources, but also in terms of acknowledging expertise and even in terms of organisational mission. It's a principle of care ethics that practices of care are driven by the needs of the cared for rather than the priorities of the carer. This means that organisations who practice this work need to be highly flexible in terms of mission so that the priorities of users can lead the development. At the De La Warr Pavilion and at the Royal Pavilion and Museums Brighton, the content of the interpretation and events was shifted away from the collections/exhibition artefacts, and the outcome was that new uses of the organisation's cultural heritage were generated. At the Peale, the organisation's cultural heritage was literally regenerated in digital form, to provide levels of accessibility that could not be replicated in the physical domain.

Conclusions

The key findings of our project were to confirm that it is possible for historic, civic museums to extend their audiences by using digital tools to augment their activities that are normally based in and around physical premises and collections. Measures of success included extending the geographic reach of programming; quantification of audience engagement with digital activities including numbers of accesses or time spent using the offering as one indicator of the perceived value of the content; and finally, enhanced confidence of audiences that the organisation shared the priorities of the community.

The most successful projects in terms of increasing visitor use of digital technology involved **optimising technology** choices, mainly by presenting content via platforms that were already in use by the intended audiences. These included mobile web-based versions of material or activities that had previously been accessible via downloaded apps or by museum-provided handheld devices; the use of replayable online broadcast services, which are most easily adapted by users for their own circumstances; and migration from a physical environment to the web-based virtual reality platform, Second Life. We also found that there were benefits to **developing inclusive**

content. This was achieved primarily as a result of consistent and responsive engagement with external experts (including experts by experience) through the different stages of planning, execution, and reflection as the content was developed. Shifting the work of developing content from the organisation itself onto external experts may challenge the structures of authority and expertise that museums have often developed. But taking on the **organisational implications** of improving inclusivity is foundational to successful inclusivity initiatives. Civic museums need to demonstrate high degree of flexibility in terms of prioritising the needs of users over established institutional missions and practices in order to establish relationships of mutual trust that underpin engagement. All of these practices can neatly be summarised as gestures of care on behalf of the institution for its audience: gestures that demonstrate consideration for their diverse and possibly unexpected needs of their civic museum.

These are the conclusions that we drew from our work in the months immediately after we completed it. The context of delivery of the programme during the height of the COVID-19 pandemic may, however, eventually provide a different perspective on the projects and their outcomes. COVID-19 significantly altered the behaviour of audiences and the way that the partner organisations were working during the period of the project delivery, especially in their use of digital communications tools. What started as responses to a crisis may become more fully embedded in the relationships between cultural heritage organisations and their local – and more distant – audiences. If this is the case, then one vital area for further development is in the area of evaluation (Economou 2016). In 2018, we planned that the evaluation of our initiatives would be via site-based interactions between organisation staff and the visitors or users, methods which we were largely unable to engage in as the project was in fact delivered. Our evaluations were based mainly on the valuable feedback from project partners who were involved in the development and delivery of the programmes (who practice research daily in their work as Emily Pringle observes in her 2019 book); and we also gained insight through thinking about our data in different ways (for example, rather than the number of users, the quality of their engagement as expressed in duration). Encouraging visitors to interact with us via chat functions during broadcasts helped to supplement the information that came through the more conventional route of formal evaluation feedback forms and interviews. The limitations on our use of audience or user data do not simply reflect an instrumental failure of our processes to recruit data that was sufficient for the purposes of evaluation, but shed light on the central problem that the study was designed to explore: that communication is at least a two-way act, and that it is through using communication tools, digital and otherwise, to invite genuine dialogue between cultural heritage organisations and their audiences that has the potential to improve their inclusivity.

These outcomes are consistent with the proposition that was the foundation of our project: that museum contributions to community "wellbeing" do not need to be focused solely on a medical model of health that seeks to establish the impact on the physical and mental health of the individual user. While medical advantages of course present a huge potential gain both for museum visitors and their hosts, this does not represent the limit of what can be achieved by conceiving of cultural heritage organisations as part of a "landscape of care". By fostering programming that enhances the reciprocal levels of social and emotional engagement between cultural heritage organisations and their users, organisations such as our partner museums can embed themselves as part of a structure which sustains, offers, and demands our participation in inclusive communities.

References

All-Party Parliamentary Group on Arts, Health and Wellbeing and What Works Centre for Wellbeing., 2017. *Arts, engagement and wellbeing*. Barnsley: Culture, Health and Wellbeing Alliance. https://www.culturehealthandwellbeing.org.uk/appg-inquiry/ [accessed 25 April 2022].

Brown, M., and Tucker, K., 2018. Unconsented sterilization, participatory storytelling, and digital counter-memory in Peru. *Conexion*, 7 (9), 55–80.

Clarke, R. and Lewis, R.M., 2016. Reconfiguring inclusion, decolonising practice: digital participation and learning in Black women's community-led heritage. *Journal of Adult and Continuing Education*, 22 (2), 134–151.

Economou, M., 2016. Evaluating digital resources in cultural heritage: lessons from the ScotDigiCH network. In: H. Thwaites, L.S. Lun and A. Addison eds, *22nd International Conference on Virtual System & Multimedia (VSMM)* 17–21 October 2016, Kuala Lumpur, Malaysia. New York: Institute of Electrical and Electronics Engineers, 1–7.

Hill, K., 2013. Manufactures, archaeology and bygones: making a sense of place in civic museums, 1850–1914. *International Journal of Regional and Local History*, 8 (1), 54–74.

Horne, V. *et al.*, 2016. Taking care: feminist curatorial pasts, presents, and futures. *OnCurating* [online] 29. Available from: https://www.on-curating.org/issue-29-reader/taking-care-feminist-curatorial-pasts-presents-and-futures.html#.YlC255LMLOQ [Accessed 25 April 2022].

Innocenti, P., 2016. Cultural networks and social inclusion of migrants in Europe: heritage, ICT, and participatory governance. *International Information & Library Review*, 48 (4), 274–286.

Kidd, J., 2019. With new eyes I see: embodiment, silence and empathy in digital heritage interpretation. *International Journal of Heritage Studies* 25 (1), 54–66.

Leigh, S., 2016. Free people's medical clinic. In: B.R. Munoz, ed. *Health* London: MIT Press and the Whitechapel Art Gallery, 85–88.

Margetis, G. *et al.*, 2021. X-Reality museums: unifying the virtual and real world towards realistic virtual museums. *Applied Sciences,* 11, 338.

Milligan, C., and Wiles, J., 2010. Landscapes of care. *Progress in Human Geography*, 34 (6), 736–754.

Morse, N., and Munro, E., 2018. Museums community engagement schemes, austerity and practices of care in two local museum services. *Social & Cultural Geography*, 19 (3), 357–378.

Nedelcu, M., and Soysüren, I., 2020. Precarious migrants, migration regimes and digital technologies: the empowerment-control nexus'. *Journal of Ethnic and Migration Studies*, doi: 10.1080/1369183X.2020.1796263

Pringle, E., 2019. *Rethinking research in the art museum*. London and New York: Routledge.

Proctor, N., 2013. Crowdsourcing – an introduction: from public goods to public good, *Curator: The Museum Journal*, 56 (1), 105–106.

Proctor, N., 2021. The collection is dead; long live the collective: rethinking the role of content and collections in the museum's purpose post-pandemic, M. Shehade and T. Stylianou eds, RISE IMET 2021, Nicosia, Cyprus 2-4 June 2021, Cyprus: CYENS 1432, 254–268.

Samaroudi, M., Echaverria, K.R., and Perry, L., 2020. Heritage in lockdown: digital provision of memory institutions in the United Kingdom and United States of America during the COVID-19 pandemic. *Journal of Museum Management and Curatorship*, 35 (4), 337–361.

'Second Life', *Wikipedia*, https://en.wikipedia.org/wiki/Second_Life [accessed November 2021].

Taylor, J., and Gibson, L.K., 2017. Digitisation, digital interaction and social media: embedded barriers to democratic heritage. *International Journal of Heritage Studies*, 23 (5), 408–420.

Thomson, L., and Chatterjee, H., 2015. Measuring the impact of museum activities on well-being: developing the museum well-being measures toolkit. *Museum Management and Curatorship*, 30 (1), 44–62.

Todd, C. *et al.*, 2017. Museum-based programs for socially isolated older adults: Understanding what works. *Health and place*, 48, 47–55.

7 Participatory polyvocal performative and playful interpreting Resnik's 4 for creative placemaking with digital tools

Tanis Grandison, Tom Flint, and Kirstie Jamieson

Introduction

This chapter presents a 4Ps framework for using digital media within creative placemaking. In so doing, it reflects upon the processes of creative placemaking and the capacity of digital media tools to support communities to explore, unpack, and construct new and relevant meanings and connections. The authors argue that digital media tools are particularly useful within creative placemaking practices when used to support social inclusion.

In the context of this chapter, inclusion through digital tools is a playful approach to facilitating young participants' engagement with counter-narratives about place. Using an empirical Digi-Mapping case study conducted in Wester Hailes, Edinburgh UK, the research described in this chapter demonstrates how inclusion through digital tools can be incorporated into creative placemaking processes to support the construction and celebration of diverse identities.

The Digi-Mapping project provided an opportunity for young participants to counter the stigma of Wester Hailes, an area of multiple deprivations according to the Scottish Index of Multiple Deprivation (SIMD 2021). The project revealed how creative and collaborative processes can provide platforms where participants are able to share contested forms of knowledge about place and enable a pluralist approach to placemaking. Moreover, the project found that digital tools supported dialogic and collaborative narratives that over time, sustained an engaged and polyvocal community. The use of Digi-Mapping facilitated "social meaning, convention, cultural understandings about role, function and nature and so on" (Harrison and Dourish 1996, p. 67) and thereby cultivated a sense of place in Wester Hailes that transformed the spaces of stigma into those of storyworlds and memory.

The Digi-Mapping project employed the tools of map-making, digital media tools such as audio recorders, tablets, and Bare Conductive TouchBoards. To support an explorative and embodied communal experience of Wester Hailes, the research developed psychogeographic tours of

DOI: 10.4324/9781003277606-7

the area to facilitate hyper-local encounters with place. While other technology such as MicroBit and Arduino were considered, Bare Conductive TouchBoards were chosen for the following reasons:

- They are relatively cheap, costing £55
- They are created with an audio focus – but are capable of other functions
- They do not require learning a programming language to start using them which is ideal for workshops with time limits.

The technology and approach of the empirical study is framed through the lens of Resnick 4P's for digital creativity. This framework was chosen because of its attention to processual modes of engagement rather than an end product. The benefits of Resnick's framework will be discussed further in the following sections.

The core contribution of this chapter is a revised 4Ps framework sensitive to the complex forms of individual and collective knowledge that is associated with placemaking. This chapter argues that the proposed 4Ps framework can be adapted to site-specific processes of unpacking meaning *with* communities *through* digital media tools. This framework will be of use to those working in critical and community heritage practice as well as those working in heritage institutions that wish to engage in Zitcer inclusive and critical practices. The research described in this chapter also contributes to the field of practice for creative placemaking. It responds to Zitcer's (2020) call for creative placemaking to continue to be successful it "needs to be institutionalized and a field of practice built" (p. 286). In this way, this chapter advocates inclusion as a means of enabling pluralities of place-based meaning. The proposed 4Ps framework described in the following paragraphs should be understood as an adaptive platform for participants to construct, perform, and share meaning about their local area. This chapter draws on both critical and community heritage practices to help understand approaches to creative placemaking and their value for exploring meaning and identity with places.

This chapter begins with a critical review of the literature. Firstly, it draws upon Resnick's 4Ps for digital creativity arguing that when combined with digital storytelling, Resnick's 4Ps can support social inclusion through pluralised meanings and acts of sharing. This inclusive approach is supported further by literature drawn from critical heritage and creative placemaking practices. Through this conspectus of literature, the authors argue that digital media is uniquely placed to facilitate complex and inclusive meaning-making. Resnick's revised 4Ps are then presented through their application within the empirical study, a six-week Digi-Mapping project in collaboration with WHALE Arts in Wester Hailes, Edinburgh, UK. Details of the participative processes, and outcomes of the Digi-Mapping media, and its tactical talking affordances are then described followed by a discussion of the findings. Drawing upon insights gained from the findings, the authors propose an amended 4Ps framework of Participatory, Performative, Polyvocal, and Playful. Finally, the chapter concludes by highlighting how this framework supports inclusion with young participants.

Literature informing this chapter

To better understand how digital media and creative placemaking can support social inclusion, it is useful to draw on two key areas. Firstly, Resnick's 4Ps for creativity, which highlights the process of creativity with digital media tools. In the paragraphs that follow, comparisons are drawn between the ethos of Resnick's framework and creative placemaking. Developing the argument for Resnick's 4Ps in creative placemaking, this chapter demonstrates how the author's attention to a processual logic can support social inclusion with digital media tools. Secondly, literature from scholars of critical and community heritage is drawn upon to provide a contextual body of work that privileges bottom-up approaches to place. The literature allows connections to be made between creative placemaking and critical and community heritage through their shared attention to issues such as communities of practice, polyvocal narratives, and digital storytelling. Synthesising the work of Resnick with critical and community heritage literature, this chapter develops an understanding of the inclusive role that digital media can play in Resnick's processual 4Ps for digital creativity; Projects, Passion, Peers, and Play.

Resnick's 4Ps for digital creativity

While creating the programming language Scratch at MIT, Mitch Resnick developed the 4Ps framework of Projects, Passion, Peers, and Play. Scratch was developed from a project perspective rather than a step-by-step learning approach. The design of Scratch and Resnick's framework is heavily influenced by constructionist learning principles (Papert 1980). For a comprehensive overview of the 4Ps refer to Resnick's book "Lifelong Kindergarten" (2017):

Projects

According to Resnick, people learn best when they are doing something that is meaningful to them. When participants are interested and engaged with something, they will continue to learn iteratively on that learning to build knowledge. He tells us that this supports construction and the processes of meaning-making through engaging in a reflective process.

Passion

Resnick states that people are more likely to meaningfully engage in things that are considered difficult when they are genuinely interested in the subject. A concept, the author refers to as "hard fun". Engaging in things people are passionate about should according to him lead participants to learn *more i*n the process as they will actively work out challenges and work longer and harder to complete tasks.

Peers

Resnick argues that peers can act as a mechanism to collaboratively problem-solve and enhance understanding. He posits that this is important as *thinking* and *doing* take place in a context. It is through the collaboration and mutual learning that engagement can be sustained, what O'Reilly-de Brún *et al.* (2017) call "meaningful engagement". According to Resnick, digital media can be a useful tool to unpack, process, and share meaning through processes of polyvocality and social action creating meaningful engagement.

Play

Kane (2006) argues that play is a vital aspect of our development through experimentation and imagination. It is not solely a form of leisure. Play challenges the status quo and using digital media can engage in counter-narratives that create a platform for empowerment and social inclusion (Sutton-Smith 1997).

Digital storytelling and social inclusion

One-way communities can come together without the need to be present in their immediate local physical spaces is through digital networks, where shared values and identity-based narratives can take new forms and reach new audiences. Papacharissi (2015) argues that in digital spaces, meaningful creation happens in storytelling acts where the creating and sharing of identities both reflect and produce a sense of community. Anderson (2009) suggests that the binary of physical/digital is less useful than seeing community space as that which is embedded in the triad of place, culture, and context. Whether physical or digital, this triad is *performed* and given form through rituals and narratives that shape people's connections, memories, and rhythms. Place is therefore shaped by both physical and digital interactions and meanings. Moreover, place is produced through storyworld conventions where fact, fiction, myth, and memory collide. For both Papacharissi (2015) and Anderson (2009) storytelling supports mutual understanding and galvanises a sense of community and a community of feeling. Storytelling can serve multiple functions for communities: a means of understanding the community's connection to an ever-changing world, a way of learning through collective memory, a form of reflection, a way of eliciting social action, and lastly as a process of understanding ourselves and our identity (Lambert 2013). Storytelling is more than the sum of its parts, as units of knowledge, it enables the retelling of knowledge through stories that retain knowledge structures and connect to other/wider/older memories.

Media creates opportunities to form new experiences and explore relationships between ourselves, to the world, our identities, and communities (McLuhan 1964). Digital storytelling can be understood as a mechanism to "*amplify the ordinary voice*" (Burgess 2006, p. 207). It is through this capacity to amplify previously marginalised voices that digital storytelling can contribute to the building and connecting of communities through a shared sense of history (Conrad 2013). Lambert (2013) argues that when using storytelling practices in community work, stories are more successful within an environment that is thought of as "safe" (p. 15). Lambert also states that one way safety is created is through the group and that everyone is in it together, sharing and listening to each other. Additionally, Schofield (2014) notes, storytelling is a vital element in the creation of memory. Storytelling conjures people rather than objects as active agents in the production of forms of heritage that connect life, beliefs, and tradition rather than relics or works of art (Davis 1999).

Digitally mediated site-specific storytelling offers audiences a chance to empathically engage with spaces and subjects in an immediate and locative way. This allows audiences a unique opportunity to draw upon other phenomenological senses beyond that of the screen. Moreover, site-specific digital storytelling can highlight connections that are meaningful between mobile devices and places rather than a focus of the screen as the site of content and engagement (Farman 2018).

According to Raley (2009), digital media, or "tactical media" can subvert or counter dominant narratives through a "micropolitics of disruption, intervention and education" (p. 1). This argument situates digital storytelling as a potent counter-narrative to discourses of deprivation and poverty that can over time stigmatise places and their communities. Hoskins (2009) highlights the link between media remediation and collective memory, in what he describes as ecologies of media/memory defined as the "mediatisation of memory" which becomes the basis for social groups and collective identities (p. 278). Building on this, Vivienne and Burgess (2013) argue that when using personal images in digital storytelling, even the processes of editing, selecting, and sharing are mediated due to their identity within social networks. When these memories are mediated, they then change our relationships with the objects and the narrative around it also changes. This echoes Assmann's (2008) claim that as memory cannot be transferred, props can instead be used in the storytelling process. Memory can be closely aligned with imagination.

Critical heritage

Winter (2013) argues that heritage has the capacity to address social issues beyond heritage. Adding the prefix "critical" to heritage highlights "the different and often contradictory understandings of the nature, ownership, value, meaning, and significance of heritage that are held by official interlocutors and unofficial sectors of the population" (Silverman 2014, p. 3332). Critical heritage not only acknowledges the traditional top-down power structure of heritage-making, but also seeks to afford communities collaborative opportunities to participate in the production of heritage meanings (Waterton and Smith 2009).

The capacity of critical heritage to recalibrate the top-down processes of heritage-making has a broad appeal to urbanists, community planners, and creative placemakers. The collaborative activities that advance more democratic heritage-making processes (Malpas 2008) include digital media which can *distribute* participation and *symbolise* diverse meanings and *enable* a collective process. Through digital media tools, meanings of heritage can be presented as contingent and playable, allowing community members to contribute to a matrix of meaning (Malpas 2008). For example, mobile phones are a powerful tool to advance critical heritage's bottom-up approach to heritage-making (Farman 2018), by distributing the capacity to engage and create contested landscapes. This can be done by creating editable interactive digital content that is specific to place. In time, this can become a pluralised record of place that is formed through an ongoing processual and contributive relation to heritage-making. Layers of distributed non-expert participant-led digital content can produce stories of space and time that have traditionally been excluded from mainstream heritage discourses and spaces.

Zavala *et al.* (2017) examine the role of community archives to challenge traditional practices that reflect community value and agency. Their research includes different types of digital archives that enabled the community to self-regulate materials. This approach led to the archives better reflecting community values, needs, and empowers individuals. According to Zavala *et al.* (ibid.) using these digital and distributed approaches can enhance trust when collaborating with larger organisations such as public libraries by breaking the assumption of control and custody of archives. Looking at the use of digital storytelling in archives, Nisi and Cesario (2021) investigated how digital storytelling can support community interpretations of intangible cultural heritage by migrant communities. The researchers sought to democratise the heritage-making process to create an interactive digital storytelling platform for oral histories. The researchers argue for approaches that include the community from the outset of the project, thereby allowing the community to develop culturally sensitive approaches that ensure the safeguarding of stories shared.

Exploring how museum and bottom-up heritage can converge through digitally mediated dialogues Galani *et al.* (2019) argue that different types of dialogue can take place using digital media:

- It can happen between institutions and people.
- It can create unofficial narratives which mean that they can be more diverse.
- These dialogues can attract new audiences.
- Dialogues do not have to happen at physical sites.

Bringing together place with digital media and engagement with critical heritage, Poole's (2018) *Ghosts in the Garden* was a collaborative museum project that involved creating a locative and GPS RFID experience using game mechanics to trigger an immersive experience of narratives of past visitors. The aim was to create a richer experience that challenged the use of ubiquitous audio guides within the heritage industry. However, the use of such technology can have its limitations. Hornecker and Ciolfi (2019) examine the role of Human-Computer Interaction (HCI) within museum spaces, arguing that, museums generally have access to more money than communities and can innovate and experiment with new and emerging digital technologies.

The success of technology as interpretation media and as modes of community engagement is precarious. Risks associated with museums' use of technology are twofold; firstly, new technology can be expensive, and secondly its goal is to attract and maintain visitor engagement and the technology may become obsolete quickly. In line with these debates, Hornecker and Ciolfi (2019) argue that museums are changing the way that they engage with publics. They maintain that museums are becoming places that create community engagement and engage in issues facing society. However, they go on to state: "the risk is that a rhetoric of social action or community empowerment is used by museums without truly being embedded in their missions and ways of working" (p. 123). Although digital media can help to create a participatory heritage, the truth is that the use of digital media tools within bottom-up approaches to heritage does not necessarily transform community content into official histories (Han *et al.* 2014). However, Schofield *et al.* (2019) contest this and state that "it is exactly in these 'non' official histories that most exciting challenges for both heritage and design exist. A significant offer of digital technologies is the opportunity to present layered, contrasting or diverse perspectives be that through existing paradigms (e.g., comment threads or wiki edit histories) or through innovative interaction design" (p. 3).

Russo *et al.* (2012) argue that by giving people the ability to creatively share in a social media setting can support the exploration of identity and create cultural participation. The potential of participatory heritage to move towards a "post-custodial, participatory paradigm" (p. 1) is within sight according to Liew *et al.* (2022). This is an important development within the heritage landscape as digital media gives form and distribution to previously hidden counter-narratives. If we consider these elements and where they overlap in relation to creative placemaking, common themes emerge.

Creative placemaking

According to the National Endowment for the Arts, creative placemaking "integrates arts, culture, and design activities into efforts that strengthen communities" (NEA 2021, p. 1). Creative placemaking seeks to engage with co-constructed meaning of place, engaging residents in creative practice to critique and enhance their built environment. Creative placemaking brings an explicit focus on participatory processes, and the use of creative arts practice to create change in an urban area. It also involves some level of curation in the way knowledge is *made public* and shared – a way of keeping track. This curation is often more focused on the relationship between people, places, ideas, and objects and is a co-produced effort between the different actors involved (Courage and McKeown 2019).

The use of creative practices that unpack collective memories, artefacts social constructs and sensory connections to places presents community members with a way of exploring and expressing their identity and connection to place individually and collaboratively. Key to the importance of these kinds of inclusive creative practices is the artist van Heeswijk's argument that the "*community is the expert in being the community*" (2012) and when done properly creative placemaking creates an "*agency of relative expertism*" (Courage 2017). The concept of "relative expertism" speaks to the turn to critical heritage and its valorisation of traditional non-experts, whose expertise is inextricably linked to lived experience and implicit working knowledge of place. In this context, everyday stories map relationships between people and place.

In creative placemaking practice, storytellers help shape the ways in which the environment can be related to a sense of self. Storytellers can conjure a feeling of place through the sharing and telling of characters' experiences. The diegetic bond between storyteller and listener reveals the "co-constructed nature of meaning" (Lambert 2013, p. 14). It is useful to consider the role of the storyteller in relation to Digi-Mapping because it brings to the fore the value of both stories and mapping in leveraging the power of the imaginary. As Duxbury *et al.* (2019) argue "imagination carries potentials for unseating convention, perspective, actuality, reproducibility, and common sense. Space for imagination can shift research and community planning from a 'reflective' stance to a more 'future forming' orientation and practice, in which life is characterized in terms of 'continuous becoming'" (p. 6). The authors argue that taken together, maps and stories are potent tools in the enabling of alternative chartings of space, time, experience, relationships, ecologies, moments, and concepts. The authors cite more benefits to the use of creative mapping activities and the potential to make "unprecedented connections between the material and the abstract, the actual and the virtual, the tangible and the intangible, the objective and the felt" (p. 6).

The storyteller and the map belong to an assemblage of tools, professions, and community members that contribute to a diverse set of creative placemaking activities. According to Duxbury *et al.* (2019), together these constituent parts form a relational community of practice (CoP) capable of offering "fresh challenges and opportunities to traditional planning methods and community self-representation" (p. 6). For Fusté-Forné and Nguyen (2018) "CoP brings together concepts of history, identity, values, practice, and community. Intangible cultural heritage (ICH) communities are networks of people whose sense of identity and interconnectedness emerge from a shared historical and geographical relationship" (p. 1).

Of pertinence to our work, Wyckoff (2014) highlights the ambiguity of creative placemaking and questions where it sits within Placemaking. He proposes four areas: Placemaking, Strategic Placemaking, Creative Placemaking, and Tactical Placemaking. These areas overlap and can create ambiguity. Creative placemaking is more than the sum of its parts and it is capable of offering alternative forms of community knowledge. However, if creative placemaking is going to continue to be successful, then new frameworks and methods are required to explore and support a processual and collaborative approach to "places-in-the-making" and support and "encourage citizen-led agency" (Courage and McKeown 2019, p. 1). When done well, creative placemaking creates an ecology of community voices wherein space is given to collaboration and the co-construction of place-based knowledge.

Synthesising the literature

Courage (2021) clearly states that creative placemaking needs to place more emphasis on the ephemeral processes, and as described above, Resnick's (2017) framework was chosen precisely because it focuses on the *process* of creativity with digital media tools. There are several elements within this framework that are particularly useful and link with creative placemaking practice. It can be argued that the process of creativity creates authentic participation particularly through storytelling. The framework embraces reflective practices which is a fundamental aspect of bottom-up approaches, investigating meanings, memory, and identity with place. Moreover, Resnick places importance on the use of "Peers" within the framework. Of relevance to this chapter is how this process sits within communities, again linking to a community of practice which is fundamental to creative placemaking.

Resnick's framework enables people who are non-experts to be part of a *community of making* which mirrors the approaches of critical heritage and community heritage. Lastly, it embraces the ethos of remediation and remixing, which can be thought of as *flow*: creating, sharing, and feedback when building on the work of others. This is similar to the flow of folklore among a group (McNeill 2013) or "lived-ness" (Krawczyk-Wasilewska 2017, p. 29). As argued by Perkin (2010) folklore and community-based expression are vital to heritage. Resnick's framework can be a way for people to digitally engage with counter-narratives, future-making, community-making, and this could lead to creating social inclusion through play.

Digital storytelling can also create safe spaces for mutual sharing, and this is key to the potentiality of critical heritage and its capacity to address issues and create social inclusion. However as outlined by Resnick, participants need to be willing to learn something hard (that they do not already know) if they are to become meaningfully engaged in placemaking activities.

Digi-Mapping Wester Hailes

Wester Hailes, according to the Scottish Index of Multiple Deprivation (SIMD 2021), sits within the top 10% of areas with multiple deprivation in Scotland, U.K. It is an area that lies approximately 5 miles West of Edinburgh city centre. It was initially built as a brutalist housing scheme in the 1960s. The original urban planning aim of areas such as Wester Hailes was to move inner city poverty to the outskirts of the city. Sites such as Wester Hailes were large-scale public housing, poorly constructed contributing to them quickly becoming an undesirable place to live (Gilloran 1983). For most of its lifespan, the reputation of Wester Hailes has often been associated with negative and dangerous connotations that have been aggregated by films such as "Trainspotting" (Hodge *et al.* 1997) and "Restless Natives" (Hoffman 1985) which mine Wester Hailes' brutalist landscape and disrepute for a debauched and criminal story world. In the 1980s, Wester Hailes and Edinburgh became the HIV/AIDS capital of Europe. This was mainly attributed to the high levels of drug abuse and violence in the area. This negative and stigmatised reputation of Wester Hailes earned it the nickname "Wasters Hell" (Matthews 2014).

However, because of the social exclusion that has consistently affected the area, Wester Hailes has had a long history of community activism and a commitment to tackling some of the struggles that the area's reputation is based upon. Within Wester Hailes, the local arts organisation WHALE Arts sits on the site of one of the old community-built huts. These huts as demonstrated in the Channel 4 documentary "The Huts" (Bradly 1985) were built by the community as community centres. Members of the community identified this as a need when it was initially built; a need that reflects the fact that Wester Hailes was given little in the way of communal amenities.

In response to both the stigma and the history of community activism, we sought to develop ways of engaging the community in critically informed narrative constructions of place. The aim of the Digi-Mapping project was to give participants an opportunity to give voice to alternative ways of knowing Wester Hailes – ways of knowing that countered the dominant stigmatised negative reputations around high crime, high poverty, and drug abuse.

WHALE arts approach

Arts organisation WHALE Arts has been resident in the local community since 1992, its mission is to be the creative heart of a vibrant community. At the inception of this project, WHALE had recently appointed a creative placemaker funded by the National Lottery. The creative placemaker's remit was to develop various projects with different groups engaging the local community with place. The creative placemaker approached the research team at Edinburgh Napier University, to collaborate on an art project that could explore the local area with children using technology.

A Participatory Action Research (PAR) approach was employed in this study as this approach is uniquely placed to shift the role of a researcher who is an outsider – someone who elicits knowledge – to one that is a facilitator of methods to enable co-produced knowledge (Fischer 2000). This approach closely ties with the ideals of creative placemaking and the approach of Resnick's 4Ps. PAR can also make use of creative methods and help to triangulate tools and methods in these knowledge co-production spaces. This means that PAR is aligned with a collaborative methodology and the values of inclusion and empowerment. Combining PAR with art-based tools "provided rich content to discuss many layers of the relations to the place" (Kunt 2020, p. 93). These types of bottom-up approaches using PAR can create empowerment and inclusion by democratising knowledge and valorising affective and emotional relations to place. Research that combines PAR with creative methods is found in the work of Kunt (2020) whose exploration of cultural heritage puts participation and polyvocality at the centre. When this is done well, O'Neill (2018) and Grandi (2021) believe that it can create alternative modes of knowledge production and support social inclusion through bottom-up practices. O'Neill (2018) argues for an embodied approach to PAR and advocates for walking research methods (WRM) that can support the creation of a social imaginary within PAR. Grandi (2021) insists that within a PAR framework, creative methods can help certain groups to feel safe and encourage participants to share a deeper and more critical understanding of topics.

The creative placemaker was partnered in the design and delivery of the Digi-Mapping workshops in schools. This collaborative research with WHALE gave young participants the opportunity to share their narratives about their local area. The tools used in the Digi-Mapping project supported critical engagements with the creative placemaker in schools with children. Collaborating with WHALE enabled the team to quickly establish trust with participants. We were transparent about our role as researchers, but having

WHALE establish the local need for the project and bring academics *to the community* allowed us to privilege the expertise of participants.

Resnick's framework had numerous influences on our approach to empirical research. The first is the core idea of focusing on the process rather than an end product. The workshops were designed to examine the ways in which participants shared meaning about Wester Hailes. Map-making was agreed to be the most suitable method for this purpose. The design of the project gave space to encourage playful practices as highlighted by Resnick, this is important in constructing knowledge. This was particularly focused on by employing psychogeography as a WRM. Participants could record content in any way they wished. It also supports storytelling by promoting genuine participation. Hosting the empirical research in schools and organising participants in groups meant that a community of practice could be created within the sessions. It also enabled participants to support and give feedback to each other, a crucial aspect when developing bottom-up approaches.

The Digi-Mapping project took place in each of the three primary schools located in Wester Hailes. Each iteration of the project lasted six weeks and consisted of one two-hour session per week during the school day. In total, four Digi-Maps were created. Central to the Digi-Mapping project was the use of psychogeography as a method to explore and interact with the local area using digital media tools such as audio recorders and tablets to take photographs. Map-making is an important mode of knowledge generation as it focuses on the creative processes of *making* the map and the multimodal types of knowledge it elicits. Data was gathered using six cameras for video observation. The project was undertaken as six distinct activities leading to a co-produced map for public display.

Week one

After an introduction to the project, participants were introduced to the term psychogeography which included a short classroom exercise understanding boundaries and types of places within the classroom. In groups, participants were asked to draw their walk to school on large sheets of paper. While drawing they were asked to think about the route they took and the things they saw on the way. Finally, they were asked to list their top places in the local area, to inform the psychogeography walk in week two.

Week two

Before this session, a walking route was planned with the creative placemaker and the participants. This was to ensure that the route was safe, manageable within the scheduled time, and incorporated places of importance to the participants. The design was influenced by Henshaw's (2015) model for the design of sensory walks. In week two participants were put into groups and went on a psychogeography walk of the local area. After a demonstration of the technology, they were asked to record stories, memories, and sounds while they were on the walk. They were allowed to move independently from the other group as each group was assigned a facilitator. They were also asked to take photos using tablets. The facilitators consisted of the research team, creative placemaker, and teacher. Their role was to supervise the participants and support them in creating content. Their role was background with the participants taking the lead in content creation and navigating the local area. If participants struggled to come up with content a dice game with questions was used consisting of the following prompts:

1 Record a sound, tell us what it is
2 Share a story about this place
3 Share a feeling
4 A story someone has told you
5 What do you smell?
6 What do you see?

Week three

Before this session, the audio recordings from week two were catalogued and categorised. Approximately 40 sounds selected for participants to use. Sounds were uploaded onto a local access HTML page on laptops. In this session, participants learned how to use Bare Conductive TouchBoards. Week three included a large amount of instruction and we found that using participant-generated content helped to maintain engagement. Bare Conductive TouchBoards are microcontrollers with micro-SD Cards. The data on the card can be mapped to capacitive touch sensors on the board which are coded via a laptop. Crocodile clips, foil, and copper tape can be attached to these sensors and sound can be heard through supplied speakers. While other technologies such as MicroBit and Arduino were considered, Bare Conductive TouchBoards were chosen for this research for the following reasons:

- They are relatively cheap, costing £55
- They are created with an audio focus – but are capable of other functions
- They do not require learning a programming language to start using them which is ideal for workshops with time limits.

In this session, participants learned how to create a circuit and how to make a drawing interactive using tin foil and copper tape. When the image is pressed it plays a recording chosen from the local website of sounds (see Figure 7.1).

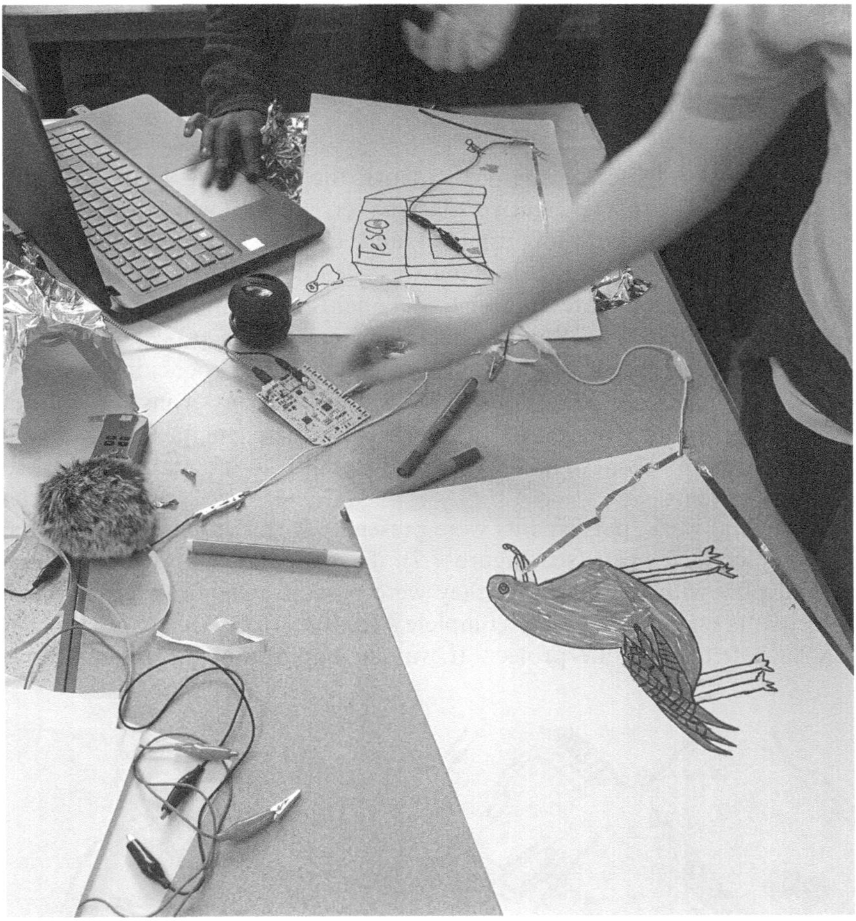

Figure 7.1 Interactive drawing with Bare Conductive TouchBoard. Photograph by T.Grandison.

Week four

Before this session, approximately 30 images were selected and printed from the tablets used to take photos of the local area in week two. In this session, participants drew pictures of the places visited on the walk using the photographs as a guide.

Week five

Before the session, further sounds were selected and added to the HTML page on the laptops. Approximately 20 drawings were selected from the previous week to use in the session. In week five participants worked in groups to select sounds for approximately three to four drawings and make them interactive. These were the final drawings and sounds that would later be used on the Digi-Map.

Week six

Before being presented to the participants, the final Digi- Map was built collaboratively with the creative placemaker. The drawings were placed and made conductive using tin foil and copper tape underneath the drawing. The foil under the drawing was then connected to the wire that was soldered to the Bare Conductive TouchBoards and all components were attached together. Building the final map was a process that took longer than the allotted times of the workshops. The process involved the use of equipment such as Stanley knives and soldering irons. It was not deemed appropriate to use the equipment with the participants. The build of the final map was designed to ensure durability so it could be displayed at various events.

In the final week, participants were presented with the finished Digi-Map that they co-developed (see Figure 7.2). This was an opportunity to first see and play with the map that they were part of collaboratively making. Participants were also asked to complete a feedback form that captured how they each felt about the project. It was an opportunity to ask questions

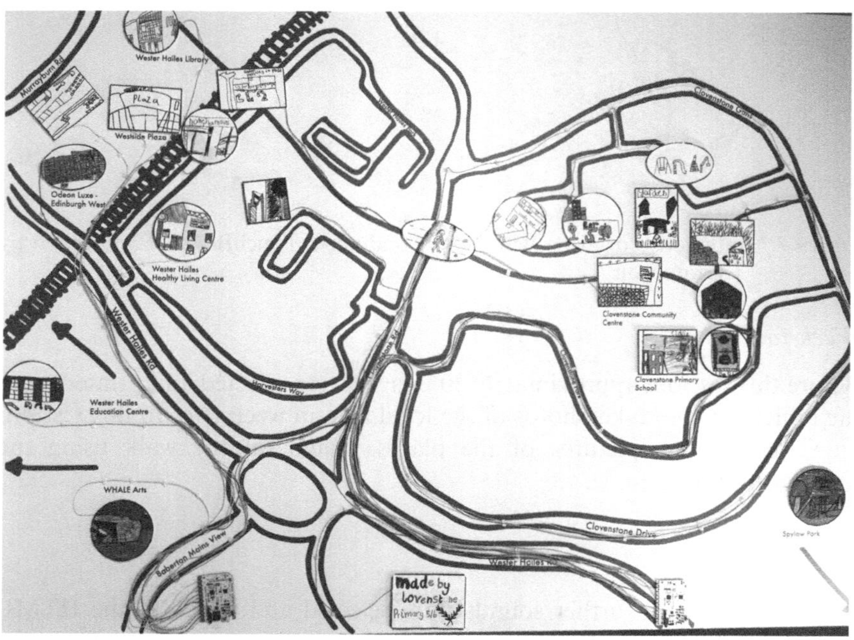

Figure 7.2 Image of final Digi-Map. Photograph by T.Grandison.

about the project, computing or more about other things that happen at WHALE and the university. Some of the feedback elicited from the participants is included in subsequent sections.

Development of a new 4Ps framework

Employing a thematic analysis approach to the gathered video data, findings were coded into categories and then coded under four main themes to define a new 4Ps framework of Participatory, Polyvocal, Performative, and Playful. A table with the coding structure can be seen in Figure 7.3.

Participatory

Participation was at the heart of this project's aims and methods. It was the most important of the 4Ps in the framework and it was through participation that the other Ps emerged. The P of Participatory in creative placemaking is identifiable through the actions of the community of practice; participants needed to be collaborative not only with the facilitator, but with each other when undertaking tasks.

The creative placemaker needed to ensure that the tasks were collaborative, but also that the tasks had an element of openness that allowed participants freedom to engage in ways that were of interest to them. This type of participatory practice can lead to the other 3Ps:

Participatory	Polyvocal	Performative	Playful
Relationships To Other Places	Storytelling	Storytelling	Routes
Detail	Democratic Process	Routes	Use of Colour
Routes	Helping Each Other	Narration	Sound Effect
Storytelling	Working things out together	Sound Effect	Singing
Democratic Process	Boundaries	Singing	Playing with technology
Helping Each Other	Interviewing	Playing with technology	Helping Each Other
Working things out together	Trigger Memory	Democratic Process	Interviewing Each Other
Interviewing			Democratic Process
Trigger Memory			Working things out together
			Storytelling

Figure 7.3 Table of coding structure.

- Polyvocality in a contested narrative,
- Performative actions in the way participants perform meaning,
- Playing and testing with the technology collaboratively to understand and appropriate.

The project design was participatory; participants were assigned to work in groups which helped to facilitate participation with each other. Examples of participation within the other Ps will be demonstrated in the following paragraphs, but it is important to note that Participation was evident in the smallest of gestures. For instance, participation was observed in the sharing of equipment during the psychogeography walks. It was also observed in the negotiating of computer sharing.

Participation and a democratic approach to knowledge were also observed in the ways in which children taught those children who had missed sessions how to work the boards. This atmosphere of support extended to children encouraging classmates to choose their own images and sounds. Referring to the map as "our map", participants at one school wrote a song about the researchers and the project and presented their map at a school assembly.

Interestingly, we can identify what Courage (2021) insists is central to creative placemaking in the activities described above. For Courage (2021) creative placemaking is a community of practice charged with the role of creating and sharing platforms that enhance empowerment and create distributed expertise (Jocson 2015). This distributed expertise was manifested in several ways throughout the Digi-Mapping project.

Sharing meaning using audio recorders provided participants with playful, performative, and collaborative interactions in week two. During the workshops, distributed expertise was evident in the ways participants documented knowledge. The groups also demonstrated distributed expertise when working with the laptops and boards; transferrable skills emerged within the group e.g., computing, wiring, file sharing, and drawing. Moreover, distributed expertise was also evident in the sociability amongst the project participants; from the way participants shared knowledge of wayfinding to agreeing on local landmarks, e.g., the canal. Interestingly, teachers commented that disruptive students who usually struggled to work in class were more engaged and felt they had something to contribute to the group. By allocating children the role of experts about their local area, the researchers also supported forms of relationships, peer-working, and sociability wherein types of expertise could be shared.

Polyvocal

Embracing polyvocality allows for contested narratives surrounding place to emerge and be shared (Farman 2018). Polyvocality is a vital component in participants' process of performative sharing. The first effect of polyvocality is the shift in expertise. From interviews with teachers, they reported experiencing a shift firstly with participants on the walk when participants told teachers the way to go, and how to understand their environment. Secondly, when using the Bare Conductive TouchBoard some participants quickly became experts, showing teachers what to do. Participant feedback also revealed a desire for polyvocality. For instance, several recorded responses included statements that articulated participants' enjoyment of hearing other people's stories.

One predominant way participants engaged in polyvocality was in the use of narration while on the psychogeography walk in week two. While much of the narration could on the surface be considered mundane, Mols *et al.* (2014) argue that it is in the mundane repetition of everyday life that meaning arises in its comparisons. We saw this when participants narrated their location. This locational information was then supplemented with memories of WHEC, a local secondary school, and memories of swimming there. We also recorded this type of narration when one participant went into extensive detail for the imagined listener, recounting the place and experience of a community garden.

Narration was also used in combination with interviews and memory. Participants created content around a patch of trees behind a boxing gym in Clovenstone. Participants mixed personal narration about a haunted wood with interviews conducted with their fellow classmates as to whether the woods were haunted or not. Within these narrative pieces, participants whispered into the microphone conveying a sense of immediate fear and danger to the imagined listener. The participatory nature of this storytelling is closely aligned with what Halbwachs (1992) refers to as the socially constructed nature of collective memory. This was observed in the ways participants shared collective knowledge about the haunted wood. Interestingly, Assmann (2008) suggests that embodiment is required for memory and because of this it cannot be transferred to other people. She argues that interaction with other people and objects, symbols, and signs is often missing from memory work. However, we observed this embodiment in the process of content production when a memory was shared by participants. Furthermore, it can be argued that participants used digital media tools to augment spaces on the walk. The multi-modal affordances of the digital tools helped to create significance and present information that could not otherwise be effectively delivered (Farman 2018).

The findings show that digital site-specific storytelling offered participants a chance to empathically engage with their urban landscape in performative and collaborative ways that elicited moments of naming and remembering. Digital tools allowed participants to ascribe local space characters through shared memory acts and personal narratives. In this way, the digital tools afforded a balance of intimacy and public distance as participants mined the capacity of digital tools to augment the meanings of Wester Hailes. During the psychogeography walk in week two, participants were able to counter the negative reputations of Wester Hailes by sharing their own connections to and identity with Wester Hailes. Participants shared *why* they loved certain areas, and *where* they liked to go in the park and the "new world" that is a wooded area. They shared personal memories of the area like swimming at the WHEC and activities at the community centre. Polyvocality such as these diverse accounts of Wester Hailes amplified the ordinary voice (Lambert 2013).

Despite the prevalence of biographical narratives and positive associations in the urban landscape, the research also found tangled references to the folklore (McNeill 2013) of the stigmatised Wester Hailes. Participants shared stories of dead bodies being thrown into the canal. Other stories identified the canal that runs through Wester Hailes as a dangerous place, where *things* can pull you under, and where you die if you fall in. It is possible of course, that these stories have been passed on to children by their parents as a deterrent to playing close to the canal. Still, through the canal's repeated mythic references participants demonstrated the canal's "livedness" (Krawczyk-Wasilewska 2017, p. 29) and reputation among the local community.

Specific sites and objects acted as triggers for memory. This was regularly observed when participants shared their knowledge through different types of recordings when visiting the Odeon cinema and the shops in the Westside Plaza mall. Participants recorded sounds that were familiar to them at those sites, such as the popcorn machine and the sound of the tills in the Home Bargains shop. Participants also shared knowledge of what shops they liked and what they regularly purchased. This knowledge was also highlighted in the participant drawings in week one. Again, mundane but potentially important details were shown in how participants drew places in their local area from memory. Examples of this included how they drew logos of shops such as Greggs, a well-known UK bakery, and Home Bargains. The size of particular objects in drawings such as the spider web climbing frame denoted their importance to participants this was also demonstrated in the use of colour in the case of the High Flats, local tower blocks.

Places not conventionally considered part of a local area can still be connected through an individual's constructed meaning of place. This was evident in week one, when a participant drew Arthur's Seat on the group map. Arthur's Seat is a hill approximately 5 miles away from Wester Hailes. The participant said that they lived in a high tower in Wester Hailes from where they could see Arthur's Seat. Indeed, the first map participants created included Spylaw Park which is not located within the Wester Hailes area and takes time and effort to visit. It was observed that other non-local places filtered into participants' imagined landscape, whether through connotation, family experience or views from windows, landmarks and destinations outside of Wester Hailes became part of participants' constructed memory of place.

Performative

When using digital media tools in creative placemaking, the team sought to ensure that there was space within the tasks that allowed participants to performatively share their knowledge through the technology, and to express knowledge in ways that were meaningful to them. While instructions were given to participants, it remained open enough that they undertook the process of tasks in ways that were meaningful. The digital media tools that were used within the sessions afforded participants a chance for play and performative experimentation with both the technology and their relations to the landscape. This playful and performative relation to Wester Hailes was both individual and collective. In the 4Ps framework, Performativity is closely linked with that of Playful.

Examining the audio recordings produced by participants revealed that meaning was processed and shared through appropriations of participants' cultural knowledge such as YouTube and popular television personalities. Findings demonstrated that giving participants space to self-express in ways that were interesting to them, revealed creative approaches to categorising, revising, and expressing meanings of place. These dynamic and performative actions are situated somewhere between culture and context (Anderson 2009) and signify a lived *felt* relation to place that is charged with intimate connections and tangled relationships across culture, memory, and community. This is the essence of Resnick's P "Passion".

It was interesting to observe the ways in which participants mobilised their cultural knowledge. Participants used a variety of objects, spaces, media, and music as mechanisms to discuss their local area. In one recording, participants assumed the role of characters like Australian documentary presenter and explorer Steve Irwin to tell the imagined listener that there were spiders and snakes in the woodland. Another participant described the same woodland as a "new world", instructing the listener to "go there". This correlates with Overall (2018) concept of mythogeography, which blends fact and fiction in creative interpretations of place. It is also a useful metaphor to describe the ways in which urban space (Smith 2010) was described during the project. For example, the woodland at Hailes Quarry Park held a sense of wonder and fantasy for participants, they conjured it as an alternative world to explore, one that belonged to layers of myth and folklore. The palimpsests (Meining 1979) of myth and local lore that participants shared through acts of augmenting reality can be understood as projections on the landscape (Mitin 2017).

Instances of creatively performing content revealed the ways in which participants sought to stage places as full of intrigue and mystery. In other ways, content was performed for imagined listeners through distinctly recognisable media formats. For instance, one group created an audio quiz and asked an imagined listener to guess the sounds. Interviewing and singing were regularly adopted as processes of remediation and participants collaboratively filtered, curated, and co-produced media (Papacharissi 2015). It was observed that participants in other groups were undertaking a similar practice; it was unclear if they were copying the first group or a spontaneous creation, or a type of meme. It was also evident that some participants considered what they were making as a type of social media content. Evidence of this was provided when participants asked for "likes" when they were creating content and when one participant stated that the stories he had shared were not "click bait". These types of media creations again demonstrate that the meaning of place is as Anderson (2009) describes: a point between culture and its context.

The psychogeography walks enabled participants to phenomenologically engage with sites of meaning. Rodaway (1994) argues that sensory experience with place can elicit hidden geographies that are driven by sensory experiences. Examples of this were particularly evident when participants performed with space to record sound effects. Participants engaged in sensory touch and audio to test objects in their local area, for their *suitability* to become an audio recording. This was taken further by one group that developed and delivered an audio quiz for the listener. They asked the listener to guess what the noise was and that it would be revealed in the next clip.

We also saw evidence of performative content when participants decided to create Audio Sensory Meridian Response (ASMR) content for the listener, signing for the recorder or as in week three, assuming the role of a YouTuber to create an instructional video. One participant performed the role of DJ and host to his own radio show. He began by telling a story, cutting to an advert break, then delivering news, then interviewing his peers.

Lambert (2013) states that mainstream culture has affected our ability to understand the effects of storytelling in everyday lived experiences alongside our processes of meaning-making and sharing. The findings from this study contradict this. What has been evidenced in the findings is that mainstream culture such as YouTube and the idea of presenting a show can be an effective means through which to construct and share meaning. These media formats were used by participants to share memories. These types of playful and performative acts of media mimicking belong to what Farman (2018) describes as a media ecology of storytelling. In the performative actions in week two of the Digi-Mapping workshop, we observed what Anderson (2009) sees as an editable relation to place wherein participants could imaginatively re-edit places.

Playful

Findings from the project demonstrated that participants mined their own cultural knowledge to meaningfully use the technology to share meanings in creative ways. These playful and collaborative experiments in representing

Wester Hailes revealed the affordances of digital storytelling for playful cooperation, playful simulation, and playful learning. Digital storytelling was used as an interpretation tool to share, provoke, and construct new knowledge about place. This was demonstrated in the findings from week two's "Psychogeography Walk" which found that although participants often established similar meanings, they were playfully performed in different ways through digital media tools.

In weeks three and five, we observed that hearing other peer stories further triggered storytelling activities between participants. This brought to the fore the social processes of the workshops which afforded an expanded polyvocality wherein the testing and challenging of dominant meanings were part of a lively and dynamic workshop space. Drawing on critical heritage theory, we can understand how the distributed knowledge (Jocson 2015) of the workshops provided the means for the social actioning of heritage (O'Reilly-de Brún *et al.* 2017). Furthermore, the playful encounters the workshops afforded created opportunities for participants to become part of a collective and reflective heritage-making community of practice. These processes supported an environment where local meanings could be shared and where participants could learn and contest new knowledge about their area.

Evidence of inclusion in the Digi-Mapping workshop

Findings from the feedback forms highlighted that the participants saw the workshops as a chance to see and understand where they lived. They heard and participated in the telling of new stories. They became aware that the capacity to be involved in "Imaginating" was part of a wider world of research and placemaking. Participant feedback revealed an appetite for knowledge and a connection between the project and a desire to learn, with one participant reflecting that it "made me want to learn science". Participants also commented that they learned new digital skills. Further, conversational feedback from teachers highlighted that the workshops had had an impact on the participants particularly those who struggled to contribute in class, or those that were considered disruptive. Teachers also noted the shift in expertise. While the teachers were part of the class, it was the school children who became experts about their local area, and it was the children that became experts in the use of Bare Conductive TouchBoards.

This was also evident when participants were able to contribute to the group work. One participant reported they "felt smart". An unexpected outcome of the project was the fact that using digital media tools helped some participants develop a more confident identity and supported them in becoming active members of the project's community of practice. Interestingly, this relation to self-esteem links back to Resnick's 4Ps framework, and the capacity of digital media tools to support the creation of a sense of self-worth.

Conclusion

With reference to empirical work in Wester Hailes, this chapter aimed to demonstrate that ephemeral site-specific participatory storytelling can be supported through digital media tools to develop ground-up creative placemaking practices. The Digi-Mapping project was a co-created partnership with the creative placemaker at WHALE Arts in Wester Hailes, a post-war brutalist housing scheme that is a recorded site of multiple deprivation (SIMD 2021). Wester Hailes has a stigmatised reputation associated with poverty, crime, and drug abuse. The newly appointed creative placemaker contacted the team for help in developing a project with school children about their local area that included the creative use of technology. The subsequent Digi-Mapping project described in this chapter was designed with specific attention to inclusive processes rather than outcomes. This attention to a processual engagement and evaluations of place was supported by a revised framework of Resnick's 4Ps, namely Participatory, Polyvocal, Performative, and Playful.

The 4Ps framework that this project has tested and reflectively developed has wider application across heritage, where it aligns with the emphasis on facilitating inclusive community engagement central to both critical and community heritage. In Wester Hailes, the framework helped to elicit types of information and meaning-making that cohere with the fundamentals of creative placemaking. Using digital media tools in combination with phenomenological approaches to walking supported the triggering of memory, the hearing and sharing of contested narratives and the performance of "Wester Hailes" through individual and collective memory.

With its capacity to support issues of social justice, community empowerment, collective action, and working and learning together, this framework may be of value to critical heritage researchers and practitioners to unpack heritage-making processes, and collaboratively share meanings about a local area. It may also be of use to those in heritage institutions that wish to engage in more inclusive community engagement and critical perspectives. Further exploration is needed to understand how digital tools can further be used to explore and critically engage with marginalised narratives about place, such examples could include augmented and virtual realities and how these can create new platforms for sharing and constructing meaning.

Acknowledgements

Special thanks to WHALE Arts and Helena Barrett-Duncan. This research would not have been possible without support from the School of Computing at Edinburgh Napier University and Edinburgh Napier University Public Engagement Fund.

References

Anderson, J., 2009. *Understanding cultural geography: places and traces*. London: Routledge.

Assmann, A., 2008. Transformations between history and memory. *Social Research*, 75 (1), 49–72.

Burgess, J., 2006. Hearing ordinary voices: cultural studies, vernacular creativity and digital storytelling. *Continuum*, 20 (2), 201–214.

Conrad, K.S., 2013. Documenting local history: a case study in digital storytelling," *Library review*, 62 (8/9), 459–471.

Courage, C. and McKeown, A., 2019. *Creative placemaking: research, theory and practice*. Abingdon: Routledge.

Courage, C., 2017. *Arts in place: The arts, the urban, and social practice*. New York: Routledge

Courage, C., 2021. Introduction. In: C. Courage, et al., eds. *The routledge handbook of placemaking*. New York: Routledge. 1–9.

Davis, P., 1999, *Ecomuseums: A sense of place*, Leicester: Leicester University Press.

Duxbury, N., Garrett-Petts, W.F., and Longley, A. eds., 2019. *Artistic approaches to cultural mapping: Activating imaginaries and means of knowing*. London: Routledge.

Farman, J., 2018. Mobile media stories and the process of designing contested landscapes. In: Z. Papacharissi, eds. *A networked self and platforms, stories, connections*. New York: Routledge, 188–202.

Fischer, F., 2000. *Citizens, experts, and the environment*. Durham, NC: Duke University Press.

Fusté-Forné F., and Nguyen T., 2018. Communities of practice, identity and tourism: evidence on cultural heritage preservation in world heritage sites. *Almatourism – Journal of Tourism, Culture and Territorial Development*, 9 (18), 1–22.

Galani, A., Mason, R., and Arrigoni, G., 2019. *European heritage, dialogue and digital practices*. 1st ed. London: Routledge.

Gilloran and Wester Hailes Representative Council, 1983. *Wester hailes ten years on: A report commissioned by the wester hailes representative council on behalf of the people of wester hailes*. Edinburgh: Wester Hailes Representative Council.

Grandi, G.L., 2021. Theatre as method: Performance creation through action research, *Action research (London)* [online], Available from https://journals.sagepub.com/doi/full/10.1177/1476750321993530 [Accessed 12 January 2022].

Halbwachs, M. 1992. *On collective memory*. L.A. Coser Ed. Chicago IL: University of Chicago Press.

Han, K., *et al.*, 2014. Enhancing community awareness of and participation in local heritage with a mobile application. In: Proceedings of the *17th ACM conference on Computer supported cooperative work & social computing*, 15–19 February 2014 Baltimore: ACM. 1144–1155.

Harrison, S., and Dourish, P., 1996. Re-place-ing space. In: Proceedings of the *1996 ACM conference on Computer supported cooperative work*, November 1996 Cambridge USA: ACM. 67–76.

Henshaw, V., 2015. Route planning a sensory walk: Sniffing out the issues. In: T. Richardson, ed. *Walking inside out contemporary british psychogeography*. London: Rowman and Littlefield, 195–211.

Hornecker, E., and Ciolfi, L. 2019. *Human-computer interactions in museums.* San Rafael, CA: Morgan & Claypool.

Hoskins, A., 2009. The mediatization of memory. In: J. Garde-Hansen, A. Hoskins, and A. Reading, eds. *Save As ... Digital Memories.* Palgrave Macmillan, 27–43.

Jocson, K., 2015. New media literacies as social action: The centrality of pedagogy in the politics of knowledge production. *Curriculum Inquiry.* 45 (1), 30–51.

Kane, P., 2006. The power of play. the play ethic. [online]. http://theplayethic.typepad.com/files/the-power-of-play.pdf [Accessed 01 November 2021].

Krawczyk-Wasilewska, V., 2017. *Folklore in the digital age – collected essays.* Kraków: Uniwersytet Jagiellonski, Wydawnictwo.

Kunt, Z., 2020. Art-based methods for Participatory Action Research (PAR). *Interactions: Studies In Communication & Culture*, 11 (1), 87–96.

Lambert, J., 2013. *Digital storytelling Capturing Lives, Creating Community.* 4th ed. New York: Routledge.

Liew, C., Goulding, A., and Nichol, M. (2022). From shoeboxes to shared spaces: participatory cultural heritage via digital platforms. *Information, Communication & Society*, 25 (9), 1293–1310. 10.1080/1369118X.2020.1851391.

Malpas, J., 2008. New media, cultural heritage and the sense of place: Mapping the conceptual ground, *International Journal Of Heritage Studies*, 14 (3), 197–209.

Matthews, P., 2014. Neighbourhood belonging, social class and social media—providing ladders to the cloud, *Housing Studies*, 30 (1), 22–39.

McLuhan, M., 1964. *Understanding media: The extensions of man*, New York: McGraw-Hill.

McNeill, L., 2013. *Folklore rules.* Utah: Utah State University Press.

Meining, D.W. 1979. Introduction. In: D. Meining, Ed. *The interpretation of ordinary landscapes: geographical essays*, Oxford University Press, 1–11.

Mitin, I., 2017. Visualizing place as palimpsest: Mental maps in Russian geohumanities. *Journal for Theoretical Cartography*, 10 (1), 25–34.

Mols, I., van den Hoven, E., and Eggen, B. 2014. Making memories: A cultural probe study into the remembering of everyday life. In: Proceedings of the *8th Nordic Conference on Human-Computer Interaction: Fun, Fast, Foundational*, 26–30 October 2014. Helsinki Finland: ACM. 256–265.

National Endowment for the Arts., 2021. *Creative placemaking.* [online] Washington DC: NEA. Available from: https://www.arts.gov/impact/creative-placemaking [Accessed 6 November 2021].

Nisi, V., *et al.*, 2021. Impalpable Narratives: How to capture intangible cultural heritage of migrant communities. In: Proceedings of the *10th International Conference on Communities & Technologies – Wicked Problems in the Age of Tech*, 20–25 June 2021 Seattle USA: ACM. 109–120.

O'Reilly-de Brún, M., *et al.*, 2017. Material practices for meaningful engagement: An analysis of participatory learning and action research techniques for data generation and analysis in a health research partnership. *Health Expectations*, 21 (1), 159–170.

O'Neill, M., 2018. Walking, well-being and community: racialized mothers building cultural citizenship using participatory arts and participatory action research. *Ethnic And Racial Studies*, 41 (1), 73–97.

Overall, S., 2018. Don't walk that way! Why heritage sites need psychogeography. In: *TAG 2017*, 20 December 2017 Cardiff: Canterbury University. 1–8.

Papacharissi, Z., 2015. *Affective publics*, Oxford: Oxford University Press.

Papert, S., 1980. *Mindstorms, children, computers and powerful ideas*. New York: Basic Books.

Perkin, C., 2010. Beyond the rhetoric: negotiating the politics and realising the potential of community-driven heritage engagement, *International journal of heritage studies*, 16 (1–2), 107–122.

Poole, S., 2018. Ghosts in the Garden: locative gameplay and historical interpretation from below. *International Journal Of Heritage Studies*, 24 (3), 300–314.

Raley, R., 2009. *Tactical media*. Minneapolis: University of Minnesota Press.

Resnick, M., 2017. *Lifelong kindergarten: cultivating creativity through projects, passion, peers, and play*, Cambridge: The Mit Press.

Restless Natives, 1985. Film. Directed by M. Hoffman, U.K: EMI Films.

Rodaway, P., 1994. *Sensuous geographies: Body, sense and place*. London, England: Routledge.

Russo, A., 2012. The rise of the 'Media Museum' creating interactive cultural experiences through social media. In: E. Giaccardi, ed. *Heritage and social media – understanding heritage in a participatory culture*. New York: Routledge, 145–158.

Schofield, J., ed., 2014. *Who needs experts?: Counter-mapping cultural heritage*. London, England: Routledge.

Schofield, T., *et al.*, 2019. Design and plural heritages. In: Proceedings of the *2019 CHI Conference on Human Factors in Computing Systems*, 4–9 May 2019Glasgow UK: ACM. 1–15.

Scottish Index of Multiple Deprivation, 2021. *SIMD (Scottish Index of Multiple Deprivation)*. [online]. Scottish Government. Available from: https://simd.scot/#/simd2020/BTTTFTT/9/-4.0000/55.9000/ [Accessed 10 November 2021].

Silverman, H., 2014. Heritage theory. In: C., Smith ed. *Encyclopaedia of global archaeology*. New York: Springer, 3332–3337.

Smith, P., 2010. *Mythogeography*. Axminster: Triarchy Press.

Sutton-Smith, B., 1997. *The ambiguity of play*, Cambridge: Harvard Univ. Press.

The Huts, 1985. Film. Directed by D. Bradley. U.K: Channel 4 – Skyline Productions.

Trainspotting, 1997. Film. Directed by D. Boyle, U.K: Miramax Films.

van Heeswijk, J., 2012. Public art and self-organisation, London [online]. Available at: http://ixia-info.com/events/next-events/public-art-and-self-organisation-london/. [Accessed: 15 January 2017].

Vivienne, S., and Burgess, J., 2013. The remediation of the personal photograph and the politics of self-representation in digital storytelling. *Journal of Material Culture*, 18 (3), 279–298.

Waterton, E., and Smith, L., 2009. There is no such thing as heritage. In: E. Waterton, and L. Smith. Ed. *Taking archaeology out of heritage*. Newcastle-upon-Tyne: Cambridge Scholars Publishing, 10–27.

Winter, T., 2013. Clarifying the critical in critical heritage studies. *International Journal of Heritage Studies*, 19 (6), 532–545.

Wyckoff, M.A., 2014. Definition of placemaking: four different types. *Planning & Zoning News*, 32 (3).

Zavala, J., *et al.*, 2017. 'A process where we're all at the table': community archives challenging dominant modes of archival practice. *Archives and Manuscripts*, 45 (3), 202–215.

Zitcer, A., 2020. Making up creative placemaking. *Journal of Planning Education and Research*, 40 (3), 278–288.

8 Uncovering the colonial legacy in a British digital archive: The Pitt Rivers Museum case

Rinella Cere, Danilo Giglitto, and Daniela Petrelli

Introduction

Archives and polyvocality

In the last three decades, the idea of cultural heritage has undergone a fundamental reconceptualisation. The traditional view of the archive was anchored to the idea of the past and its legacy as formal and conservative responsibility – a prerogative of governmental or intellectual authorities to stabilise and reassure during uncertain or dire times – and based on the assumption that ordinary people should consume it rather than producing it (Lowenthal 1985, Hewison 1987, Atkinson 2008, Wright 2009). In this context, archives were seen as an authoritative field, wary of nonprofessional endeavours, and firm in holding the right to tell history and preserve heritage (Flinn 2012).

This vision has been gradually yet radically delegitimised because of two main occurrences in the cultural heritage sector at large. First, a new scholarly trend built on the idea that bottom-up approaches to cultural heritage's identification, collection, and management – involving both the contribution of local communities (Giglitto 2017, Nitzky 2013) as well as the perspectives of people whose histories and records have been subsumed in archival repositories (Mason and Baveystock 2013, Beel *et al.* 2015) – has taken over (Flinn 2012, Robertson 2012). Second, the advancement of digital technologies has fundamentally contributed to the establishment of this new paradigm, mostly by suggesting the take-up of the new possibilities in terms of dissemination and access granted by new technologies to switch the focus to the grassroots level (Affleck and Kvan 2008, Flinn 2010, Brown and Nicholas 2012, Tait *et al.* 2013). These two trends are occurring within the paradigmatic shift proposed by the critical heritage framework, which challenges the "authorised discourse" approach where heritage is interpreted via experts' perspective that tends to privilege prestigious, universal, and grand narratives (Smith 2006), neglecting the role of non-dominant groups such as ethnic minorities (Berkhofer 1995). As alternative discourses do exist, clustered around

DOI: 10.4324/9781003277606-8

different communities (defined by geography, ethnicity, culture, belief, etc.), critical heritage calls into question the concept of consensual heritage that underpins a single, authorised interpretation (Smith 2006).

Plurality of values is important if heritage must become an expression of social inclusion rather than a means to assimilate and dissimulate different, potentially dissenting voices (Smith 2006). By opening up to multiple interpretations, memory institutions' role shifts from that of being "guardian of collections" to "ambassador of cultural values and significance" (Thomas 2016). European cultural heritage institutions are increasingly addressing topics of race, religion, diversity, gender representation, colonialism, and social injustice (Van Huis 2019), counterbalancing grand narratives with history from below, while fostering an interplay of viewpoints in polyvocal frameworks (Berkhofer 1995). With the challenge to the traditional approach to the "authorised voice", the idea of heritage started to be investigated in the context of complex social processes and political actions (Smith 2006); however, most of the efforts at the level of cultural institutions have revolved around exploring how to enhance their societal role by adopting more participatory approaches to diversify the audience they aim to engage, with special attention to traditionally excluded communities (Sandell 2002, Simon 2016). We argue that diversifying audiences carries little value if not accompanied by an attempt to also expand the cultural representation held in memory institutions.

Although the interest in this direction is increasing, a systematic effort is needed to address the power imbalance and the historical imperialist narratives embedded in GLAMs (Galleries, Libraries, Archives, and Museums) of former colonial powers (Chambers *et al.* 2016). The concept of heritage as a process of contemporary interpretation of the past is particularly significant for colonialism-related heritage whereupon today's sensitivity changes the way a nation looks back. European media archives hold and curate recordings of former empires, and many have been propelled to examine such heritage, imbued with an imperialist mindset, in an attempt to decolonise and challenge it, sometimes through the voices of grassroots movements (wa Thiong'o 1981, Kurtz 2006, Agostinho 2019, Van Bockhaven 2019, Odumosu 2020). However, such dissonant voices, often rich in personal accounts and memories, do not re-enter the archive, but live on the Internet, for instance on social media or YouTube (Gebeil 2016).

Therefore, while memory institutions, postcolonial scholars, and grassroots activists are all pulling in the direction of decolonisation, the path is far from straightforward. Through a case study, we propose an epistemological approach looking at the relationship between anthropology and colonialism as the basis through which to generate a systematic way to uncover colonial legacies in archives hosting audio-visual material from the colonial era.

Anthropology and colonialism

Important critical research and writings have been done in recent decades about the complicated (and sometimes direct) relationship between anthropology, ethnography, and colonialism, but despite this, anthropology has not yet been able to shake off entirely its problematic origins in the colonial context, not least because it still relies on foundational epistemologies connected to the writings and collections (objects, photographs, films) by early anthropologists about groups and societies that were subjected to colonial rule. Appropriately, Pels and Salemink point out that "the emphasis on the 'big men' of anthropology in disciplinary histories obscures the way in which ethnography was linked to the construction of colonial and neo-colonial societies" (Pels and Salemink 1994, p. 1).

The chronological correlation between anthropology's birth as an academic discipline with the apex of many 19ths century colonial empires is not just a mere temporal coincidence, as in many cases colonial authorities facilitated anthropologists' fieldwork in exchange for information about the colonised. In some other cases, there was a more direct relationship, with colonial administrators turned anthropologists.

The critique of the collusion between the discipline of anthropology and colonial powers has accelerated in recent years through the lens of decolonial and postcolonial theories to encompass the collections amassed and the archives and museums that hold them. This will necessitate a process not only to rewrite the history of anthropology but to attend to the paradigmatic shift required for a new epistemology that accounts for the "stolen" knowledge. This process will require many different types of critical interventions, at the archives and at the museum level, for example, the contestation of what is considered a shared cultural heritage and/or the highlighting of the connection between colonialism and contemporary forms of racial oppression. Alongside, there is the yet unresolved question of returns, and here too we have seen institutions taking a different stance as to the appropriateness of restoring the objects to the people to whom they belonged.

Some key works from the second half of the last century are worth mentioning as they set in motion the epistemological shift. A very early example came via the French writer Michel Leiris (2005) in his article entitled "L'ethnographe devant le colonialisme" ("The ethnographer facing colonialism"), an essay addressing the ethnographer to call on the "segregation and other practices which testify the persistent racism" (p. 117) perpetrated by the colonial powers. For Leiris, any ethnographer with a professional consciousness must undertake this task, even when dependent on those very same colonial powers, especially if they are truly attached to the human groups studied.

Not long after Claude Lévi-Strauss will write about the contemporary crisis of anthropology in the context of decolonisation and the disappearance of the traditional object of study along with the ideological discourse that sustained it: "Anthropology must transform its very nature and must admit that logically and morally, it is almost impossible to continue to view societies as scientific objects, which the scientists may even wish to preserve, but which are now collective subjects and claim the right to change as they please" (Lévi-Strauss 1961). Our intervention and interpretation of the anthropological films at Pitt Rivers Museum also want to address this question: what has been recorded in the frame and how can its status be changed from preserved object to collective subject in the analysis of the cultures represented?

Leclerc (1972) speaks openly in his book about the ethnocentric and ideological character of the anthropological viewpoint even in its endeavour to acquire a "good ethnographic consciousness" (p. 30) that can only be achieved through "epistemic decolonisation" (p. 142). A similar critique on the problematic relationship between anthropology and colonialism has been addressed by Diane Lewis (1973) in her classic piece on anthropology and colonialism where she stated outright that "anthropology is in a state of crisis" (p. 581) and followed up the opening statement with a detailed account of the contradictions inherent in ethnographic fieldwork carried out under the auspices of colonialism and the unacknowledged racist implications of the anthropologist's work: "The noting of differences between two groups is not in itself racist, but invariably acquires such a connotation in the context of colonialism" (Lewis 1973, p. 584).

In 1994, Pels and Salemink published an article in *History and Anthropology* entitled "Introduction: five theses on ethnography as colonial practice". This lengthy article provided a sharp critical overview of the different roles played by ethnography in the colonial apparatus but it also interpellated the relationship between colonialism, academic anthropology, and ethnography (Second Thesis), with the latter, along with the fieldwork, becoming the adopted mean by which anthropologists constructed their knowledge: '[E]thnographic knowledge, constructed on the basis of extended fieldwork by a trained anthropologist, constituted a claim to authority that enhanced the anthropologists' monopoly of this kind of knowledge. Fieldwork became the hegemonic form of ethnography for most anthropologists' (p. 10). The Third Thesis traces the ongoing relationship between ethnography and colonialism even through "theoretical innovations" in the discipline of anthropology, such as holism, relativism and functionalism (p. 11). Thesis Four and Five are of particular importance to the discussion in this chapter about ethnographic film and the Pitt Rivers' archive for different reasons; Thesis Four focuses on the "materially mediated" context of the "production and consumption of ethnography", a context that is very much relevant to the anthropologists looked at here, both in terms of their original filmic production but also in terms of the films finding their way into the archive and the subsequent trajectory into digital forms, along with the questions of access and reuse by digital "artisans".

Thesis Five is especially relevant to the discussion in this chapter about ethnographic film and it is worth quoting in full: 'Ethnography was mostly relevant for colonial society, not in terms of the truth or falsity of its representations, but because it instituted representation as such (both in the literary and political sense) (Pels and Salemink 1994, p. 19). Representation that meant the "fixing of identity to a specific territory" which previously had no such fixity; the drawing of boundaries around groups was both an ethnic as well as a territorial ethnographic classification. This process has also been referred to as "tribalization"; ethnographic mapping contributed to the creation of ethnic groups and minorities within what was to become the nation-states after decolonisation. The political question about representation is key to the polyvocal interpretation of the anthropological films deposited at Pitt Rivers Museum, there is evidence of "ethnographic mapping" about territorial and ethnic groups' boundaries for colonial control: "control through representation" (p. 21).

The Pitt Rivers Museum

The museum

Pitt Rivers Museum, part of the University of Oxford, owes its existence to the rise of disciplines like anthropology and ethnography and prior to that, archaeology. Its foundational history is connected with the man whom the museum is named after, an officer in the British Army, amateur anthropologist, archaeologist, and collector. In the documents deposited in the museum about its history, in the first box of documents (there are 31 boxes), it states that Pitt Rivers wanted that his extensive collection then deposited at South Kensington Museum be transferred to the British Museum. Nothing came of this transaction as the two conditions he proposed: "adequate space" and "sole control with power to act during his lifetime" were clearly not palatable to the then British Museum's administrator and himself a collector, Augustus Wollaston Franks. A year later in 1881, negotiations began with the University of Oxford, and then, by the end of the decade, a Victorian Neo-Gothic Building had been erected to house both the Natural History and Pitt Rivers Museums.

The chronology and context of Pitt Rivers Museum's foundational history are important for two reasons in this chapter. First, it was established during the decades when the British Empire was at its utmost expansion, and secondly, it was intrinsically connected to the rise of the disciplines associated with its collections of objects, manuscripts, photographs, and films, the latter the specific subject of analysis of this chapter. The colonial mindset often cited in connection with the work of early anthropologists, ethnographers, and explorers, has received serious criticism from formerly colonised groups, often the "object" of these studies, and whose lives and artefacts became "collections". Criticism also alighted from anti-colonial and postcolonial scholars and intellectuals trying to disentangle the discipline from its colonial legacy, as Tim Ingold pointed out recently: "Britain had its empire and turned to anthropology for guidance on native social institutions to help in the administration of colonial policy." (Ingold 2018, p. 77).

Today, there is also an ongoing public debate about the "raison d'être" of these collections, specifically related to stolen sacred objects and even human remains in the context of colonial violence and a call for returning wherever possible to their source communities and nations. Activists are also increasingly calling for a total decolonisation of the ongoing colonial mindset. The museum itself has taken up this challenge and has begun a process of undoing the imprimatur of its collections and interpretation. Apart from the obvious and much-publicised withdrawal of the display of the "shrunken heads" (Batty 2020), the museum introduced a host of parallel activities, for example, the webinar about "The Emotion of Removal" in June 2021. On the museum floor, this included inserting reading labels that address the colonial legacy of the museum and the objects displayed, in consultation with some of the communities of origin, in order to (re)write their forgotten and unique history as well as to consider their restitution.

The digitised film collection

In 2014, the museum digitised part of its film collection, which is now available on the Vimeo video sharing platform. There are a total of 68 films linked on the PRM website under "Film Collection", and the majority of these are from the earlier half of the 20th century. This major digitisation project has undoubtedly allowed for more public access to films about representations of communities and groups of people, their traditions and cultures, which would otherwise have not reached us. However, very little information is available in the metadata to explain the historical context of the filming and in the introduction to the content of the film collection on the website. The museum describes them as having been "acquired for teaching and research purposes" and originally part of larger deposits and donations of objects and photographs.

The films we subjected here to the critical analysis are also highlighted in the description on the website as having "significant historical importance" and being "unique" (Pitt Rivers Museum n.d. b). These are the films of Ursula Graham Bower, Beatrice Blackwood, and Frederick Spencer Chapman, all from the 1930s and 1940s. The idea of "uniqueness" and "historical significance" is what we will try to unpack in this chapter, as all these films were made with different purposes in mind, although undoubtedly with some sophisticated filmmaking skills on the part of the three individuals concerned.

As is often the case in filmcraft, there are also surprising ways in which the final films counters unwittingly established and dominant narratives, in this case, narratives of empire. Equally, however, some of the sequences in the films also reproduce that narrative of empire and the political motivation behind the filmmaking, especially in the case of Chapman Spencer and Graham Bower. This will call into question their classification as visual anthropological and ethnographic documents even if they ostensibly fit into that category. Another question surrounding filmcraft is the amateurish nature of some of these films, at times bordering on tourism and leisure-style filming, notwithstanding the limited technology of the time. There is an evident unevenness in quality in some of the films we analysed. In filmic terms, there is an absence of information about the technologies behind the filmmaking, that could have helped explain some of the choices made in the filming in terms of shots, editing, and montage.

There is also an absence of critical material on the circumstances of this filming, although some of the information is available separately on the website under the names of the individual anthropologists and filmmakers. The visual shortcomings arising out of these colonial-related filmic texts will be unravelled below but it is worth pointing out at the outset that the people filmed were not seen as subjects in their own right and their cultures were rendered picturesque. As it has been pointed out by many decolonial and postcolonial scholars and activists, "patterns of objectification and exploitation for personal career benefits are very ingrained in the profession" (Asad 1979, p. 313). Equally, in early anthropology, the ethical protocols for seeking consent were not in place.

These are important critical issues when looking at some of the early films realised whilst Britain still had an extensive empire and deposited at PRM. The films are sometimes difficult to classify in an anthropological sense many of them were not even made for the field of anthropology, but rather for political purposes as in the case of Graham Bower and Spencer Chapman; this entanglement between colonial administration and anthropology is a legacy visible in the filming itself.

Methodology

In looking at the anthropological audiovisual material hosted in the Pitt Rivers Museum's archive, we carried out a film analysis looking at the content, proposed narrative, aesthetics, and symbolic meaning of the films (Mikos 2013). We also cross-referenced the films with biographic information about the anthropologists as well as the monographic material released by the anthropologist themselves. Our analysis led to the formulation of five postulates underlying the colonial legacy in anthropological digital archives.

As the archive hosts 68 films, we had to make a sample of films to analyse. In doing so, we proceeded by selecting three prominent British anthropologists that operated during the same period and under the privilege of British colonial endeavours, but that extensively differed from each other in terms of gender (two women and a man), expertise (namely, the extent of

Table 8.1 List of films included in the analysis

Anthropologist	*Film*	*Length*	*Year*	*People/Place*
Ursula Graham Bower	Apatani Part 1	4:37	ca. 1946	Apatani (India)
	Apatani Part 2	2:53	ca. 1946	Apatani (India)
	Apatani Part 3	19:22	ca. 1946	Apatani (India)
	Naga Part 1	1:13	1939	Naga (India)
	Naga Part 2	3:26	1939	Naga (India)
	Naga Part 3	2:12	1939	Naga (India)
	Naga Part 4	3:55	1939	Naga (India)
	Naga Part 5	3:56	1939	Naga (India)
	Culture and Crafts in Manipur, northeast India (1939) – Part 1	27:08	1939	Naga (India)
	Culture and Crafts in Manipur, northeast India (1939) – Part 2	23:07	1939	Naga (India)
Beatrice Blackwood	A Stone Age People in New Guinea (1936–7)	26:24	1936–1937	Anga (Papua New Guinea)
Frederick Spencer Chapman	Tibet film #1	18:05	1936–1937	Tibet
	Tibet film #2	18:01	1936–1937	Tibet
	Tibet film #3	18:01	1936–1937	Tibet
	Tibet film #4	18:02	1936–1937	Tibet
	Tibet film #9	14:21	1936–1937	Tibet
	Greenland (1934) & Tibet film #10	18:02	1934 and 1936–1937	Greenland and Tibet
	Tibet film #11	18:02	1936–1937	Tibet

previous anthropological training and professional background), interests, place of fieldwork, and ethnographic style. The reason is that by looking at such different figures operating in similar contexts it would be easier to investigate what ideas and patterns intersect with the colonial context. The choice fell on Ursula Graham Bower, Frederick Spencer Chapman, and Beatrice Blackwood. Table 8.1 shows the list of film samples for the analysis, while the next section provides more details on the three anthropologists and their films.

Analysed films and anthropologists

Of the three individuals whose films have been analysed, only one could be described as having formally trained as an anthropologist,

Beatrice Blackwood. The other two, Ursula Graham Bower and Frederick Spencer Chapman, may be perhaps described as "having fallen" into anthropological and ethnographic research via their personal interests (steeped in class privilege), in adventures the former and in nature the latter. However, in both cases, the term adventurer has been applied. By her own admission, Ursula Graham Bower went to Northeast India by "accident" on an invitation of a friend whose brother was in the Colonial Office (Macfarlane 1985a, 1985b), while Spencer Chapman's visit to Tibet was as an employee of the British Government delegation in a political-related "mission" to "establish permanent British representation in Lhasa"[1]. On the other hand, Beatrice Blackwood gained her anthropology diploma at Oxford University in 1918 and alongside her fieldwork worked for the institution in many different departments and guises until her official retirement in 1959, and unofficially well beyond that, right up to her death in 1975. In the reorganisation of the departments, she was transferred from the Human Anatomy Department to Pitt Rivers Museum as "Demonstrator in Ethnology".

"A stone age people?": Beatrice Blackwood

In the digitised film collection, there is only one film by Beatrice Blackwood about the fieldwork she undertook in New Guinea amongst the Anga people. The film is titled *A Stone Age People*, which is edited together from three short reels in black and white with metadata from Blackwood's own fieldnotes describing the content. In them, she details the visual content of the footage; the daily activities of the group referred to as "domestic scenes of KUKUKUKU life". Noteworthily, even by her own admission the terminology KUKUKUKU, long discarded, is not how the people she lived with addressed themselves. Studies on Blackwood are at pain to point out that she was not keen on the requirements dictated by the "paymasters" at Oxford and the museum, or on being subject to pressures from the colonial office. Larson describes her somewhat romantically in these terms:

> In Melanesia, she had immersed herself in village life, realizing that anthropologists must work hard to break down the barriers—physical, cultural and linguistic—between them and their subjects. She had resented having to interact with, and compromise for, the colonial community in New Guinea; she had resented the pressure to travel in order to collect artefacts or anthropomorphic data: she had been happiest when she could have "my natives to myself". (Larson 2011, p. 88)

Nonetheless, however much Blackwood tried to think herself outside the colonial constraints of the time, and in line with what Leiris called the "professional consciousness" mentioned above, she was undoubtedly facilitated in her ethnographic fieldwork by that very same context, not least because the field trip to New Guinea was financed by the museum and was ostensibly conceived to serve the purpose of enlarging the collections: "As a result of this trip well over 2,000 objects were accessioned into the collections at the Pitt Rivers Museum" (Pitt Rivers Museum 2005).

The description and language used in "my natives to myself" also connote a relationship of possession that objectify the groups she was studying and as a consequence deprived them of any agency. The film itself, which is under 30 minutes, is only a small part of the visual account of her overall fieldwork with the Anga people, and we will discuss below the question of authenticity and filmcraft in the film.

The "Naga Queen": Ursula graham bower

Ursula Graham Bower was a prolific photographer and filmmaker; in the interview conducted by Alan Macfarlane in 1985, she stated that she had taken about 2,000 films on the culture of the Zemi Nagas (Macfarlane 1985a, 1985b). The film currently digitised stand at 10, three on the Apatanis, five on the Nagas, and two more on the culture and crafts in Manipur, Northeast India, as shown in the table above. The interview covers her entire life, beginning from her origins as an upper-class woman, albeit "impoverished", to her involvement in World War II and her eventual return to the UK after the war. In the course of the interview, her "uncomplicated views" about her relationship with the groups of people she lived with and filmed, her own position as a white woman, undoubtedly part of the British colonial empire, become a mythologised narrative of courage, strength, and adventure. More than that, as encapsulated in the sentence she utters in the interview about how she was perceived by the people she met: "... they couldn't be more delighted to be honoured with the presence of an unescorted young lady". The theme of the adventurous British woman is a constant refrain throughout the interview that masks the coloniser–colonised relationship at play in this narrative.

The title "Naga Queen", acquired during a further trip to Northeast India, among Manipuri, is also an example of the collusion between her and the colonial service. Movements that were likely spurred by rebellion against colonial powers but that have been recorded as "millenarian movements" drawing on fanatical religious sources, had apparently replaced their captured and imprisoned leader, a young woman they believed to be their goddess, with Ursula. To give her her due, she was not particularly keen on this but the advice from the colonial office was such that this would make her a better "informer" on any problems arising in the district. One of the many examples where anthropologists, especially amateur ones such as Graham Bower, could serve the colonial power and its ideology.

"Mission' to Lhasa": Spencer Chapman's Tibet

The motives behind the Gould "mission" to Lhasa were political and undoubtedly stemming from the previous century colonial and commercial expansionist British government project (Mckay 2003). No details of this transpire on the website metadata but surprisingly some of the sequences in Spencer Chapman's silent films speak volumes as we will see in the analysis below. The photographic material connected with the mission has been digitised and is available on the PRM website under the title: The Tibet Album, British Photography in Central Tibet 1920–1950 (Pitt Rivers Museum 2006). For this "mission", Frederick Spencer Chapman collaborated along with other members as photographer and filmmaker as well as Secretary to Gould[2]. The idea of him having lived an adventurous life is also present in the short biography available on the PRM's website, albeit without the gendered preoccupations we have seen for Ursula Graham Bower (Pitt Rivers Museum 2006).

Unlike the reports and the photographs, the films were not the main source of information required by the British Government, and it appears as if they were more complementary to the photographic production, much of it based on Spencer Chapman's own interests in the natural landscape of Tibet, especially its flora and fauna, its people, its religious architecture, and Buddhist customs. Only a few sequences are dedicated to the official gathering and meetings, although occasionally difficult to distinguish the temporal from the religious powers. Perhaps in the case of Spencer Chapman, given the specific political context and his role on the trip, we may not properly talk of anthropology and ethnography, even though the audio-visual material is deposited in the archive of Pitt Rivers Museum. We can however still draw a parallel in terms of British political interests and the gathering of information and what has been described on the PRM's website metadata as "unprecedented in the history of British representations of Tibet" (Pitt Rivers Museum n.d.a). The film collection digitised to date is composed of 11 films in their near entirety about Tibet, with just a short film about a steamer boat called Lady Sybil and many shots connected with the voyage to Greenland, mixed in with shots of Tibet, probably because taken on the same roll of film.

The colonial legacy in anthropological archives: A framework

The five postulates

In identifying patterns and commonalities within the films, and by cross-referencing these with additional material about and/or from the three anthropologists that complemented our observations, we have identified five postulates that constitute the basis of our framework aimed at uncovering the colonial legacy in anthropological audiovisual material. These are:

1 *Anthropological subjectivity*, referring to the self-perception of the anthropologist making the film.
2 *External perception*, referring to the tone of externally-attributed perceptions, both in the field of anthropology and outside.
3 *State of exception*, referring to the way in which the fieldwork might have been conducted that was not (entirely) abiding by the existing social conventions, rules, and customs.
4 *Authenticity and filmcraft*, referring to the overall quality, informativeness, and ethnographic values of the films.
5 *Use and reuse*, referring to the way the films are conceptualised and presented when re-proposed in more recent or contemporary settings.

These postulates can be interwoven on several different levels to feed the depiction of composite descriptions. In the next section, we will apply this framework to films selected for analysis.

Feeding the framework

Postulate #1: Anthropological subjectivity

We define our first postulate, the *Anthropologist subjectivity*, as having four specific features: self-interest, intrusiveness, othering of cultures, and romantic view of self among "the noble savage". All three individual filmmakers construct a narrative about themselves and their relationship with the subject they are filming. What we refer to as the anthropological subjectivity is interwoven with ideas of self and "other" and the inevitable construction of this "colonial-anthropological" mode in the films: the idea of cultures "stuck" in time, which one can "intrude upon" as a necessity for undertaking fieldwork and which are perceived as requiring study and preservation. The relationship which ensues is always one where the "primitive is defined in an inverse relationship to civilised [sexuality]" (Stallabrass 1990, p. 108). Indeed, as Leclerc (1972) commented in his book on anthropology and colonialism, what is missing is the Western understanding of the specificity of [African] cultures as "real knowledges" and as "branches of universal knowledge", in other words what he also termed as "the narcissistic monologue of the west" (p. 119). The Western subjectivity plays out differently in the three sets of films not least because the context and interaction between the filmmakers and the people filmed are very different. For example, it is less in evidence in the films of Spencer Chapman, whose subjectivity is translated into his predominant interest in filming nature rather than people and customs, but also because we do not have any writing from him that articulates a relationship of "possession" (as with Blackwood) or as having a special place within the groups and cultures filmed (as in Graham Bower).

Postulate #2: External perception

Our second postulate, *External perception*, refers to the narrative that has been constructed over the years about these three individuals, both within the field of anthropology and in the public and mediatic spheres. In this process, a whole host of aggrandising terminologies have been adopted to describe their persona and their work which have ignored the colonial context in which they operated. In the case of Graham Bower, the descriptions extended to a full-blown mythologising exercise connected to how she herself thought she was perceived by the Naga group she lived with; the 1985 interview with Cambridge anthropologist Alan Macfarlane (Macfarlane 1985a, 1985b) does nothing to dispel the myths, if anything, it reinforces the idea that she was an exceptional woman, a quasi-heroic figure for having chosen to live with the exotic 'other' rather than live out the comfortable life of an upper-class English woman. A more recent account, part of the 2019 Pitt Rivers Museum exhibition "Intrepid Women: Fieldwork in Action, 1910–1957", depicts her somewhat differently and mentions how in later life she rallied for the Zeme Naga and their discontent with the British and Indian administration (Pitt Rivers Museum 2018). Blackwood was also one of the six women anthropologists in this exhibition, which is framed around the prejudices and obstructions towards women studying anthropology at the turn of the 20th century, undoubtedly worthwhile research, but which again does not provide any consideration of the colonial context or signals to the connections between patriarchy, anthropology, and colonialism. Terms like pioneer, legendary figure, and brave are used often in the external perception without attending to the negative meaning they carry in the British imperial history of the 19th and 20th centuries. Spencer Chapman also received much public and media attention over the years and, similarly, his exploits were referred to as heroic, especially in relation to World War II. Likewise, Spencer Chapman published a number of books on his voyages and missions, and one, in particular, a 1940 publication, was directly connected with the Mission to Lhasa in Tibet and the films deposited in the Pitt Rivers Museum archive.

Postulate #3: State of exception

We have called our third postulate *State of exception*, by which we mean that the fieldwork conducted by the anthropologists – and already referred to above as being problematic in its very nature – was justified on the basis of the "superiority" of Western science methods and the ensuing suspension of non-Western rules, what Tomaselli has called the "victorious 'scientific' order of knowledge" (Tomaselli 2001, 178). The scientific status, along with the colonial context, allowed the anthropologists to ignore questions of consent around local rules, transforming live cultures, people, and their craft into collectable for museums, whilst boundaries were either ignored, misinterpreted, or even belittled. The fieldwork practice that today demands express permission was not part of the consideration of the early anthropologist. In the films we have analysed, we have come across numerous instances of the practice of the "state of exception", especially in relation to the absence of permission to film people, their sacred surroundings, and intimate ceremonies. In the films of Graham Bower and Blackwood we have instances of people, often women, fleeing in front of the camera. In others, we have a sense of a passive resigned attitude to the filmmaker, or of people intrigued by the technology while others adopt a more performative stance; this is particularly the case in the films of Chapman, possibly connected with the demands of the political mission, as many shots are clearly of Tibetan dignitaries with their British counterpart. Even these, however, connotes a state of exception in the way the people and surroundings are rendered picturesque and hence not a political body in Western terms.

Postulate #4: Authenticity and filmcraft

The visual content of the body of films analysed has generated this fourth postulate, which attempts to combine observations about the question of *Authenticity and filmcraft,* the latter denomination adopted in part to denote the different levels of skills of these "amateur" filmmakers, all of them however with a keen sense of the visual if not of the montage process. Arguably, their main aim was to provide authentic visual documentation about the culture they were encountering and studying. The films are silent, so the visual element is the determinant of the interpretative process. In terms of filmcrafting, we have identified two elements: the staging and even direct intervention for the camera of indigenous people and activities and the aestheticisation of their lives and cultures, what we also call along with Leiris, the "eye of the ethnographer" (Leiris 2005). Coupled with filmcraft is the idea of capturing the authenticity of the other, which the constant fascination with exoticism and primitivism reinforces and with a preference for the most remote, distanced, and uncontaminated societies possible, temporally and spatially. Blackwood's images about the Anga people in New Guinea (*A Stone Age People*) do not show "performative primitives" (MacCannell in Tomaselli 2001) but the insistence of the camera's eye on people and objects (stone age tools) replicates Western stereotypes about these contemporary people as of the past. On the other hand, Graham Bower's extensive filming of the Apatani and the Naga filmcrafts most of her subjects and their culture through visibly performative actions, down to approval from the filmmaker. The filmcraft of Spencer Chapman's films is less ethnographic in style. The sequences of Lhasa buildings, its inhabitants, and the various meetings with dignitaries required by the political mission (which are still shot with evident performative actions), are interspersed with long shots of the natural environment. Filming nature rather than people and their customs was an obvious preference of Spencer Chapman, who indulged in high-level and skilful documentarist shots of the Himalayas and the animal kingdom (especially birds). The main connection of the films with anthropology seems to be mostly stemming from the fact they are included in an anthropological collection, raising some doubts over their intrinsic anthropological value.

Postulate #5: Use and reuse

Use and reuse refers to the way the films are conceptualised and presented when re-proposed in more recent or contemporary settings. This postulate has looked at the ways in which these films have been recirculated and interpreted, including the more recent process of their digitisation and their availability via the PRM's website on Vimeo. The films have been reused on television programmes and documentaries; an early example was Graham Bower's films featured in the 1956 BBC series *Travellers' Tales*, produced and narrated by David Attenborough (1956–1959). The specific episode was titled "The hidden Valley of the Apa Tani"; it was one of nearly thirty episodes with exotic and racist titles, such as "Savage New Guinea". Blackwood and Graham Bower's photography and film work has been reused more recently in the 2011 documentary *Captured by Women* (2011) by anthropologist and filmmaker Alison Khan. This documentary, as already mentioned above, offers an insight into the difficulties of women achieving recognition at the turn of the 20th century but does not delve into the visual representation of their anthropological work or into the colonial context which facilitated their visits and fieldwork. Spencer Chapman was the subject of the TV Series "This is your life", broadcast in two episodes in January 1964. The programme concentrated on his life as a soldier in Malaysia during World War II rather than on his work as a photographer and filmmaker. While postulate #2 concentrates on the perceptions about the three anthropologists and their work, *Use and reuse* explores how the narrative surrounding them is still reproduced through the use and/or reuse of their audio-visual material, which not also replicates the same aggrandising and flattering portraits, but also deliberately or negligently ignores the colonial context.

Digital archives and colonialism: A way forward

The development of the analytical framework has provided us with a much-needed tool to interpret critically ethnographic and anthropological films produced during colonial times. On the surface, the films appear to reveal hidden cultural treasures, whether it be people and their ways of life or their material and spiritual culture; however, delving into the production and aesthetics of the film exposes all the Western bias as well as the colonial power relations in place. In this exercise, we have hoped to accompany the access already provided by the archives themselves, in our case through digitisation, with a decolonial methodology that interrogates not only the films themselves but their wider significance as part of the contested origins of the discipline of anthropology and ethnography and the colonial-related cultural heritage more generally.

The framework – with its five postulates arising out of considerations on the individual involved, the films themselves, their reception, their use/reuse, and the historical context – is also meant as a contribution to the epistemological shifts referred to above. First, the absolute necessity to reverse the dominant Western paradigm which generated the idea and practice of racial supremacy, even if disguised in scholarly and scientific pursuits. Second, the urgency of providing a framework that allows for broader and more diversified interpretation of digital archives by uncovering the bias informing their foundation. As Fanon put it so well as far back as the early 1960s, "Racism is never a super-added element discovered by chance in the course of the investigation of the cultural data of a group". (Fanon 1970, p. 46). Anthropological archives hold this data in many forms which now requires not only an acknowledgement of its multiple ties with the colonial legacy but a granular revision and reinterpretation of their collections stemming from the imperial past, which to date remains a work in progress.

Conclusions

This chapter has illustrated an analytical framework that may facilitate the identification of colonial legacy in audiovisual material. While the framework was developed for analysing ethnographic material, several of the postulates may be adapted to different disciplinary contexts and types of audiovisual material. For instance, the filmmaker's subjectivity and their externally attributed perception may serve as tools to investigate potential biases in other forms of audiovisual cultural representations. Similarly, how filmcraft may push deliberate agendas or unconscious biases in light of a claimed authenticity – together with the way in which the material is received, recirculated, and re-narrated – may also offer fruitful critical lenses.

With this in mind, within the context of the European-wide project "Polyvocal Interpretation of Contested Colonial Heritage (PICCH)", we are working on enriching the framework. Next, the framework will be used to analyse the audiovisual material of two other European digital archives: the colonial propaganda films hosted at the Netherlands Institute for Sound and Vision and audiovisual material related to the Algerian war of independence from colonial France hosted at the French Institut National de l'Audiovisuel. The findings of this new film analysis will inform the framework both by adding new postulates or expanding the existing ones.

Notes

1 Frederick Spencer Chapman (1907–1971). Available from: https://tibet.prm.ox.ac.uk/tibet_Frederick_Spencer_Chapman.html [Accessed 10 March 2022].

2 Basil Gould was the political officer that led the mission to Tibet; Frederick Spencer Chapman was his "private secretary".

References

Affleck, J., and Kvan, T., 2008. A virtual community as the context for discursive interpretation: A role in cultural heritage engagement. *International Journal of Heritage Studies*, 14 (3), 268–280.

Agostinho, D., 2019. Archival encounters: Rethinking access and care in digital colonial archives. *Archival Science*, 19 (2), 141–165.

Asad, T., 1979. Anthropology and the colonial encounter. In: J. Huizer and B. Mannheim eds. *The politics of anthropology. From colonialism and sexism toward a view from below*. The Hague: Mouton Publishers, 85–96.

Atkinson, D., 2008. The heritage of mundane places. In: B.J. Graham and P. Howard, eds. *The Ashgate research companion to heritage and identity*. Aldershot: Ashgate, 381–396.

Batty, D., 2020. Off with the heads: Pitt Rivers Museum removes human remains from display. *The Guardian*, 13 September. Available at: https://www.theguardian.com/culture/2020/sep/13/off-with-the-heads-pitt-rivers-museum-removes-human--remains-from-display

Beel, D., *et al.*, 2015. The geographies of community history digital archives in rural Scotland. *Scottish Geographical Journal*, 131 (3–4), 201–211.

Berkhofer, R., 1995. Beyond the great story. *History as text and discourse*. Cambridge: Harvard University Press.

Brown, D., and Nicholas, G., 2012. Protecting indigenous cultural property in the age of digital democracy: Institutional and communal responses to Canadian First Nations and Māori heritage concerns. *Journal of Material Culture*, 17 (3), 307–324.

Chambers, I., *et al.*, eds., 2016. The postcolonial museum. *The arts of memory and the pressures of history*. London: Routledge.

Fanon, F., 1970. *Toward the African revolution*. Harmondsworth: Penguin Books.

Flinn, A., 2010. Independent community archives and community-generated content: "Writing, saving and sharing our histories". *Convergence: The International Journal of Research into New Media Technologies*, 16 (1), 39–51.

Flinn, A., 2012. Archives and their communities: Collecting histories, challenging heritage. In: G. Dawson, ed. *Memory, narrative and histories. Critical debates, new trajectories*. Brighton: the University of Brighton, 19–35.

Gebeil, S., 2016. Les mémoires de l'immigration maghrébine sur le web français de 1999 à 2014. *Les Cahiers du numérique*, 12, 115–138.

Giglitto, D., 2017. *Using wikis for intangible cultural heritage in Scotland: Suitability and empowerment*. Thesis (PhD). The University of Aberdeen.

Hewison, R., 1987. The heritage industry. *Britain in a climate of decline*. London: Methuen.

Ingold, T., 2018. *Anthropology. Why it matters*. Cambridge: Polity.

Kurtz, M., 2006. A postcolonial archive? On the paradox of practice in a Northwest Alaska project. *Archivaria*, 61, 63–90.

Larson, F., 2011. "Did he ever darn his stockings?" Beatrice Blackwood and the ethnographic authority of Bronislaw Malinowski. *History and Anthropology*, 7 (2), 75–92.
Leclerc, G., 1972. *Anthropologie et colonialisme*. Paris: Librairie Arthéme Fayard.
Leiris, M., 2005. *L'occhio dell'etnografo. Razza e civiltà e altri scritti 1929–1968*. Turin: Bollati Boringhieri.
Lévi-Strauss, C., 1961. Today's crisis in anthropology. *The UNESCO Courier*, November.
Lewis, D. 1973. Anthropology and colonialism. *Current Anthropology*, 14 (5), 581–602.
Lowenthal, D., 1985. *The past is a foreign country*. Cambridge: Cambridge University Press.
McKay, A., 2003. 19th century British expansion on the Indo-Tibetan frontier: A forward perspective. *The Tibet Journal*, 28 (4), 61–76.
Mason, R., and Baveystock, Z., 2013. What role can digital heritage play in the reimagining of national identities? England and its icons. In: M. Anico and E. Peralta, eds. *Heritage and identity: Engagement and demission in the contemporary world*. London: Routledge, 15–28.
Macfarlane, A., 1985a. Interview with Ursula Graham Bower, Part 1 of 2 [online]. YouTube, Prof Alan Macfarlane – Ayabaya. Available from: https://www.youtube.com/watch?v=oKy3I5afxEA [Accessed 8 April 2022].
Macfarlane, A., 1985b. Interview with Ursula Graham Bower, Part 2 of 2 [online]. YouTube, Prof Alan Macfarlane – Ayabaya. Available from: https://www.youtube.com/watch?v=RSMhZqf2FiY [Accessed 8 April 2022].
Mikos, L., 2013. Analysis of film. In: U. Flick, ed. *The SAGE handbook of qualitative data analysis*. London: Mikos, 380–393.
Nitzky, W., 2013. Community empowerment at the periphery? Participatory approaches to heritage protection in Guizhou, China. In: T. Blumenfield, and H. Silverman, eds. *Cultural heritage politics in China*. New York: Springer, 205–232.
Odumosu, T., 2020. The crying child. On colonial archives, digitization, and ethics of care in the cultural commons. *Current Anthropology*, 61 (22), 289–302.
Pels, P., and Salemink, O. 1994. Introduction: Five theses on ethnography as colonial practice. *History and Anthropology*, 8 (1–4), 1–34.
Pitt Rivers Museum, no date a. Lhasa Mission Diary 1936–1937. Available from: https://tibet.prm.ox.ac.uk/mission.php.html [Accessed 4 April 2022].
Pitt Rivers Museum, no date b. Film collections. Available from: https://www.prm.ox.ac.uk/film-collections [Accessed 26 April 2022].
Pitt Rivers Museum, 2005. Beatrice Blackwood. Available from: https://www.prm.ox.ac.uk/b-blackwood.html [Accessed 4 April 2022].
Pitt Rivers Museum, 2006. Frederick Spencer Chapman (1907–1971). Available from: https://www.prm.ox.ac.uk/event/intrepid-women [Accessed 21 April 2022].
Pitt Rivers Museum, 2018. Intrepid women: Fieldwork in action, 1910–1957. Available from: https://tibet.prm.ox.ac.uk/tibet_Frederick_Spencer_Chapman.html [Accessed 4 April 2022].
Robertson, I.J.M., ed., 2012. *Heritage from below*. Farnham: Methuen.
Sandell, R., 2002. *Museum, society, inequality*. London: Routledge.
Simon, N., 2016. *The art of relevance*. Santa Cruz: Museum 2.0.

Smith, L., 2006. *Uses of heritage*. Abingdon: Routledge.
Spencer Chapman, F., 1940. *Lhasa the Holy City*. London: Chatto &Windus.
Stallabrass, J., 1990. The idea of Primitive: British Art and Anthropology 1918–1930. *New Left Review*, 183, 95–115.
Tait, E., *et al.*, 2013. Linking to the past: An analysis of community digital heritage initiatives. *Aslib Proceedings*, 65 (6), 564–580.
Thomas, N., 2016. The return of curiosity. *What museums are good for in the 21st century*. London: Reaktion Books.
Tomaselli, K., 2001. The semiotics of anthropological authenticity: The film apparatus and cultural accommodation. *Visual Anthropology*, 14 (2), 173–183.
Van Bockhaven, V., 2019. Decolonising the Royal Museum for Central Africa in Belgium's second Museum Age. *Antiquity*, 93, 1082–1087.
Van Huis, I. (2019). Contesting Cultural Heritage: Decolonizing the Tropenmuseum as an Intervention in the Dutch/European Memory Complex. In Dissonant Heritages and Memories in Contemporary Europe, edited by Lähdesmäki, T., Passerini, L., Kaasik-Krogerus, S., & Iris van, H., 215–248. New York: Palgrave Macmillan. doi: https://doi.org/10.1007/978-3-030-11464-0_8
wa Thiong'o, N., 1981. Decolonizing the mind. *The politics of language in African literature*. London: James Currie.
Wright, P., 2009. *On living in an old country*. Oxford: Oxford University Press.

9 Reframing ephemera: digitisation, community music-making, and archival value(s)

Charlotte Armstrong, Rachel Cowgill, Alan Dix, Christina Bashford, Rupert Ridgewell, Maureen Reagan, Michael Twidale, and J. Stephen Downie

Introduction: the internet of musical events

Socio-musicologists such as Christopher Small (1998) and Tia DeNora (2000) define music as a social activity in which everyone has a role: experiencing music is a social action that is interwoven with our personal lives, individual and collective identities, memories of shared events, and intergenerational dynamics within our communities (Dix *et al.* 2014, p. 4). Live musical performances play a powerful role in defining human communities across the globe, yet such intangible temporal/spatial experiences tend to leave only faint traces on the historical record, even in modern times. While musicologists have used some types of concert ephemera to capture the nature and identity of musical events, the sources, such as they are, remain frustratingly partial. The term "ephemerality" derives from the Greek for "lasting one day" and denotes a state of being "of the moment" – that is, short-lived, and contingent on a particular event, individual, or social context. Ephemera are therefore things in the process of dying, that are easily discarded, and that do not hold their value; yet they are also often imbued with affective currency and associated with aesthetic experiences way beyond the everyday (Edenheim 2014, Abbate 2017, Russell, 2018). These qualities and contradictions carry forward into musical performance, which Carolyn Abbate (2017, p. 82) regards as "ontologically ephemeral (even though it can of course be recorded)". In contrast with the interpretation of texts, she argues, "the forms of knowledge that honour ephemera like a musical performance are elusive" (p. 82), and this at least partly accounts for musicology's past tendencies to overlook performances in favour of staking a claim on the relative clarity and fixity of the score.

Traditional archival values – by which collections and archives survived or not on the basis of being judged "worth preserving" (Evans 1997) – have been closely allied to canonic musical values in the West and Global North, particularly to ideas of durability, significance, and timelessness, and according to whether a composer was deemed to be writing for immediate commercial

DOI: 10.4324/9781003277606-9

success or for posterity (generally mapped onto an over-simplified popular/classical musical divide). Lydia Goehr highlighted this connection in the title and central arguments of her influential book, *The Imaginary Museum of Musical Works: An Essay in the Philosophy of Music* (1994). With the cultural/critical turn in the humanities, however, musicology's construction of its field began to move away from music as texts towards music as events, to music as social discourse, and to reception-oriented accounts of music and meaning-making, as marked in several signal anthologies (Bergeron and Bohlman 1992, Cook and Everist 1999, Scott 2000, Clayton *et al.* 2003).

Scholars began to recognise the potential of capturing and analysing the exceptionally rich, formulaic data on performances that were available in runs of programmes and other music-related ephemera (see Bashford 2007 and 2008), and in 2003, the International Association of Music Archives, Libraries and Documentation Centres set up what would become its Study Group on Access to Performance Ephemera: "a forum for discussion of strategies to encourage the improvement of access to performance ephemera (including programmes, posters, flyers, and tickets) both nationally and internationally, and where appropriate to develop common approaches and/or standards" (IAML 2019). Hitherto, with notable exceptions, ephemera had been treated as something of a nuisance – items are often bulky, repetitious, printed on paper of assorted sizes (frequently disintegrating), and require time and specialist knowledge to catalogue that many archives do not have. It is no surprise, therefore, that the survival of significant runs of ephemera has been more the exception than the norm. The Concert Programmes Database project, established in 2004, began to list, initially at collection level, deposits of concert programmes in European libraries, archives, and museums as "a resource for the history of musical life from the 18th century to the present day" (CPD 2022). What started to emerge was a potentially whole new history – or indeed histories – of community musical engagement and participation that by virtue of ephemera could begin to be built from the ground up.

In recent years, the emergence of critical archival studies has moved the debate further in these directions, inspired first by Foucault (1971), and then by Jacques Derrida's *Archive Fever* (1996). Here, Derrida draws attention to the violence at the heart of archiving, arguing that recording memories and narratives in the archive leads to the repression and suppression of alternatives, and of other ways of building and telling such stories. Around the same time, José Esteban Muñoz pointed out, as Gillian Russell expresses it, "how 'anecdotal and ephemeral evidence', including performance and documents normally classified as 'ephemera' such as photographs, tickets, posters, album covers, flyers, personal memorabilia – could 'grant access to those who had been locked out of official histories'" (Muñoz 1996 cited Russell 2018). It seems hard to overestimate the joint impact of these critical voices on archive studies decades later: Victoria Hoyle, quoting Michelle Caswell (2021), describes it as "'a field on fire', amid a radical and liberatory challenge to its core principles galvanised by 20 years of critical approaches to dominant epistemologies" (2022).[1] New debates and fierce self-scrutiny abound among the archives community to make progress on representation – who is included and who is excluded, who gets to participate, and who is able to advocate for themselves within the context of the archive (Hoyle 2022). What has been apparent is a remarkable opening out of archival values; no longer does power flow in a sealed loop – the researcher drawing authority for her work from the archive, and bestowing authority in return; instead, archives have become what Elizabeth Yale (2015, p. 355). describes as "communal resources, sites at which personal, civic, and national memories can be accessed, and from which they can be brought before the public, to constitute the affective glue that holds a community together".

This chapter explores community archives of musical ephemera in the UK as sites of "post-custodial" collecting and preservation that can radically transform approaches to digitisation, community music-making, and archival value(s). The ephemera in question pertains to several former chapters of the British Music Society (BMS), which was established in 1918 by the progressive musical author, educator, and organist Arthur Eaglefield Hull (1876–1928). Hull's aim was to restore international collaboration and exchange between British and overseas musicians after the twin catastrophes of the Spanish Influenza and World War One. The BMS served as a celebration of musical volunteerism and promoted the unique value of amateur committees in cultivating rich musical communities. Hull was a skilled administrator who developed a robust organisational framework for the BMS and set up chapters in towns and cities throughout the UK and internationally. Many of these chapters remain active today, and while they may have limited knowledge of their shared origins, they have amassed significant archives over the past century that shed light on the rich history of this extraordinary initiative and the broader role of music in community life from local to global.

The Internet of Musical Events: Digital Scholarship, Community, and the Archiving of Performance (InterMusE) is a 2-year project funded by the Arts and Humanities Research Council's "UK-US New Directions for Digital Scholarship in Cultural Institutions" scheme. The project brings together a team of scholars from humanities and computing backgrounds to work with three former chapters of the BMS: the Belfast Music Society (BeMS), British Music Society of York (BMSY), and Huddersfield Music Society (HMS). As they emerge from a period of acute social and economic instability that was felt by cultural institutions around the world in the last few years, these societies are eager to document and interpret their collections, and InterMusE is working with them to capture and link different forms of data relating to musical events with a view to creating a dynamic, open-access digital archive of musical ephemera. In doing so, the project aims to harness the capacity of digital technologies to enable collaboration with members of the public in environments that are often relatively poorly equipped and under-resourced. It serves as a testbed for some of the issues outlined thus far: adopting a deeply collaborative methodology based on principles of co-design and democratisation, and disrupting what Laurajane Smith (2006, p. 11) refers to as an "authorised heritage discourse" which privileges the power and knowledge forms of large (and therefore "worthy") institutionalised cultural agencies and relies on dominant claims of technical and aesthetic expertise. Instead, we view preservation as a form of reactivation: our research and its outputs will be developed by and with members of these music-making communities as they reflect on their identities, take stock of their histories, and plan for their future.

Amateurism and expertise in collaborative community archiving

Given the emphasis of InterMusE on co-production between university researchers and participants who are highly knowledgeable and engaged members of the public, ideas about amateurism and expertise are central to our project. Today, amateurism in the arts has been defined on the one hand as the consequence of passionate engagement and an alternative to established artistic knowledge and practices. In this sense, it is sometimes associated with innovation and radicalism. On the other hand, amateurs may take on the role of guardians or gatekeepers of traditional artistic forms (Morris Dancing, for example) who are "legitimated not by their high aesthetic value, but as important markers of national or community identity" (Holdsworth *et al.* 2017, p. 7). But these definitions fail to capture the kind of amateur culture represented by the BMS: these societies have programmed high-profile, professional performers from around the world, initially guided by a national advisory committee, in many cases for more than a century.[2] At the same time, they are run predominantly by volunteers, many of whom are local aficionados of classical music with extensive knowledge of their societies' histories. In this sense, they are characterised by the aspects of passion and voluntarism often associated with amateurism.

While the BMS has its roots in Hull's vision of a dynamic amateur-led culture in the early 20th century, InterMusE is not only concerned with amateurism alone in a musical sense. The project brings together an interdisciplinary team spanning musicology, computer science, archival theory and practice, librarianship, and music professionals. Within this team, some are experts in historical musicology, some in collections management and cataloguing practices, and others in the designing and building of technologies and applications. A further spectrum of knowledge and expertise exists within the music societies themselves, which comprise performers, archivists, administrators, fans, aficionados, and audiences. InterMusE brings these groups together to enrich and consolidate the historical record of live musical performance both within and beyond these concert-giving communities, helping them to organise and interpret their collections and to understand and communicate their histories. To do so requires the coming together of "expert" and "amateur" perspectives on both the collections and preservation practices of the societies and on the digital techniques and technologies that will shape our collaboration and formation of a dynamic and enriched digital archive. In taking a holistic view of these activities as part of a broader outcome of establishing a culture of participation and co-production, we have found cause to interrogate the very concepts of "amateurism" and "expertise" and their usefulness for defining the types of knowledge and experience brought together in our project. Here, we take cues from Hoyle, who writes that in reimagining archival values to create more equitable and participatory preservation cultures, "[t]he distance between 'expert' and 'non-expert' perspectives has to be repeatedly collapsed, so as to facilitate the co-construction of new realities" (Hoyle 2022, p. 233).

Acknowledging the need to embrace the intersections between academic and public approaches to the archive, we sought to establish a foundation for democracy and participation at the start of the project by conducting informal introductory interviews and collection assessments with our stakeholders. In doing so, we hoped to foster peer relationships, develop a shared vision, and gather requirements for the project's outcomes. These interviews confirmed that the lines between expertise and amateurism are not clear cut, mirroring the findings of Ruth Finnegan in *The Hidden Musicians*, which explores the unique and "highly significant" interrelationship between these two concepts in the context of local music-making (Finnegan 2007, p. 13). Finnegan identifies the participants in her research as being on the "amateur rather than the professional end of an overlapping and complex spectrum, taking account of the variations along this continuum" (13). For the author, the issue lies not in distinguishing between these two terms, but rather, in exploring the absence of a distinction between them (14). In some ways, this concept of a "continuum" of amateurism and expertise is useful for conceptualising how we might integrate different levels of knowledge and experience into the range of activities that comprise our project, including archiving.

While the societies we are working with would self-identify as "amateur" in terms of their archiving, in many cases, there is an acute understanding of archival values and processes that would typically be associated with professional practice. A database created by the archivist of HMS serves as a striking example of this phenomenon. It contains over 3000 entries cataloguing the dates, venues, performers, works, and composers of every performance at the society since its inaugural season. This data is derived from the society's expansive programme collection. The archivist has supplemented the data with notes and cross-references to relevant performance reviews (Armstrong *et al.* 2021, p. 45). This form of systematic cataloguing is akin to expert-level archival practice and demonstrates understanding of the importance of provenance, as well as other important archival concepts and values. This shows how the boundary between "expert" and "amateur" can become blurred in the context of this project and how these kinds of terms may not be so useful after all. The concept of a continuum provides an alternative to the implicit hierarchy in these terms, as well as in concepts such as "top-down" or "bottom-up".

Archiving the local

Our initial interviews with representatives from BeMS, BMSY and HMS shed light on the importance of local perspectives in shaping the archival values of these communities. The process of collapsing or reimagining traditional archival methods and concepts encompasses issues of socioeconomic status, political leaning, and associated conceptions of cultural value, and the BMS's role as a network of local concert-giving institutions is particularly important in this regard. Musicologists have recognised the rich insights to be gained by looking beyond London to trace networks of performers, audiences, and venues in and between cities, towns, and villages across Britain (Cowgill and Holman 2007). There has been an emphasis on place and performance in digital musicology since its emergence in the early 1990s. Significant studies of concert life in the Western classical tradition, such as the Concert Life in 19th-Century London Database and Research Project (1993) and the Concert Programmes Database Project (2004–2007), have drawn systematically on historical newspapers and periodicals, transcribing large bodies of data to map supply and demand, structures and networks, and changing orders of magnitude. While ground-breaking, these studies have largely focussed on high-profile concert venues in metropolitan hubs. By placing emphasis on live performances happening outside of capital cities and major conurbations, InterMusE celebrates the importance of amateur, local, and community-focused musical events on which so much of local cultural life depend. This move towards the local also has important implications for co-production projects like our own that seek to produce research outputs with – rather than for or about – non-academic communities.[3]

A newfound focus on localism in cultural heritage studies points to the significance and value of communities outside of urban centres in replacing "top-down" approaches to heritage with more inclusive and participatory cultures. John Schofield has been an important voice in theorising this shift, advocating for "a new approach to cultural heritage [...] that is participatory, bottom-up and fundamentally grounded in local concerns and interests" (Schofield 2014, p. 2). Understanding these local concerns and interests has been an important part of our work to date. Our interactions with members of the music societies have highlighted that each chapter has developed distinct perspectives, not only on their role within the broader BMS, but also with regard to their participation in the project. Many of these unique perspectives stem from factors of locality. BMSY has strong links to the university and mostly comprises middle-class members, many of whom are former members of university staff. The society's chair was unaware of the shared heritage with HMS and BeMS and is keen to forge closer ties and develop a relationship of active collaboration. Having postponed their 100th concert season due to COVID restrictions, BMSY hopes to incorporate participation in InterMusE activities as part of their commemorative centenary season. As the founding chapter of the BMS, HMS has a special interest in the establishment of the organisation by Hull (who lived and worked in Huddersfield) during the 20th century. The society is proud of its heritage, having maintained an unbroken record of performances since 1918 until its forced closure in 2020 with the outbreak of the COVID-19 pandemic. HMS's archivist has suggested that their participation in the project presents an important opportunity to continue Hull's vision for shared knowledge and collaboration with other chapters in a digital age. There is a sense of a deep connection between the HMS and the local community, with the society's archivist having produced articles for local publications, including the journal of the town's local history society. Another key motivation for participating in the project is the desire to capture audience reactions to and recollections of HMS's concert history, which is documented in an almost complete run of programmes and related materials. BeMS shares a notably complex relationship with the broader BMS in light of the region's protracted political crises and associated negotiations with the idea of "Britishness". The society's 100-year-long history of chamber-music provision in the city is particularly meaningful given the troubled history of the region, and the society is eager to celebrate this legacy alongside other planned centenary celebrations.

Despite their distinctive local concerns and interests, the societies have also faced shared challenges. All three faced prolonged closure during the pandemic, and some have cited subsequent difficulties in engaging live audiences in light of anxieties about public health. This raises important questions about the sustainability of small, underfunded local venues, and this sense of precarity is encapsulated by InterMusE participant David Byers (2020) in his history of the BeMS featured on the organisation's website:

> For the [BeMS], survival has long been an essential requisite. In the face of challenges, international, national and local (the Second World War, Great Depression, strikes, 'The Troubles') – not to mention geographical add-ons like weather, travel problems and additional costs, a.k.a. 'financial constraints' – it had sustained a regular subscription series of chamber music concerts in the image conceived by its founders, 75 years earlier. […] But long before the financial crisis of 2008 and the pandemic of 2020, questions were being asked about sustainability and even the contemporary relevance of the [BeMS]. In December 1989, a Music Ireland article about the [BeMS]'s 70th birthday recognised its funding shortfall, rising costs (artists' fees, venue costs, etc.), public expectation

for the 'big' (equals expensive) names, and the drawbacks of being run on a voluntary basis.

This extract points to the way in which circumstances at a local or regional level can interact with and even expound national and global challenges. It also points to the importance of lived experience in shaping motivations for archiving.

Sharon Webb (2022, p. 442) refers to community archives and heritage projects as being driven on the one hand by a desire to redress the omission of certain voices and perspectives in formal histories, and on the other hand by a desire to celebrate or commemorate the stories of traditionally marginalised or overlooked groups. While Webb refers specifically to LGBTQI+ communities whose histories have been hidden by institutional neglect, we can certainly observe the existence of similar motivations within these chapters of the BMS, whose role in established historical narratives of musical performance may be regarded as peripheral. The societies have a vested interest in preserving the record of their societies for the long term, but their motivations for doing so are not always shared and may encompass an enthusiasm for enriching explorations into family history, enhanced publicity, and increased funding opportunities, or a desire to secure a legacy for their personal investment into preserving materials. In his assertion that "heritage is for everyone", Schofield (2014, p. 1–2) points to local and "everyday" concerns as an important driving factor in establishing new approaches to cultural heritage that are both relevant and sustainable. It is important that our work considers this diversity of local interests and perspectives, both in terms of building our digital archive and facilitating its use by and value to the societies and their communities. Rather than assuming a position of power or influence and simply granting community members a tokenistic level of control over this process, the success of the project will be reflected in the active participation of the community in developing the archive and determining its use. For a community to do so "on their own terms" is a defining characteristic of community archives, according to Andrew Flinn *et al.* (2009, p. 73). To be able to foster a collaborative archival culture like this depends on our understanding of the different approaches to collection and preservation in the societies. As a starting point, knowing what kinds of materials are valued by the community and why can play an important role in shaping common goals and understanding how different forms of amateurism and expertise might need to come together to achieve them.

Anatomy of a music archive: valued collections and community values

In March 2021, we carried out collection assessments with each society by interviewing the individuals responsible for the collection and, where material has been deposited in a repository, by consulting existing catalogues (Armstrong *et al.* 2021, p. 44–45). Ephemera such as concert programmes and season brochures feature heavily across all three societies' collections. There are also correspondence items, a number of newspaper reviews (often stored as cuttings), and administrative records such as subscriber lists, minutes, and financial records. As noted, some of the collections have been deposited in local libraries and archives, but many materials are kept in private homes or society offices. The decision-making around what to deposit and what to keep close at hand is of interest to us as it can reveal the existence of certain tensions around the perceived trustworthiness of formal repositories and a desire to maintain access to valued collection items (Armstrong *et al.* 2021, p. 45–46). One society member has chosen to keep the society's concert programmes in their possession, revealing a sense of attachment between the custodian and the collection, while acknowledging that it may be safer if deposited in a library. We are also aware that the collections of the societies are expanding year on year as items are discovered and passed on from members of the community.

This sense of collective responsibility for preservation, as well as the value that is placed on the items by members of the community, has evidently been a factor for many years. An important moment towards what Michelle Caswell (2014) denotes "archivization", or the process by which records are collected, preserved, and identified as archives), is revealed in the minutes of a 1961 BMSY committee meeting: "Dr Summers said he wished there was a list of all the Programmes performed over the years and was promptly proposed as Archivist and the Secretary promised access to the Minutes for the purpose of the preparation of such a History" (Anon 1961). Across the three societies, the custodians of the collections have been compelled to archival action, not only taking responsibility for physically gathering the material, but also taking steps to catalogue the collections and record the provenance of the materials. This suggests a desire to both document history and ensure its usefulness and accessibility for future generations. We refer to this acknowledgement of value and the associated desire to preserve and make accessible the collections as an "instinct to archive". This instinct is based on the custodians' personal investment in the material and their stake in ensuring its preservation. In this way, community values (and the perceived value of the community) are intricately bound up with archival practice. Returning to Webb's ideas (2022), we might also explain this instinct to archive as a (perhaps unconscious) social or political act that seeks to reframe the history of a music-making community that has been overlooked or subordinated in musicological discourse: "recast histories and their making challenge and seek to undermine both the distortions and omissions of orthodox historical narratives, as well as the archive and heritage collections that sustain them" (Flinn *et al.* 2009, p. 3–4).

It is clear, then, that the record of the community reflects its values. Our responsibility as facilitators of the project is to honour these values when designing for participation. To do so requires our understanding of how the material has been collected. In the chapter "Collecting Reconsidered", Susan Pearce (1994, p. 194) identifies three modes to which most collections belong: objects as "souvenirs", as "fetish objects", and as "systematics". The author defines systematic collecting as the selection of examples that are "intended to stand for all the others of their kind and to complete a set" (p. 201). While systematic collecting is perhaps favoured by formal heritage institutions such as museums and galleries, souvenir and fetish modes of collecting may lend themselves to so-called "ground-up" or community archives. Souvenirs are memorabilia or personalia relating to a noteworthy person or group of people. This mode of collecting is particularly significant in the context of music archives, as these types of objects are often associated with particular events (concert programmes, for example). Pearce uses the term "fetish" to describe the collection of objects not for their relation to specific geographical or social context (as with souvenir collecting), but for either their perceived value or the value that may be attributed to their accumulation. She suggests that, while souvenir collecting may serve as a way to commemorate or authenticate the experiences of the collector, fetish collecting may represent the collector's attempt to define themselves in terms of their possession of certain materials. As an example, the author points to sets of materials known for their association with a past collector, such as named collections that have been donated to museums or galleries.[4] However, fetish collecting is a useful concept for describing the approach to archiving within the BMS chapters with whom we are working. There has long been a sense within these institutions that what they are doing is of significance and worthy of preservation. All three societies have instinctively collected a range of ephemera and administrative records in order to secure a legacy for their work, and to do so has often required considerable personal investment on the part of members of the community.

Both of these modes have significance for music archives in that they place emphasis on the people responsible for the collection and curation of objects and the role of the objects in reflecting personal or social values. Christopher Tilley's (2012, p. 60) "objectification processes" is a useful concept here, referring to "what things are and what things do in the social world: the manner in which objects or material forms are embedded in the life worlds of individuals, groups, institutions or, more broadly, culture and society". In revealing something about the "life worlds" from which they originate, the objects collected by the societies also play a key role in capturing otherwise ephemeral events like live performances. This is especially true of programmes and reviews. "Souvenirs are intrinsic parts of a past experience", Pearce (1994, p. 195) writes, "but because they, like the human actors in the experience, possess the survival power of materiality not shared by words, actions, sights and the other elements of experience, they alone have the power to carry the past into the present". In that they act as "samples of events which can be remembered, but not relived", this type of material and the associated mode of collecting encapsulates key ideas about the ephemerality of performance and the role of the archive in capturing it. A notable example of this kind of collecting is the Manchester Digital Music Archive (MDMArchive), an online initiative that invites members of the public to deposit self-digitised materials relating to the musical culture and social history of Greater Manchester. The MDMArchive is an exemplary model of the democratised and co-produced community archive, thus discrediting Pearce's claim that "[s]ouvenirs discredit the present by vaunting the past, but it is an intensely individual past – no one is interested in other people's souvenirs" (p. 195). The materials gathered within this archive play a significant role in shaping and solidifying the collective identity of the communities involved in the initiative. Furthermore, it demonstrates that the very act of collecting can be an important factor in establishing a sense of togetherness and permanence for community groups.

Negotiating the politics of co-production

InterMusE concerns and attempts to consolidate an ecosystem of people, places, objects, and meanings that have formed around live musical events. In taking a holistic view of the project's outputs and the role of our stakeholders in shaping them, we draw on Flinn's concept of the "community of the record", which refers to all who come into contact with an archive, whether directly or indirectly. For Flinn (2010), recognising the importance of this community – an "untapped" source of knowledge, in his view – is a key component of a "successful democratised and participatory archive". This perspective sheds light on the role of communities in creating a collective or shared identity through archival processes. In a sense, our role is to create spaces for shared practice within this ecosystem. Literature on co-production has often pointed to the value to be derived from collaboration between groups traditionally considered to be "expert" and members of a given community. For Keri Facer and Kate Pahl (2017, p. 2), collaborative partnerships between universities and community groups can be understood as "a means of creating greater 'impact' on the social world", "a way of enhancing the quality of knowledge", "a form of democratic recalibration of knowledge production" and "a way of generating more robust products and services". For InterMusE, co-production also means the coming together of experiential expertise and scholarly perspectives, a form of radical collaboration that produces different kinds of knowledge, expertise, and values for everyone involved.

While its benefits are clear, co-production is not without its challenges, and establishing a welcoming and inclusive participatory culture is not always straightforward. Where co-production initiatives bring together academic and non-academic communities, there can be tensions around the value of different outputs for different groups. For example, while there is a discernible move away from the academic reliance on monographs and articles, the diverse and often creative outputs of co-produced research may pose challenges for those working in academia, where success is still predominantly measured in published outputs. A related issue is that of conflicting interests. Co-production doesn't necessarily imply consensus, and as such, there is a need to consider how we acknowledge and honour differences in perspectives (including with, within, and between participant groups) without silencing or levelling participants. Complexities may also occur as a result of the tendency for academic participants to view the co-production process as a form of research in itself, which may result in community participants feeling commodified as research objects.

The solution to many of these challenges lies in the shift from "hierarchical" or "power-over" to "horizontal" or "power with" relationships. One clear mechanism for driving such a shift is communication: as researchers, we need to be cognizant of the issues at play and, crucially, willing to discuss them openly with project participants. While our introductory interviews and collection assessments proved valuable in establishing a foundation for trust and reciprocal exchange with stakeholders, we were conscious that systems of hierarchy and power dynamics within the music societies themselves may have prevented us from reaching everyone within the community of the record. Since this time, we have held open group consultations or "information sessions" with the societies, during which we have sought to establish a relaxed environment for participants to share ideas, insights, and concerns. In some cases, issues we had anticipated and prepared to address were revealed to be of no concern to participants, while other issues that had not occurred to us were highlighted. Once again, this showcases the diversity of perspectives at play within the societies and points to the importance of facilitating participation as broadly as possible. As the following sections demonstrate, designing a "people-first" participatory culture requires us to create a diversity of opportunities, think carefully about our means of engagement, take a critical view of the technologies we are utilising, and above all, centre the voices of our participants.

From crowdsourcing to co-ownership

Debates about the ethics of participant labour and the risk of lingering power dynamics between university researchers and community participants are crucial in the context of InterMusE. While co-production initiatives often situate themselves as grounded in an ethics of equality, mutuality, and reciprocity, participatory interventions can promote imbalances of power between different stakeholders and perpetuate bias and about the value of certain contributions over others. To illustrate this point, Turnhout *et al.* (2020, p. 16) describe a traditional "top-down" model of participation in which one group (they use the term "elite participant") maintains influence over both the co-production processes and the designation of value on the outputs of such processes. This is due to the nature of the institutions that typically take on a leadership role in co-production initiatives (government agencies, large NGOs, universities), who "have more time and resources available, often initiate [the] processes, define the scope for participation, have more knowledge and skills, and are, for all these reasons that resonate with social-cultural biases, better able to articulate a contribution that is considered relevant and important" (Turnhout *et al.* 2020, p. 16). This "top-down" model of participation is often found in crowdsourced digital archiving projects, many of which comprise three key steps:

1 A large (i.e., "worthy") institution has a collection of raw digitised material such as old maps or handwritten letters. Often, there is no existing way to automatically extract structured information, but it is relatively simple for a human to do so.
2 An interface is created (usually web-based) that presents relatively small, homogeneous tasks that require little expertise.
3 Volunteers (the crowd) are recruited to take part in the effort in order to support the worthy cause of the institution.

There are variations of this model for other types of activities. For example, volunteers may gather primary data by photographing historic monuments or supplying local dialect/slang terms for common words. In some cases, participants may receive monetary rewards (as in Amazon's Mechanical Turk) or the required task may be performed as a side effect of another activity, for example, the text and image recognition tasks in ReCAPTCHA (Von Ahn, L. *et al.* 2008). Critically, however, there exists a chasm between the relatively mundane activity of the crowd and the substantive goals of the institution. This model provides a classic example of alienation (Hansson *et al.* 2019), and indeed, the term "human computation" has been used to liken the human participants' role to that of a cog within the computational machine (Quinn and Bederson 2011).

Citizen science projects such as Gardenwatch provide an alternative to the top-down crowdsourcing model. Here, local data collection is more common and there is a more balanced dynamic between crowd and institution due to the mutual benefit to be derived from the tasks: spotting a bird in the garden or counting bees on a local moorland is not just about supplying raw data, but something pleasurable in itself that connects participants to the local environment. Platforms such as iSpotNature (Silvertown *et al.* 2015) and Zooniverse (Simpson *et al.* 2014) take this a step further by enabling individuals and groups to create their own projects while in the process adding to large datasets. This places value on the knowledge and expertise of the crowd (experiential or otherwise), thus providing a counter to the traditional "power over" model found in both co-produced research and crowdsourcing initiatives. Moreover, such a model emphasises the co-ownership of the project by participants and the institution.

InterMusE aims to apply similar principles to the digital archiving of musical ephemera. There are many examples of small groups creating their own archives or collection resources using the likes of community history Facebook pages and websites (Our Place 2022). These kinds of community-produced collections open up access to smaller and more obscure documents (such as performance ephemera) that may lay beyond the bounds of interest or processing capacity for formal archives, the scholarly equivalent of O'Reilly's (2005) long-tail characterisation of Web2.0. However, we hope to create ways to bring local collections together to produce a national or even international picture. The associated coming together of community members and university researchers offers often overlooked opportunities for collective knowledge enhancement and the celebration of shared interests. Moreover, while there is clearly local value to local collections, there is also value and empowerment in knowing that local efforts are contributing to global knowledge.

The initial scanning of documents within the InterMusE project demonstrates how this may work (Figure 9.1). A local musical society might scan it own programmes or other documents using a low-cost book scanner or smartphone scanning application. This may be sufficient for use on society websites or for sharing between members interested in the history of the society. These types of scans will also be of sufficient quality for volume Optical Character Recognition (OCR) to enable locally and globally accessible text searches, which could be useful for a society member who is researching family history, for example. Elsewhere, a university researcher may come across these scans and find that they are of interest for an academic study. It may be that the community scan is sufficient, but it may be that a higher-quality scan is needed. The scholar sends the required document for higher-resolution scanning, which is then connected to or fed back into the (potentially decentralised/virtual) repository so that both future scholars and local society members can access these higher-quality scans when available.

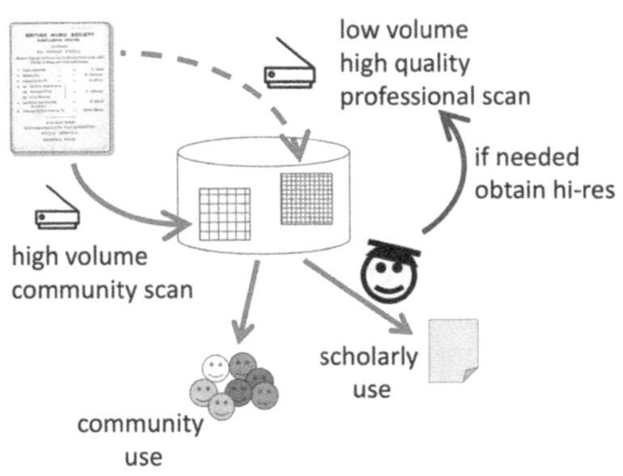

Figure 9.1 An archive that is open and scholarly, local and global.

While this vignette (Figure 9.1) is about raw scanning, it is possible to imagine similar use cases for various forms of interpretation, annotation, or markup of digitised collections. For example, local members might link named performers to Wikipedia entries or VIAF identifiers, allowing cross-referencing and connection to other databases. A scholar might use this volume data to find documents of interest, but may wish to verify critical linkage for themselves, for example, asking whether the "B. Britten" mentioned in a concert programme is a well-known composer or a lesser-known local performer. Having verified this, this information should ideally be available for future users. Note that we are seeking to neither privilege the local societies nor the scholar, but rather realise that each has different goals and needs for the materials and brings different knowledge and skills to its creation and interpretation.

As the societies we are working with have substantial repositories of paper documents, scanning and primary digitisation is a key objective. There is value in this on its own, especially when coupled with OCR to enable free-text searching of documents. However, at this stage, they still constitute piles of documents. To become a living resource, they need to be annotated, structured, linked, and above all, used. Use cases are at the heart of many agile software-development methods. Rather than producing a system from start to finish and then deploying it, the development is split into small units, each of which produces useful functionality so that the system is deployed stage by stage, and is usable from the beginning. There are arguments for working like this in scholarly archives (Dix *et al.* 2014), but even more so for community heritage. For those engaging with the archive in their spare time as a hobby or personal interest, it is unreasonable to expect a complete pass at collection, curation, and cross-indexing before the data is used. Instead, we expect that the normal patterns of data augmentation will be based on specific uses: an anniversary brochure, a personal family history, a series of weekly Facebook posts about interesting stories in the records. This emphasises the need for infrastructure, tools, and processes that embrace incremental enhancement, co-ownership, and collective use.

Storytelling and enacted curation

Another key component in establishing an effective culture for co-production is our ability to harness the expertise within the societies. This expertise also plays a key role in the use of digitised materials. However, we have found that there is a tendency for perceptions of amateurism and expertise to create barriers to participation among local communities. This echoes Schofield's observation that, in the context of cultural-heritage management, "stakeholders other than authoritative, elected or appointed heritage experts often feel unconfident or unqualified to articulate views on the heritage they value, perhaps because they are not familiar with the professional language of heritage, or are wary of expressing personally held views in the context of rational or 'scientific' enquiry" (Schofield 2014, p. 1). This chimes with our own experience of engaging members of the societies. Some individuals have expressed a reluctance to play an outward-facing role (for example, by speaking alongside academic researchers at community events), understandably being more comfortable taking on a "background" role in project activities. At times, however, this is at odds with the nature and significance of their contributions. This may result in the academic researchers on the project team having to "speak for" the society members, and as a result, other community members may not see themselves represented and may become reluctant to participate. On the one hand, we might accept this bind as an inevitable dynamic of co-produced research. Our responsibility is to the communities, and as such, our role is to facilitate participation on their own terms. This issue does beg the question as to whether we have a role in empowering these communities to embrace and showcase their expertise. However, this assumes a degree of authority on the part of the academic researchers and may invoke a sense of hierarchy that we are trying to avoid.

We have found that participants feel more at ease in drawing on their expertise in the form of storytelling, and one of the key ways in which data is both used and connected is through stories. Narrative and storytelling have always been an essential part of community history. The Oral History Society (2022) cites examples as far back as the 8th century and Sharpless (2008, pp. 7–32) looks back to Heroditus in the 5th century BCE. This accelerated during the 19th century, especially in relation to folk tales and songs. However, the emergence of audio recording and especially magnetic tape recording created the modern field of oral history. Digital technology has further transformed the collection and curation of audio material (Lambert and Frisch 2019) including geo-coding stories whilst walking (Zembrzycki 2013). In presenting oral histories for public access, the spoken word is often illustrated in professionally edited multimedia presentations, with the voice overlaying still images. We wanted to create something similar, but with the ease of pointing at people in a photograph or names in a document. When talking to someone about their archives of photos or documents and they look at an example, they will instantly start to tell you about the people, places, and events represented, linking them to other documents. Often, these stories constitute a form of primary data in themselves, particularly in the case of older members of a musical society who may be able to recall specific concerts or members of the committee now deceased.

We have found that looking at documents is often the key to unlocking these stories, and in another community heritage project, we developed a tool called TalkOver (Figure 9.2). The TalkOver application allows photos to be uploaded and shown on screen. The person with stories (an archivist, or another member of the community), then simply touches (for tablet) or mouse-clicks (for laptop) the photo whilst talking about it, just as you might

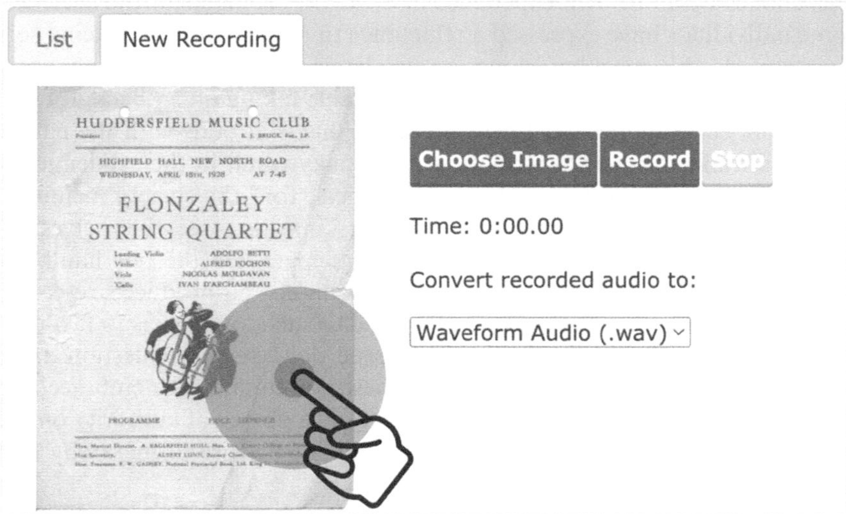

Figure 9.2 TalkOver application records touch points on the photo whilst talking.

point to the physical photograph. The system records the location of these touchpoints alongside the audio and then highlights them with a small glowing circle as the audio is replayed. Note that this (i) creates an enriched recording, which can be embedded directly, for example, in a web page; (ii) is an annotation of the archive contents that is available for future use; and (iii) forms a basis for additional annotation, for example, linking to named people based on the audio annotation. Whilst TalkOver was originally produced for a different context, the music society representatives instantly saw potential uses for it, for example, by having members of their society talk about old concert programmes or meeting minutes. This highlights the way in which co-creation for one community can lead to results that are of broad use.

Conclusion: properties of an open and scholarly archive of music ephemera

The above scenarios bear witness to Lisa Darms' (2015) assertion that "the innate qualities of an archive are not rigidity or bureaucratic order-making, but rather fluidity and even a kind of productive chaos". Modelling new approaches to the open-access presentation of musical ephemera based on digitally enabled collaboration, InterMusE is identifying key properties of digital archives that are valuable for both community meaning-making and scholarly research. They are inevitably heterogeneous in terms of the kinds of data and documents they comprise, as well as the levels of quality and the density of linkage and annotation. The archive needs to support incremental change and update, not just in terms of the growth of the items stored, but also the level of detail of structural markup and annotation. These changes also need to be auditable, maintaining the provenance of when and who added or updated items, so that users of the archive can understand their authority, validity, and availability. To be useful, local archives need to be connected both internally and to external data sources that can enrich collections and make them more findable (Fair Principles 2022). Finally, and perhaps most importantly, the archival processes at play need to be accessible, not demanding that community archivists learn complex ontologies, but instead making it easy to link emergent local folksonomies of tagging and labelling to more traditional forms when needed. The tools and technologies to support this also need to be accessible in the widest sense, enabling use by individuals across the community of the record, regardless of their age, disability, technological skill, and indeed, access to digital technology. Together, these qualities enable us to bring an intentionally diverse array of source types into dialogue with each other, creating relationships between them, interrogating them, and experimenting on them to unlock new musicological and technological insights. Such an approach holds the potential to reframe musical ephemera as a means through which to consolidate and enrich the historical record of live musical performances both within and beyond our local cultural institutions.

Notes

1 We are grateful to Victoria for allowing us to read her book manuscript before publication.
2 Before the BMS was dissolved in 1933, it published catalogues of British composers, and an annual British Music Bulletin (later the British Music Bulletin and The Music Bulletin).
3 We use 'academic' and 'non-academic' here to refer to the profession, rather than to denote scholarly rigour.
4 Fetish collecting therefore ties in with ideas about colonial collecting and appropriation, now part of broader debates about how cultural institutions can instigate processes of restitution and repatriation, as explored by Dan Hicks (2020).

References

Abbate, C., 2017. Overlooking the ephemeral. *New Literary History*, 48 (10), 75–102.

Anon, 1961. Minutes Of The British Music Society Of York Committee Meeting, 9 May 1961. York: Borthwick Institute for Archives, BMS 1.

Armstrong, C., Rachel Cowgill, Alan Dix, Christina Bashford, D Stephen Downie, Mike Twidale, Maureen Reagan, and Rupert Ridgewell (2021). 'Towards a Foundation for Collaborative Digital Archiving with Local Concert-Giving Organisations'. 8th International Conference on Digital Libraries for Musicology, 41–49. https://dl.acm.org/doi/10.1145/3469013.3469019

Bashford C., 2008. Writing (British) concert history: The blessing and curse of ephemera. *Notes*, 64 (30), 458–473.

Bashford, C., 2007. Educating England: Networks of programme-note provision in the nineteenth century'. In: Cowgill, R., and Holman, P. eds. *Music in the British Provinces, 1690–1914*. Ashgate, 349–376.

Bergeron, K., and Bohlman, P.V., eds., 1992. *Disciplining music: musicology and its canons*. University of Chicago Press.

Buffel, T., 2018. Social research and co-production with older people: Developing age-friendly communities. *Journal of Aging Studies*, 44, 52–60.

Byers, D., 2020. The BMS – its fourth quarter century: 1996–2021. Available from: https://www.belfastmusicsociety.org/about-us/our-history/the-bms-its-fourth-quarter-century-1996–2021/ [Accessed 12 April 2022].

Caswell, M., 2014. *Archiving the unspeakable: Silence, memory, and the photographic record in Cambodia*. University of Wisconsin Pres.

Caswell, M., 2021. *Urgent archives: Enacting liberatory memory work*. Routledge.

Clayton, M., Herbert, T. and Middleton, R., 2003. *The cultural study of music: A critical introduction*. Routledge.

Concert Programmes Database, 2022. Available from: concertprogrammes.org.uk [Accessed: 28 March 2022].

Cook, N., and Everist, M., eds., 1999. *Rethinking music*. Oxford University Press.

Cowgill, R., and Holman, P. eds., 2017. *Music in the British provinces, 1690–1914*. Ashgate.

Darms, L., 2015. Radical archives: introduction by Lisa Darms. *Archive Journal* 5 [online]. Available from: https://www.archivejournal.net/essays/radical-archives/ [Accessed 31 March 2022].

DeNora, T., 2000. *Music in everyday life*. Cambridge University Press.

Derrida, J., 1996. Translated by E. Prenowitz. *Archive fever: A Freudian impression*. University of Chicago Press.

Dix, A., *et al.*, 2014. Authority and judgement in the digital archive. In Proceedings of the *1st International Workshop on Digital Libraries for Musicology (DLfM '14)*. ACM, USA, 1–8.

Edenheim, S., 2014. Lost and never found: The queer archive of feelings and its historical propriety. *differences* 24 (3): 36–62.

Ehrlich, C., 1985. *The music profession in Britain since the eighteenth century: A social history*. Clarendon Press.

Evans, R.J., 1997. *In defence of history*. Granta.

Fair Principles, 2022. [online]. Available from: https://www.go-fair.org/fair-principles/ [Accessed 30 March 2022].

Finnegan, R., 2007. *The hidden musicians: Music-making in an English town*. Wesleyan University Press.

Flinn, A., 2010. An attack on professionalism and scholarship? Democratising archives and the production of knowledge. *Ariadne* 62 [online]. Available from: http://www.ariadne.ac.uk/issue62/flinn [Accessed 28 February 2022].

Flinn, A., Stevens, M., and Shepherd, E., 2009. Whose memories, whose archives? Independent community archives, autonomy and the mainstream. *Archival Science* 9, 71–86.

Foucault, M., 1971. Translated by R. Swyer. *The archaeology of knowledge*. Tavistock.

Goehr, L., 1992. *The imaginary museum of musical works: An essay in the philosophy of music*. Clarendon Press.

Graham, H., Vergunst, J., and Curtis, E., eds., 2019. *Heritage as community research: Legacies of co-production*. Policy Press.

Hansson, K., Ludwig, T., and Aitamurto, T., 2019. Capitalizing relationships: Modes of participation in crowdsourcing. *In Computer Supported Cooperative Work* (CSCW), 28 (5), 977–1000.

Hicks, D., 2020. *The Brutish museums: The Benin bronzes, colonial violence and cultural restitution*. Pluto Press.

Holdsworth, N., Milling, J., and Nicholson, H., 2017. Theatre, performance, and the amateur turn. *Contemporary Theatre Review* 27 (1), (2017), 4–17.

Hoyle, V., 2022. *The remaking of archival values*. Routledge.

IAML, 2019. Study group on access to performance ephemera [online]. Available at: iaml.info/study-group-access-performance-ephemera (Accessed: 28 March 2022).

Lambert, D., and Frisch, M., 2019. Digital curation through information cartography: A commentary on oral history in the digital age from a content management point of view. *The Oral History Review* 40 (1), 135–153.

Lloyds Bank, 2021a. 2021 UK consumer digital index [online]. Available from: https://www.lloydsbank.com/banking-with-us/whats-happening/consumer-digital-index.html [Accessed 22 March 2022].

Lloyds Bank, 2021b. 2021 Essential digital skills report [online]. Available from: https://www.lloydsbank.com/banking-with-us/whats-happening/consumer-digital-index.html [Accessed 22 March 2022].

Maloney, L., and Schofield, J., eds., 2021. *Music and heritage: New perspectives on place-making and sonic identity*. Routledge.

McVeigh, S., 1993. *Concert life in London from Mozart to Haydn*. Cambridge University Press.

Muñoz, J.E., 1996. Ephemera as evidence: Introductory notes to queer acts. *Women and Performance: A Journal of Feminist Theory*, 8 (2), 5–16.

O'Reilly, T., 2005. What is web 2.0 [online]. Available from: https://www.oreilly.com/pub/a/web2/archive/what-is-web-20.html [Accessed 28 March 2022].

Our Place, 2022. Music memories database [online]. Available from: https://ourplace.whereweare.org/music-memories/ [Accessed 13 April 2022].

Pearce, S.M., 1994. Collecting reconsidered. In: S.M. Pearce, ed. *Interpreting objects and collections*. Routledge, 192–204.

Quinn, A.J., and Bederson, B.B., 2011. Human computation: A survey and taxonomy of a growing field. In: *CHI '11: Proceedings of the SIGCHI Conference on Human Factors in Computing Systems*, 1403–1412.

Ridgewell, R., 2003. Concert programmes in the UK and Ireland: A preliminary report. IAML (UK & Ireland) and the Music Libraries Trust.

Russell, G., 2018. Ephemeraphilia: A queer history. *Angelaki: Journal of the Theoretical Humanities* 23 (1), 174–186.

Schofield, J., 2014. Heritage expertise and the everyday: Citizens and authority in the twenty-first century. In: Schofield, J., ed., *Who Needs Experts? Counter-mapping Cultural Heritage*. Routledge.

Scott, D.B., ed., 2000. *Music, culture, and society: A reader*. Oxford University Press.

Sharpless, R., 2008. The history of oral history. In: R. Sharpless, T.L. Charlton, and L.E. Myers, eds. *Thinking about oral history: Theories and applications*. Altamira Press, 7–32.

Silvertown, J., *et al.*, 2015. Crowdsourcing the identification of organisms: A case-study of iSpot. *ZooKeys* (480), 125–146.

Simpson, R., Page, K.R., and De Roure, D., 2014. Zooniverse: Observing the world's largest citizen science platform. In: Proceedings of the *23rd international conference on world wide web*, 1049–1054.

Small, C., 1998. *Musicking: The meanings of performing and listening*. Wesleyan University Press.

Smith, L., 2006. *Uses of heritage*. Routledge.

Swansea University, 2020. Digitally included? [online]. Available from: https://www.swansea.ac.uk/science/computationalfoundry/festival-of-ideas/festival-2020/#th-june-digitally-included=is-expanded [Accessed 31 March 2022].

The Oral History Society, 2022. The history of oral history [online]. Available from: https://www.ohs.org.uk/about-2/ [Accessed: 7 February 2022].

Tilley, C., 2012. Objectification. In: Tilley, C., *et al.*, eds *The Sage Handbook of Material Culture*. Sage, 60–73.

Turnhout, E., *et al.*, 2020. The politics of co-production: Participation, power, and transformation. *Current Opinion in Environmental Sustainability*, 42, 15–21.

Vergunst, J., Graham, H., 2019. Introduction: heritage as community research, in: Heritage as Community Research. Policy Press, pp. 1–24. https://doi.org/10.1332/policypress/9781447345299.003.0001

Von Ahn, L., *et al.*, 2008. Recaptcha: Human-based character recognition via web security measures. *In Science*, 321 (5895), 1465–1468.

Webb, S., 2022. Preserving queer voices. In: T. Stylianou-Lambert, A. Bounia, and A. Heraclidou, eds. *Emerging technologies and museums: Mediating difficult heritage*. Berghahn Books, 42–64.

Weber, W., 2016 (1975). *Music and the middle class: The social structure of concert life in London, Paris and Vienna between 1830 and 1848*. Routledge.

Westphal, A.J., *et al.*, 2006. Stardust@ home: Virtual microscope validation and first results. In: *37th Annual Lunar and Planetary Science Conference*, 2225.

Yale, E., 2015. The history of archives: The state of the discipline. *Book History*, 18, 332–359.

Zembrzycki, S., 2013. Bringing stories to life: Using new media to disseminate and critically engage with oral history interviews. *Oral History*, 41 (1), 98–107.

10 Sami traces: Diversity and curatorial workarounds in image archives

Vendela Grundell Gachoud, Anna Näslund Dahlgren, and Karin Hansson

Introduction: Cultural heritage in motion

Cultural heritage is that which remains to tell a story of human life at a certain point in time and space, a story often framed by a dominant narrative. Among the artefacts and practices chosen to convey this life, photographs offer a trusted yet fragile repository. The photograph keeps and transforms the memory of what it holds. Artefacts and practices live on in images circulating beyond their origin, reaching new contexts where their meanings multiply. Digitalisation adds to this transformation. In the shift from analogue archive to digital database, metadata that describes content and context becomes crucial for identifying images. This article elucidates the tension around identification and identity in the image archive online. The photograph here (Figure 10.1) exemplifies this tension since its metadata both enhances and obscures its roots among the Sami. The Sami is an ethnic minority originating among nomads in Mesolithic Fennoscandia, modern-day Sapmi where territorial and cultural conflicts with the Swedish state are ongoing since the 16th century. The image appears in the presentation of the Swedish National Heritage Board (Riksantikvarieämbetet) on the social media site Flickr Commons, where it serves to amplify the diversity of the archive's users and uses (Boman 2020). The SNHB (RAÄ) is the government agency for cultural heritage in Sweden since 1630 (SNHB web a, b). As such, it is committed to the Universal Declaration on Cultural Diversity which promotes a unique, varied, and dynamic embodiment of identity – situating diversity as a spectrum of perspectives, echoed in everyday vernacular (UNESCO 2001: §1–4, 6–7, 11; OED 2020).

From circa four million photographs – private and institutional collections of items, monuments, buildings, and people in urban and rural landscapes since the 19th century – the SNHB have digitised approximately 200,000 photographs since 2000 for their online image database Kulturmiljöbild, of which circa 1% is presented on Flickr Commons for the public "to share, to comment, tag or just enjoy!" (SNHB web: b). Sharing archival images online enables extensive circulation and reuse of cultural heritage. As Figure 10.2 discloses, relatively many viewers see the relatively

DOI: 10.4324/9781003277606-10

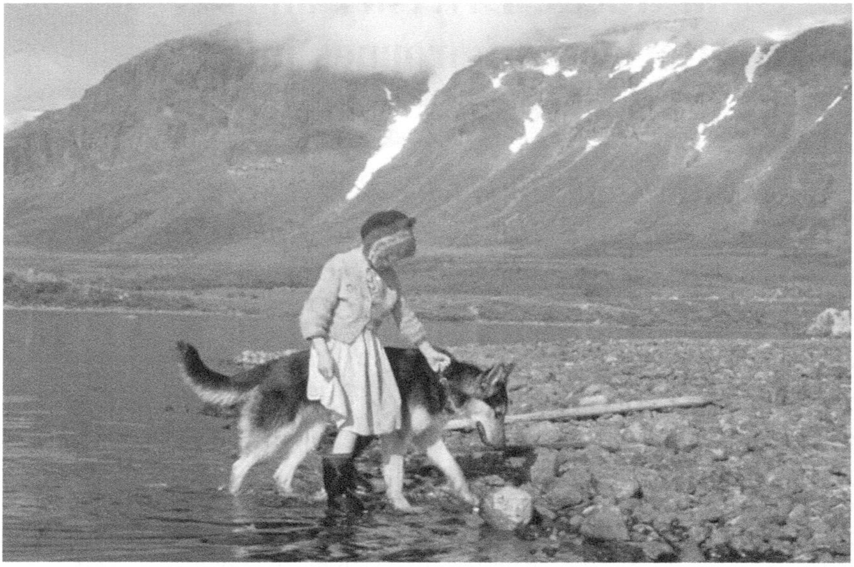

Figure 10.1 Björn Allard: *Girl and dog, Satisjaure (Satihaure), Gällivare, Lappland, Sweden* (1958). SNHB, Flickr Commons 2020 (public domain).

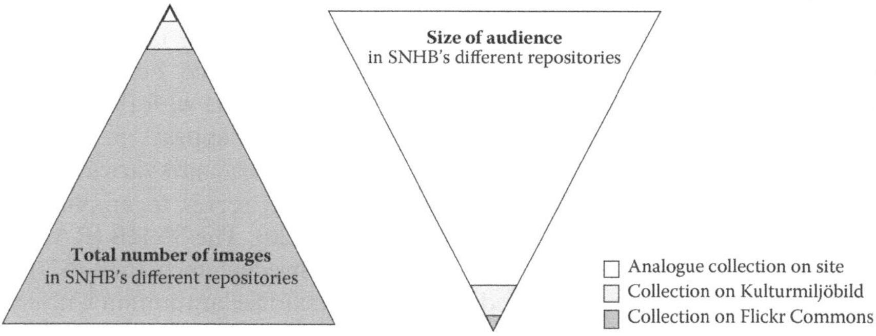

Figure 10.2 Left: Visualisation representing the relative relations between images in the analogue archives of the Swedish National Heritage Board, images digitised in Kulturmiljöbild and images published on Flickr Commons. Right: Visualisation representing the public exposure of the collections of the Swedish National Heritage Board, where the smallest amount of the images on Flickr Commons has the largest public exposure.

few images that the SNHB shares on Flickr Commons while very few see most of the images in their analogue collections. Our analysis articulates the representational politics of a leading cultural heritage institution in this gap between analogue archive and digital display.

This study addresses images of cultural heritage as cultural heritage since their contents and contexts of circulation and display keep public memory alive in a digital world where visuality is vital to stay relevant in a community. We argue that metadata is key to this process because it governs access to historical narratives, the current understanding of cultural heritage in the past, and the current production of future cultural heritage. However, if metadata is incorrect, insufficient, or otherwise problematic, it is hard to even retrieve the image compared to an analogue archive. Metadata lets us find the image and interpret it through a description: what is not described does not exist in digital reality. Figure 10.1 fronts an album on the SNHB's Flickr Commons site, where it gives the only directly visible cue to the Sami – the red hat in the mountainous landscape – but it is not described as Sami in a clear searchable way. This observation prompted our inquiry since it flags a mismatch between image and metadata. A description fitted to fixed classification modes may imply a dominant narrative with biased or omitted information that simplifies the multiple complex narratives that images reflect and generate. This narrative affects not only minorities that it may exclude – it affects everyone. On the one hand, the inclusion of materials into an archive depends on a decision of what not to include. On the other hand, exclusion is problematic for an archive bound to UNESCO's pluralistic stance on diversity as a spectrum of perspectives. To account for this tension, this chapter considers how metadata, particularly user-generated descriptions, shapes the conditions of cultural heritage images in an online archive since the issue of diversity is explicit yet also contested there.

The aim is to analyse how metadata shapes the conditions of cultural heritage representation, with a focus on Sami cultural heritage in the online image archive of the Swedish National Heritage Board. By tracing these images across the in-house database Kulturmiljöbild and the social media platform Flickr Commons, we investigate how the mediation of the images on these different sites becomes a workaround for diversity: i.e., a means to resolve or bypass limitations to the spectrum of perspectives expressed in descriptions of images. The following cases point out how metadata gains the potential to either enhance or obscure diversity as it steers what we find when searching for images in online archives.

This study relates to research that critically discusses metadata as a tool or obstacle for diversity, set against an "authorized heritage discourse" by which official institutions hegemonically affirm or ignore certain heritages (Smith 2009). It connects and expands findings about descriptors that characterise diversity. On the one hand, these descriptors expose biases in both existing and absent categorisations (Loukissas 2017) and thus counter the erasure of marginalised identities (Clarke and Schoonmaker 2019). On the other hand, institutional and crowdsourced image descriptions may support "counter-data" (Cairns 2013; Liew 2016; Alemu 2018) but also reproduce biases (Miltenburg 2016). In a Swedish context, our inquiry fits a paradigm of normative criticism that redirects attention to people outside dominant heritage narratives (Bernsand and Narvselius 2018) – narratives where heritage institutions play a nationalist role by featuring Sami cultures imagined as foreign (Harding 2020). Since we home in on metadata and diversity regarding image sharing online, our study complements Sami-related research which mainly concerns colonialism (e.g., Eriksen 2018; Overud 2019) and conservation (e.g., Pinto-Guillaume 2017; Porsanger and Virtanen 2019) with some focus on museum practices (e.g., Swensen 2017; Horsberg Hansen 2020). In doing so, we also contribute to broader research on photographic documentation of the Other (e.g., Smith 2013; Turner 2016).

With this study, we respond to urgent and topical developments for the Sami and the SNHB. In November 2021, the Sami parliament signed an agreement with the Swedish government for a truth commission on violations in Sapmi, for which the Swedish church has issued an official apology – while racism, territorial disputes, and other signs of colonial trauma persist. One step towards recognition, which underlines visual culture in this slow and fragile process, is that Sami cultures feature in dedicated local institutions like the Ájtte museum in Jokkmokk, in mainstream art institutions like Sven-Harrys konstmuseum in Stockholm, and at international events like the Venice Biennale where the Nordic countries will be represented solely by Sami artists in 2022. Given the traction of digital access, the Sami presence online is key. As Kulturmiljöbild closed in June 2021 – its contents partly remaining in the databases Kringla.nu, K-samsök, and Forndok – we highlight a minority material at a moment when it gains the majority's interest yet also risks losing the narratives it participates in. The images from Kulturmiljöbild on display on Flickr Commons situate the Sami and the Swedish as specific yet integrated collectives, representatives of a dominant narrative which they also criticise.

This study enriches the understanding of cultural heritage narratives in motion, supporting the UNESCO diversity plan that emphasises knowledge, best practices, and policy as "awareness-raising modalities and patterns of cooperation" (2001: §1–3, 14, 19–20, quote: §2). The online context remains crucial since it governs access to media production, dissemination, and literacy in digital communication networks (Ibid: §9–12). As these networks integrate social and technical norms pervading human lives, the assumed neutrality of data is exposed as false (e.g., Kember and Zylinska 2012; Gitelman 2013; Mauthner and Gárdos 2015). This critique, against the ways that big data generates seemingly neutral generalisations about a presumed "mass", points to the discursive power of the archival apparatus (e.g., Schwartz and Cook 2002; Bonde Thylsdrup *et al.* 2021) and how it necessitates a plurality of narratives around archival images online to avoid reducing them to an ungraspable "mass" photography (e.g., Rubinstein and Sluis 2013; Baylis 2014). Metadata establishes and maintains the integration of technical and social norms, so central for the reproduction of culture embedded in technology that it steers how images are found and used online (Dahlgren *et al.* 2020). Grounded in a mixed-media method for representational politics, the main contribution of this article is an innovative combination of visual and textual analyses elucidating an under-researched empirical material.

Theoretical perspective: Democracy, visuality, and identity formation

We approach the nexus of metadata, diversity, and cultural heritage images online within a framework of democracy and identity formation where participation and performativity are key (Hansson and Näslund Dahlgren, forthcoming). In a report on the role of cultural heritage work for social development, the SNHB states that a focus on identity, social cohesion, and inclusion – and, thereby, on social hierarchies as well as the ownership of, and access to, heritage – guides contemporary interpretations of the past and what its traces represent (SNHB 2016: 41–43, in Bernsand and Narvselius 2018: 68). This stance aligns with a heritage politics informed by normative criticism that "enables emancipation and representation of previously silenced and invisible perspectives and identities [but] introduces normatively loaded rhetoric to heritage work, often in the form of binary oppositions" (Ibid: 68, 88). Our framework follows this discourse as it targets image descriptions whose biases implicate social hierarchies, while we take care not to repeat divisive language.

In line with Fraser (2005), we understand the democratic effort of cultural heritage institutions as a process of recognition, redistribution, and representation – firstly, acknowledging varying worldviews to incentivise participation; secondly, providing means, skills, time, and networks to enable participation; and, thirdly, facilitating the (self-)expressions of a plurality of identities to make participation meaningful to the participants. This three-part theorisation proves useful in research on how archives shape the social equality of different publics by controlling representations that affect participation in cultural heritage (Waterton and Smith 2010) and how digital practices facilitate such participation in marginalised communities (Were 2015). We specify this model with regard to visual culture by emphasising performativity (Austin 1962; Butler 1988). Tying into the discussion on the integration of technics and aesthetics, we understand visuality as a dynamic between, on the one hand, the multisensory experiences and expressions that shape how we embody our subjectivity and, on the other hand, the socio-cultural structures that shape our embodiments not least by technological means (Marks 2002; Mirzoeff 2006). In this view, photographs invite a gaze that both illustrates discourses and generates them since they describe a reality which they also affect through the description (Iversen 2007; Schneider 2011). This process becomes pertinent when photographs represent people defined as vulnerable, situating the body as a site for ideological moulding and resistance (McRuer 2006; Andrews 2011; Ellcessor 2016). We argue that images and their metadata shape such ideological embodiments, and thus shape and perform social relations by affecting the reality that they describe. This framework sharpens our research question with an emphasis on visuality as key to a democratic participation in representational politics: how does metadata shape the conditions of cultural heritage representation, so that the visual framing of a plurality of heritages in online archives may facilitate diversity?

Material and methodology: Metadata extraction and close reading

The datasets for this study comprise images and image tags from the SNHB collection on Flickr Commons and Kulturmiljöbild. In doing so, they capture the organisation of the archive within and across two different sites with different policies and practices regarding metadata: one image database at a central administrative agency for cultural heritage and one corporate social media platform for image-sharing. Flickr offers free image use as a Web 2.0 business while the SNHB does so under governmental decree. As one of 116 institutions, notably from the global North/West, the SNHB joined Flickr Commons in 2009, one year after it launched with the aim to "increase access to publicly-held photography collections, and to provide a way for the public to contribute information and knowledge" (Flickr web: a). At the time of writing, the SNHB holds the largest Swedish account with 20100 followers and 20.3 million visits, 1957 images, 29 albums, 2259 tags, 1600 geotags, and 45 group memberships (SNHB web: b). The SNHB gains traction from the user interaction on Flickr, while Flickr's mix of personal and institutional users builds the brand.

What unites these two sites is accessibility. The Flickr platforms mainly operate through an Application Programming Interface (API) that lets members freely access most data (Flickr web: b). The API, which identifies unique users and images, turns Flickr into a participatory space while content turns into a malleable material: "With over 5 billion photographs (many with valuable metadata such as tags, geolocation, and Exif data), the Flickr community creates wonderfully rich data" (Flickr web: c). This issue is pertinent since we extracted the SNHB's tags using flickr.tags.getListUser, an API-based tool available in Flickr's pool for applications developed by members. On the part of the SNHB, all metadata is created by antiquarian Anna Boman at the SNHB Archives, who took part in the SNHB's initiative on Flickr Commons since the start in 2009, and who was the curator and manager since it became permanent in 2010 until her retirement in 2021. Any additions from users have been filtered by Boman following the SNHB's metadata template: a short description in Swedish and English; geographical and topographical information; the image's medium, photographer and year; and a link to Kulturmiljöbild – all this is copied from Kulturmiljöbild, except the descriptions that may vary between platforms (Boman 2020).

To account for the precarious process of representing cultural heritage online, we combined quantitative and qualitative methods within the emergent field of critical data studies, where the focus lies on "the nature of data, how they are being produced, organized, analysed and employed, and how best to make sense of them and the work they do" (Kitchin and Lauriault 2014: 1, in Loukissas 2017: 652). Tying into quantitative analyses of cultural heritage collections online (e.g., Saleh 2018; Freire *et al.* 2020), our inventive approach includes visual interpretation to target "data discrimination" such as biases, omissions, and stereotypes (Noble 2018). We combined automated extraction of image tags with two qualitative approaches in the format of a cross-disciplinary case study (Flyvbjerg 2011). Firstly, a semi-structured interview with curator Anna Boman to clarify the institution's views on participatory incentives, technical affordances, and curatorial strategies that affect issues around diversity (Boman 2020; Kvale and Brinkmann 2014). Secondly, a close reading of Sami-related images and metadata to clarify their *punctum*: i.e., the decisive detail that "pricks me (but also bruises me, is poignant to me" (Barthes 2000: 26–27). Together, these approaches illuminate how a key local institution engages in the production and preservation of cultural heritage in an online setting with global reach – an institution with a clear cultural heritage mission that dominates Sweden's representation on Flickr and therefore can, and should, affect diversity issues for a wider public.

After mining all image tags used by the SNHB on Flickr Commons – 2259 tags for 1957 images in September 2020 – we selected markers of identity that indicate diversity such as gender, ethnicity, role, age, profession, nationality, and appearance in actual and symbolic representations. We tested the relevance of our delineation by analysing the first 10% of the tags and then selected 308 tags for further inquiry. These sometimes occur in several categories, overlapping with a porousness that erodes descriptive conventions like gender binaries. The initial quantification indicated the Sami trace since we noticed images that contained Sami content – locations, buildings, objects, and clothes – which the metadata did not describe. To follow this trace through potential gaps in the metadata, we conducted searches using the keywords "sami", "sapmi", "same", and "samisk" which define the Sami material in English, Sami, and Swedish since they refer to people, places, objects, and practices in this cultural context. The word "sami" refers to Sami culture in the native tongue and in English; the Sami word "sapmi" refers to the Sami people and their traditional location; the word "same" is a Swedish derivation of Sami and Sapmi; and the word "samisk" is the Swedish adjective referring to Sami culture (SIC web: a). To approximate identical search conditions in Kulturmiljöbild and Flickr Commons, given that the former is organised in categories and lacks the latter's interactive elements, we used the free text search tool rather than specifying e.g., objects. We also analysed an album of photographs by Björn Allard, documenting Sami culture as part of the SNHB's culture-historical

Table 10.1 Methodological outline

Step 1	Semi-structured interview regarding incentives, affordances, and strategies with Anna Boman, antiquarian at the SNHB, and curator of the SNHB account on Flickr Commons.
Step 2	Extraction of image tags from the account of the SNHB on Flickr Commons using Flickr API.
Step 3	Identification and analysis of identity markers in the image tags on Flickr Commons using uncontrolled terms, i.e., terms chosen freely by taggers.
Step 4	Image search on Flickr Commons using the keywords "sami", "sapmi", "same", and "samisk". Analysis of results in comparison with results of tag extraction from Flickr Commons.
Step 5	Image search in Kulturmiljöbild using the keywords "sami", "sapmi", "same", and "samisk". Analysis of results in comparison with results of image search on Flickr Commons.

surveys and archaeological excavations due to territorial regulations when power construction expanded in northern Sweden in the 1950s and 1960s. The cover image of Allard's Flickr album is *Girl and Dog* (Figure 10.1), which prompted our study. All data – interview notes, images, and tags in figures and tables – are available in individual and compiled formats at the Harvard Dataverse Repository (HDR 2021).

Results: Biases, workarounds, and interventions

The information drawn from our interview with curator Anna Boman threads together the subsequent steps: tags on Flickr Commons, keywords on Flickr Commons and Kulturmiljöbild, and the Allard album. According to Boman (2020), the SNHB aimed to make the archives accessible by participating on Flickr Commons as an image communication service with the benefits of social media interactivity – broadening the audience with a representative overview that shows images in context and broadening the context by enabling downloads, comments, and crowdsourced details about copyright free images. A broad appeal is created with the visual efficacy of attractive images showing people and environments from different places, i.e., showing diversity insofar as they include marginalised groups and draw visitors from 70 countries (Ibid). A negotiation around inclusion plays out within and between text and image – an interplay not without resistance.

Image tags in the SNHB archive on Flickr Commons

The 10% most frequent tags capture a dominant institutional narrative around nature and nation (Figure 10.3). The SNHB asserts itself with the two most frequent tags, #riksantikvarieämbetet (1957) and #theswedishnationalheritageboard (1947), that, together with links to Kulturmiljöbild, lead users away from the multilateral sharing of images towards the unilateral

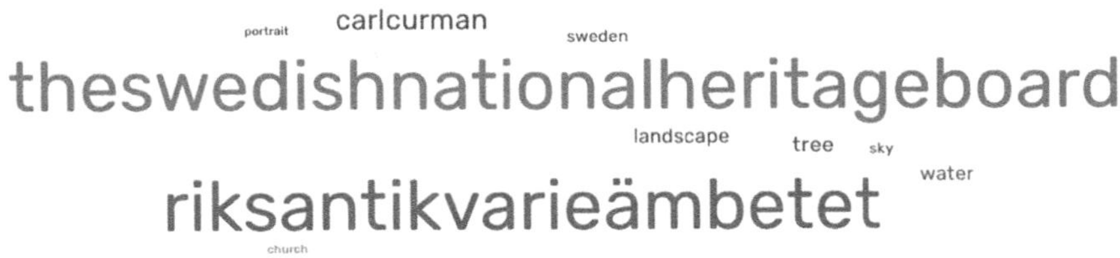

Figure 10.3 A visualisation representing the top ten tags in the Swedish National Heritage Board's account on Flickr Commons in September 2020.

manifestation of the in-house database. Among the top ten, the four tags referencing nature – #trees (104), #water (93), #landscape (90), and #sky (65) – also proliferate on both sites, as does the context of #sweden (79) and the Swedish #church (63). The third most frequent tag, #carlcurman (160), is occasioned by the first album published by the SNHB on Flickr Commons, featuring Spanish snapshots by physician, artist, and photography amateur Carl Curman. Tying in with #portrait (55) in tenth place, these tags reflect institutional priorities in both the source archive and its social media display.

The 308 tags are predominately referring to white European men (Table 1–2, HDR 2021). Men have 90 tags compared to 43 for women, occurring 409 times compared to 126. For instance, 50 men and 17 women are named. A euro-centric view is established as 58 tags refer to nation 2257 times, of which 2200 refer to four northern countries. Ethnicity is referenced only 13 times with ten tags that pertain to four images of Roma and Sami people. This scarcity is an indication of how biases against minorities may exist in both present and absent metadata, notable as an implicit exclusion if not as an explicit prejudice (Loukissas 2017: 656). A similar scarcity concerns class although hierarchies permeate designations of social roles from the anonymous #farmer to the named #consulmollén to outliers like #fortuneteller, perhaps positioned at the opposite end of the social ladder as #saint. Roles and professions appear in 60 tags, overlapping with gender in tags such as #fishermen and #waschfrauen (laundry women) – an intersectional variety also noted in 60 tags describing bodies. The representational dimension of being documented in everyday life also emerges in tags such as #standing (24) and #fishing (4) while the eight references to smiles converse with outliers such as #holdinghands and #frown – tags which support the claim, made by e.g., Gräslund Berg *et al.* (2013), that personal details are best captured methodologically by tracking verbs.

Biases related to gender, ethnicity, and nationality are unsurprising in an archive like the SNHB's where diversity has been neither a social reality nor a political priority during its four-centuries-long history. The marginalisation through tags is a societal factor, not an institutional choice. The biases in the tags also reflect specific institutional histories. The SNHB's first published album with Curman drew extensive media attention that affects the categories of gender and nation. This example points to a representative relation between tags and content. In contrast, the SNHB's presentation contains 308 images in 12 albums by photographer Berit Wallenberg who is only tagged once. The display of several albums by one woman makes the archive seem diverse, exemplifying the curatorial aim to promote groups whose marginalised status deny due representation as the SNHB curator puts it:

> The images on Flickr Commons show different environments, buildings and persons, from different societal groups. To some degree, different ethnic groups (like Sami and Roma). I have considered diversity and variation during the image selection and show that this diversity also exists in the archival collections. Social differences are a fact, not the least in earlier times, and to display this is unproblematic to me. The photographer at a certain time looks at the motif with the eyes of that time when he or she takes their picture, which also becomes a document of time in the case when a value is part of the representation. (Boman 2020)

The intention to include diverse material governs which images to display in which way. Yet, reinforcement is needed if metadata, or lack thereof, risks reducing the image's searchability and narrative by describing less than what the image conveys. The scarcity of tags that include marginalised groups is significant of a metadata practice where most tags are scarce – 1561 tags occur only once. Recurring tags make it easy to find images yet produce a dominant narrative through repetition, while rare instances add a variation that is key to diversity as a spectrum. As the quote above indicates, the SNHB's display on Flickr Commons is curated to convey a variation that ideally is both representative and diverse. Yet, a scarcity of recurrent tags raises the risk of missing cross-references within and beyond the platform which, in turn, may impede accessibility. However, the frequency problem is mitigated by language. Boman acknowledges that "language is cultural heritage too", noting how the metadata reflects a blend between the unified style of the government agency and the differing styles of the descriptors. Consistency is ideal, yet the SNHB language policy is implemented through personal decisions adapted to the online context: correct, comprehensible, accessible – nice and easy-going if appropriate (Boman 2020). Language thus affects diversity through voice, tone, and content. For instance, the specific "laundry women" above could have been generic "workers".

According to Boman, the SNHB's aim to reach more users online is reflected by the fact that Flickr users have contributed information about 231 images, i.e., 12% of the collections, including tags in other languages than Swedish (2020). This outcome of the institution's crowdsourcing initiative indicates that users are vital for enabling their own access to cultural heritage. Crowdsourced metadata may alleviate the problem by giving a more inclusive entrance to a less inclusive archive bound to intentions of both diversity and representativity. Here, this entrance is conditioned by an interface adapted to the fast visual cues of online interactivity. As Boman puts it, "the images must work on a site like this [and] you work with what you have" (Ibid). Consequently, the display remixes the images in a mosaic of contrasts – light and dark, city and countryside, colour and greyscale, different activities – attracting and shaping the user's gaze because "it's good for the eye to readjust [...] you see better if the images are varied" (Ibid.). Allard's image *Girl and dog* makes this point clear as a centrally placed album cover keeping the gaze with iconic intensity. As a Sami-related image that lacks Sami-related metadata and therefore does not appear in our search, it also makes clear that metadata directs what the eye can see. A visual diversity created through visual binaries may enforce social binaries – to include images of people because of their difference may "readjust the eye" for pleasure rather than for inquiry. However, the "remix" is key to reaching new users – whose devices reshuffle image relations when the mosaic changes with various dimensions and configurations.

All in all, this shows how metadata amplifies diversity but also amplifies a need to address the socio-technical condition of cultural heritage images. To address biases through the interface, visual literacy is key: if not for our visual memory of the girl and the dog, we may not have interrogated the metadata – which makes the few Sami images hard to find.

Sami traces in the SNHB archive on Flickr Commons

Our keyword search on Flickr rendered 22 hits comprising three graphical reproductions, nine photographic postcards, and ten original photographs (Table 3, HDR 2021). The graphical reproductions are two etchings from 1790 to 1800 (Images 1, 4) and a lithograph from the late 19th century (Image 7). The etchings depict Sami people engaged in crafts and reindeer herding in a camp with Sami huts in a forested mountain area in Lapland and Härjedalen, while the lithograph depicts Jukkasjärvi church in Lapland with a group of Sami watching as one of them approaches the entrance. The nine postcards (Images 5, 10–12, 14, 15, 18, 20, 22), produced 1930–1959 for the publishing company Almquist & Cöster, also convey Sami culture in transition as traditional practices intersperse with modern accommodations. The ten original photographs depict Jokkmokk old church circa 1860 (Image 19), Handöl Sami chapel circa 1900 (Image 6), Kolåsen Sami chapel circa 1940 (Image 17), a prehistoric Sami grave near a settlement at Durrientjahke (Durrienjokk) in 1921 (Image 16), and a waterfall in the national park Stora Sjöfallet in 1961 (Image 21) – the two first ones include a few people in Sami dress. Five photographs (Images 2, 3, 8, 9, 13) were taken by Björn Allard during the SNHB's archaeological surveys in northern Sweden in 1958, depicting Sami locals tending to animals and fishing nets at a camp located in the world heritage nature reserve Laponia. These five images belong to the same album as the aforementioned *Girl and dog* which should appear in our search but does not.

The images are accompanied by 57 tags that occur 114 times in total (Table 4, HDR 2021). With their references to the SNHB, to landscape and to people – 44, 28, and 14 respectively – these tags continue the archive's main narrative on Flickr Commons. Likewise, most tags are in English with a few in Swedish, German, Spanish, and Portuguese. Image 10 has the most tags, 18, followed by Image 17 with 12, and Images 3, 12, and 18 with 11. These statistics concerning metadata become pertinent when considered together in the Sami context. Out of 22 possibilities, Sami-related tags occur four times in three images. Image 6, entitled *Handöl Sami Chapel, Jämtland, Sweden*, is tagged #samipeople; Image 17, entitled *Kolåsen Sami Chapel, Kall, Jämtland, Sweden*, is tagged #kolasensamichapel; and Image 19, entitled *Jokkmokk Old Church, Lappland, Sweden* is tagged #sami and #sapmi (Figure 10.4). The first one appears in the search for "same" but not for "samisk", the latter two do not appear neither for "same", "samisk" nor "sapmi". If these occurrences are too few to carry the knowledge production of the images in these posts, they matter to the knowledge-producing process around Sami cultural heritage in relation to other posts that feature the Sami without tagging it.

Three posts exemplify the knowledge production on Sami issues here, in conjunction with the user activity noted in the statistics about tags, views, and comments. Images 10, 14, and 18 depict Sami schools in Lapland, photographed for Almquist & Cöster in the 1940s and 1950s. Image 10, entitled *Sami school in Vaisaluokta, Jokkmokk, Lappland, Sweden*, portrays a group of young children in traditional Sami dress standing with a woman

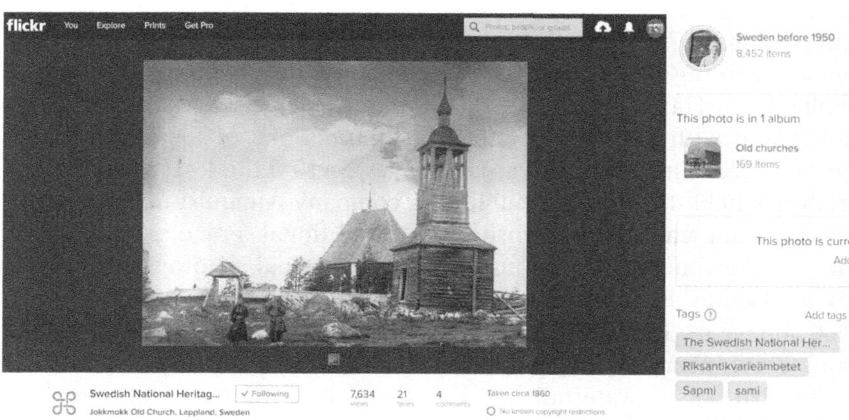

Figure 10.4 Unknown photographer: *Jokkmokk Old Church, Lappland, Sweden* (circa 1860). Screenshots. SNHB, Flickr Commons 2020 (public domain).

outside a Sami hut; Image 14, entitled *School huts for Sami children, Jukkasjärvi, Lappland, Sweden*, captures a similar group outside a row of school huts in a modern style (Figure 10.5); and Image 18, entitled *Interior of Sami school in Vaisaluokta, Lappland, Sweden*, shows eight Sami children inside a school hut. These images are the most visible among the 22 hits, respectively viewed 36353, 32534, and 28895 times and chosen as favourites by 93, 78, and 55 users. The institutional framing and the user response keep

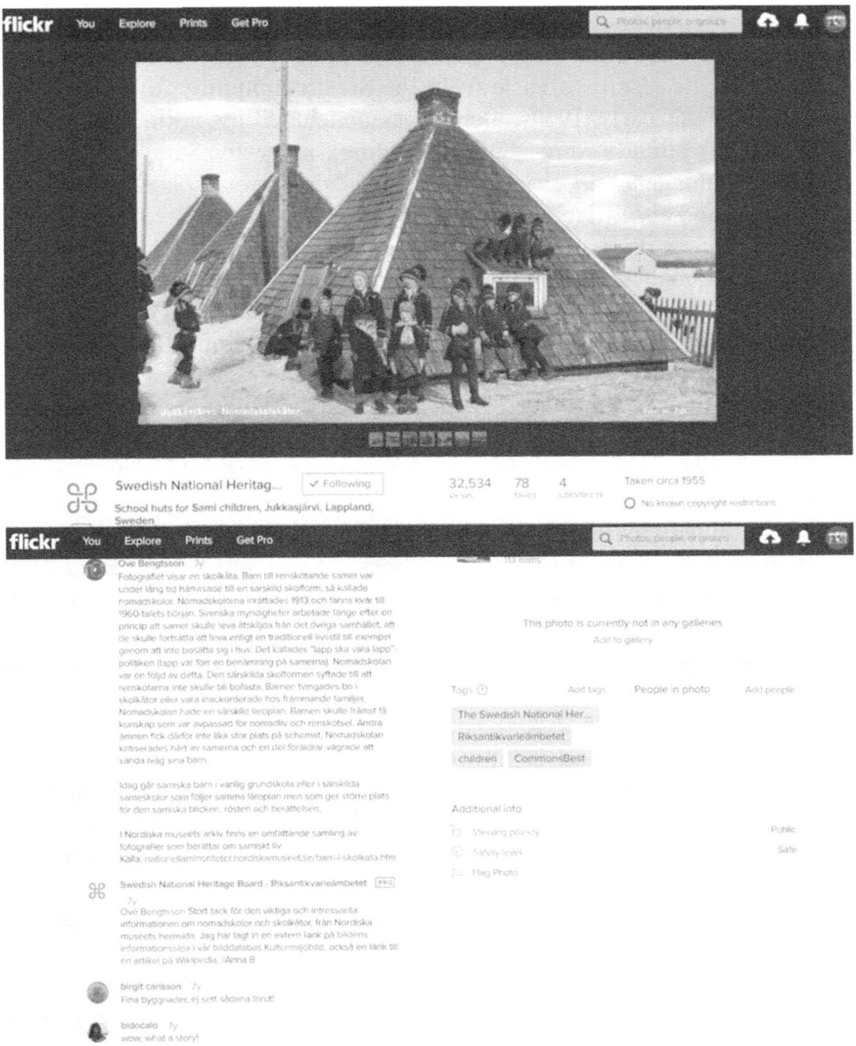

Figure 10.5 Hjalmar Falk: *School huts for Sami children, Jukkasjärvi, Lappland, Sweden* (1950–1959). Screenshots. SNHB, Flickr Commons 2020 (public domain).

a positive tone and focus with tags, captions, and comments that convey light-hearted reminiscing about the school years.

In contrast, Image 14 gives pause to generic childhood memories (Figure 10.5). One user, the SNHB administrator Ove Bengtsson writing privately here, details the history of the Sami schools. Bengtsson describes how the Swedish government established nomad schools in 1913 specifically for children of reindeer-herding Sami to keep their traditional lifestyle separate from the rest of society, based on a policy known as "*lapp* should be *lapp*" where *lapp* is now considered a derogatory word for Sami. To this end, the nomad school forced children to stay in the school huts or with other families while following a curriculum designed for nomadic reindeer herding. Despite severe criticism from the Sami community, the policy was upheld until the early 1960s. Bengtsson concludes by noting that Sami children today attend ordinary primary school or specific Sami schools that follow the same general curriculum yet that "gives more space to the Sami gaze, voice and narrative". The post also provides a link to the Nordic Museum, cited as the source of this description about Sami schools through both text and images. In response to this post, the curator Boman discloses that she has added the link, as well as a link to an article on Wikipedia, on the image's page in Kulturmiljöbild to include this "important and interesting information". While this post on Flickr Commons lacks the link and further information, the other two posts do include links to Wikipedia for further reading.

Although the posts about Image 14 are seven years old – an eternity online – they still exemplify an exchange between users and institutions that can be continued anytime to keep adding knowledge around this image and others, within and between multiple online archives and social media platforms. It is evident that threads of comments like the above connect users with images that share similar content – images that therefore may share similar issues around interpretation and function across various contexts of display.

In the final two sections, we demonstrate how metadata supports an exchange between users and institutions by first focusing on the album by Björn Allard where Sami content is present yet elusive due to the metadata, and then comparing Flickr Commons and Kulturmiljöbild. Allard's album consists of 63 photographs from 1957 to 1963, organised chronologically and geographically starting with the SNHB's expeditions to Sweden's northernmost region of Lapland where Sapmi is mainly located. The images have 79 tags that occur 260 times in total: six in Swedish, 15 in German, and 57 in English with overlaps for four multi-lingual words. No Sami-related tags occur, though Sami content occurs in at least the first 24 images (Table 5, HDR 2021).

The tags underscore two tendencies in the SNHB's presentation on Flickr Commons. Firstly, the omnipresent tags #theswedishnationalheritageboard and #riksantikvarieämbetet serve the institution's recurrent references to itself. Secondly, features and activities in nature – fishing, landscape, trees – appear in 44 tags combined with six tags referring to animals, 12 tags referring to people, and single tags such as #fischernetze and #reflections. While corresponding to imagery prevalent in the archive as instances of administrative metadata, the tags on Flickr Commons lack the formal consistency of the database though the information about the images is copied from the latter. The lack is due to structural differences between Kulturmiljöbild and Flickr Commons, entailing a shift from tight categorisation to free tagging which Boman (2020) recalls as a challenge: "A certain suspicion against crowdsourcing and with 'losing control' over how and where the images would be used, since the SNHB previously has delivered (i.e., sold) images only to known clients with an explicit area of use". Less consistency and control may enable users to contribute unexpected aspects otherwise restricted by governmental policies. Since all metadata must be approved by the curator, a gatekeeper of institutionally sanctioned knowledge who also favours remix, the inconsistencies emerging in our analysis leave uncertainties that are both problematic and productive.

Three posts stand out as examples of unexpected tagging in the Flickr album. Image 46, entitled *Farmstead, Åkerslund, Prästtomta, Östergötland, Sweden*, is tagged #path, #road, #winding, #landscape, #trees, and #grass – the addition of "winding" gives a poetic note to generic landscape features. Image 34, entitled *Mountain cattle, Hökvattnet, Jämtland, Sweden*, is tagged #fjäll (mountains), #cows, #painted, #white, #black, and #fjäll-cows (*sic*) – the black and white cows are what is "painted" here. Image 49, entitled *Garden of a small farmstead in Smedsbo, Östergötland, Sweden* is tagged #cabin, #middle, #nowhere, #landscape, and #greenery – a humorous twist, even without the missing "of" between "middle" and "nowhere". These posts exemplify that tags produce knowledge beyond a strict information value, both controlled and uncontrolled. The tags appear at once random and intentional as they follow the syntax of a sentence where you add a word for each thing that you value enough in the image to point out in a tag. As part of a metadata strategy, especially subsumed under institutional policies, these tags are superfluous: they do not add facts, they confuse coherence, and nobody would search for "nowhere". Yet, they hint at the person behind the tag, who contextualises the image in a personal way that an institutional metadata producer does not. While the institution contributes facts through the image's title and caption, this tagger contributes a connection to other users based on the experience of familiarity or estrangement with which you describe a place as "the middle of nowhere". In doing so, experiential and interpretive aspects of tagging become equally important as user expertise that the institution acknowledges in their pursuit of reaching out online. Users mainly specify details about dates and places (Boman 2020) yet here add five tags about tractors (Image 35) and ten tags about airplanes (Image 11). The lack of institutional control over the metadata gives users a chance to add tags that assert expertise and experience outside a dominant cultural heritage discourse.

Our analysis shows how users' expertise and experience may include the Sami to accommodate more diverse search needs beyond what users are currently expected, enabled, and encouraged to find – though searchability does not follow automatically. In 18 of Allard's images, references to the Sami enrich the otherwise consistent nuance and specificity of natural detail – but without mentioning the Sami. A richer knowledge appears in brackets containing Sami location names: "Satisjaure (Satihaure)", "Saggat (Sakkat)", and "Hälla (Hielle)". The first location is a lake in the nature reserve "Sjaunja (Sjávnja)", likewise presented with brackets in the caption, which states that the area is part of the UNESCO World Heritage site Laponia. The second location is a lake, featured with an archaeological surveyor from the SNHB on the shore and at a Stone Age settlement as well as with a house, fishing-nets, and rose root. The third location features a Stone Age settlement with SNHB surveyors mapping the site. Archaeological work recurs in 20 of the 63 images. Sami-related knowledge is also indicated in Allard's images number 5, 6, 7, and 10 which include "sami" in the title (Table 5). With a focus on Sami huts and camps, these titles conform to the emphasis on nature dominating the tags of the SNHB account. However, the captions mention the specific Sami hut *goahti* with the designation of the sites as a world heritage. While these *goahti* are not tagged, they do appear when searched for the specific term. Images 5, 6, and 7 do not appear in the search for the term "sami" but Image 10 does so even without the tag. However, Image 1, *Girl and dog*, is presented without Sami references (Figure 10.6). The traction gained by the Sami images – drawing the most views, tags, comments, and favourites – may thus be an inadvertent effect of being placed first in the album in an eye-catching layout rather than an intended effect of an efficient metadata structure. Nevertheless, this user interaction motivates improving the searchability to represent and enhance the Sami presence in this archive.

Sami traces in the SNHB archive in Kulturmiljöbild

Our keyword search on "same" at Kulturmiljöbild rendered 33 hits (Table 6, HDR 2021). Images 8–15 (KMB in Table 6), from 2004, are close-ups of tree trunks located to Nilasjokk, categorised as a Sami settlement in Arvidsjaur. This category is a sub-category of "nomadic industry", in turn a subcategory of "construction work". The classification has pragmatic and symbolic implications as Sami material is placed in an indirect and inferior search route. Moreover, the caption explains that the Sami used the inner bark of pine for various purposes such as food. The past tense signals that this practice and its cultural context are outdated. Images 36–47 (KMB in Table 6), from 2008, also evoke pastness. The caption describes how the lake Stora Lulevatten is surrounded by hearths

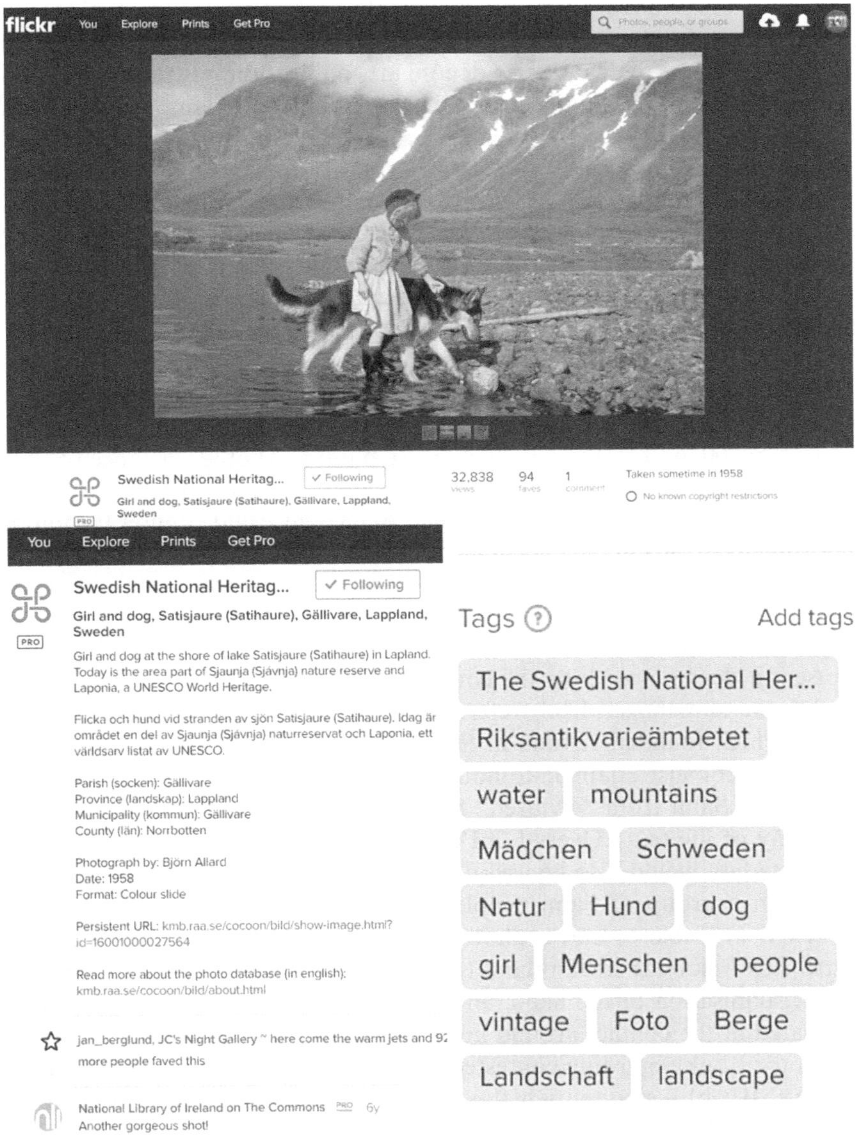

Figure 10.6 Björn Allard: *Girl and dog, Satisjaure (Satihaure), Gällivare, Lappland, Sweden* (1958). Screenshots. SNHB, Flickr Commons 2020 (public domain).

where Sami huts once stood. This description is less problematic since the categories confirm the historical setting. In addition, the historical framing is situated in the present with links to online maps that show the geographical position of the site and the photographer.

Four images are from Gällivare: three depict the sculpture *Same* from 1957 by Allan Wallberg for the municipal building park (48–50 KMB in Table 6) and one the Sami flag at the settlement Östra Ritjemjåkk in 2008 (51 KMB). While the categories denote art, public administration, and environment rather than Sami culture, the flag is linked to maps and captioned to stress its importance to all Sami peoples as part of a world heritage. Among the remaining ten images, two 18-century etchings that depict people in Sami camps (53, 57 KMB) and two postcards that capture Sami families in a hut and on the ice (59, 61 KMB) recur from our search on Flickr Commons. While assigning value to the content with map links to Sapmi and the keyword "national interest", the categories again point away from the Sami towards generic labels of art, family, and landscape – often under the heading of "other".

We identify three more postcards from this collection which depict Sami school huts, and Sami people respectively moving and exiting a building (Images 58, 60, 62 KMB). Two include map links. Another instance of self-reflection at the SNHB is that the captions rephrase the words printed on the postcards from "*lapp*" to "*same*" – a way to recognise and counter the initial bias, evident in the interface yet not transparent on the part of the institution who fashions the collection and its artefacts to an updated online context. Similarly, Image 62 (Figure 10.7, KMB in Table 6) has the printed caption "*Lappar hos 'Disponenti'*". While the institution's caption has been rephrased, it does not address the context of the word *disponenti* – *disponent* means general manager, likely referring to the state-owned mining company LKAB which founded Kiruna in Sapmi. The first LKAB *disponent*, state-employed geologist Hjalmar Lundbohm, advocated for the policy that separated the Sami from "civilized" Swedish society to maintain their "natural" way of life (e.g., Overud 2019). To address the knowledge produced with metadata would also be useful in the two last posts, depicting an altar cross with a group of Sami people in prayer created for Kiruna church (63 KMB in Table 6) and a photograph of Sami huts and people at the chapel site Ankarede in Jämtland (80 KMB in Table 6). Neither mentions the christianisation of the Sami, an initiative ongoing since the early 1600s implicated in the conflict around governmental interest in Sapmi.

A note or link regarding contested topics – e.g., to the Sami Information Centre (SIC: b) – may enrich the knowledge production, now following keywords and categories which inadvertently condone a narrative that, despite pointing to "national interest", turn Sami schools into "construction work", Sami reindeer herding into "animals" and Sami miners into "winter motif".

Among the 39 hits for the search on "samisk" were depictions of Sami spiritual practices (Table 7, HDR 2021). Images 27 and 39 (KMB) show church towns in Malå and Vilhelmina, probably in the late 1970s. The Sami presence in Vilhelmina is situated by a caption that points to traditional huts serving as church buildings but no explanation is given for

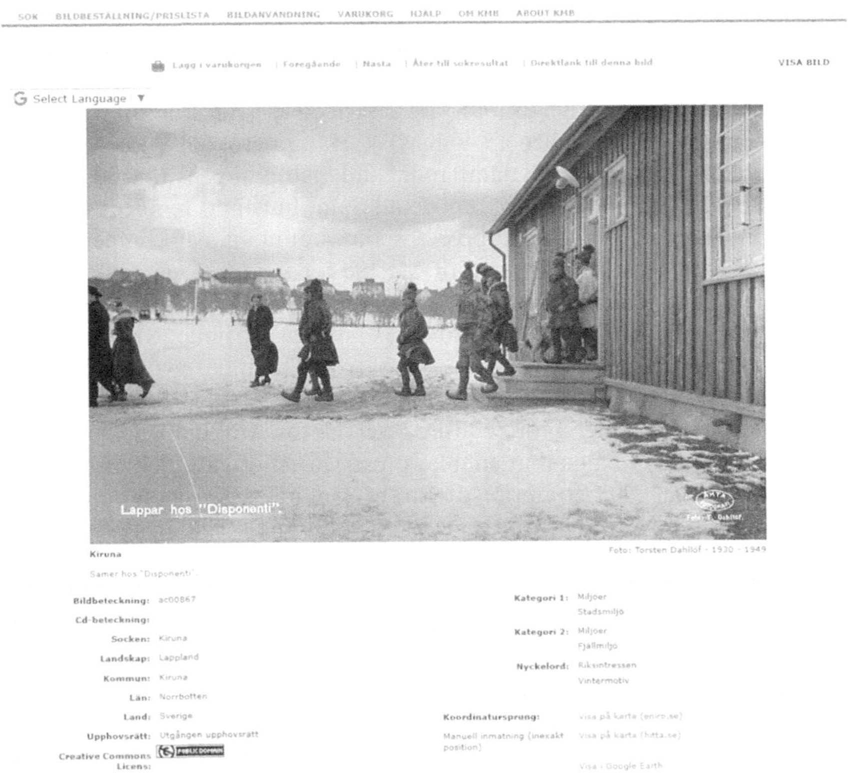

Figure 10.7 Torsten Dahllöf: *Kiruna. Samer hos "Disponenti"* (1930–1949). Screenshot. SNHB, Kulturmiljöbild 2020 (public domain).

similar repurposed huts in Malå. Both are categorised as "construction work" – and the Malå site is specified as "*lappstad*", repeating the derogatory term to signify the buildings erected close to a church where the Sami stayed during visits. The former is accompanied by the keyword "national interests" and by links to maps as well as to the register compiling cultural heritage constructions in Sweden – the latter is not. There are also three posts featuring Sami sacrificial sites in Lapland, photographed in 1994–1995 in Saivorova in Gällivare (13 KMB) and in Offerskalet in Vilhelmina (37–38 KMB). The categorisation of these images emphasises ancient folklore, and no metadata conveys the Sami's current activities though the photographs are quite recent. One related photograph (31 KMB) recurs from our search on Flickr Commons, depicting a Sami grave at Ropen in Lapland 1926 near the settlement Durrientjahke (Durrienjokk). The image is categorised as "ancient monument" while the Flickr Commons tags only refer to the SNHB.

The post links to online maps and to the database Fornsök. Among the 39 hits are also depictions of a runic calendar (1–4 KMB) and a money bag (16 KMB), both described as having Sami origins yet neither categorised as such.

Twelve images, from 1995 to 1996, are described as a Sami cultural heritage environment: Kroktjärnvallen (5–9 KMB), Hamptjärn (33–34 KMB) and Maskien (35–36 KMB) in Jämtland, and Atoklimpen (28–30 KMB) in Lapland in Table 7. The captions detail Sami huts and reindeer herding, using Sami names like Aatoeklibpie for the mountain Atoklimpen where the Sami village Vapsten is located or Meskie for the Maskien area with remains of ancient settlements. A related photograph (32 KMB) depicts the village Strimasund in Lapland described as an area, Strijmie, with Sami settlements and monuments. All images, except from Hamptjärn, are categorised as Sami settlements. The keyword "nature reserve", added for Hamptjärn and Maskien, is exchanged for "culture reserve" for Atoklimpen – a classification ascertaining a value that enables preservation of entire environments. Ten images from 2008 comprise disparate examples of water industry in Sapmi and in the world heritage area Laponia: a Sami fishing shed in Sádis (Satis) in Gällivare (10–12 KMB) and the Akkat power plant in Jokkmokk (17–23 KMB). The latter is categorised as "construction work" yet also as "painting" because of the large-scale decoration that, according to the caption, "connects to the Sami life and culture which continues to shape this part of Sweden".

Five of the 39 hits on Kulturmiljöbild can be compared to the Flickr posts. The Sami flag (15 KMB), and two postcards depicting Sami school huts in Jukkasjärvi (24 KMB) and a Sami family with reindeer and a dog in Kiruna (25 KMB) recur on Flickr Commons. The caption for Image 24 is rephrased from "nomadic" to "Sami" huts and links are added to Wikipedia and the Nordic Museum while the classification confirms the Sami presence. The caption for Image 25, *Lappland*, is extended but the classification, underlined by the Flickr tags, emphasises "animals", "environments", and "winter motif". One more postcard (26 KMB in Table 7) resembles the Flickr Commons selection but does not appear in our search on Kulturmiljöbild. Again, the classification includes "Sami settlement" and the caption, "*Lapparnas visthus*", is rephrased to describe Sami larders in Kiruna. Lastly, Image 14 (KMB in Table 7) here resembles Image 13 on Flickr Commons (FC in Table 3) – people tending to fishing nets, photographed by Allard in 1958. The caption places them in the Sami summer settlement Aleskätje in Laponia, marked by the keyword "world heritage". While the Sami word *vierme-tsakkeh* is used to point out the fishing-net crutches, the categories describe generic features and activities rather than cultural specificities.

Allard's image *Girl and dog* did not appear when we keyword searched Kulturmiljöbild. Neither the caption nor the tags on Flickr Commons (Table 5, Figure 10.6) convey the cultural context, yet include Sami

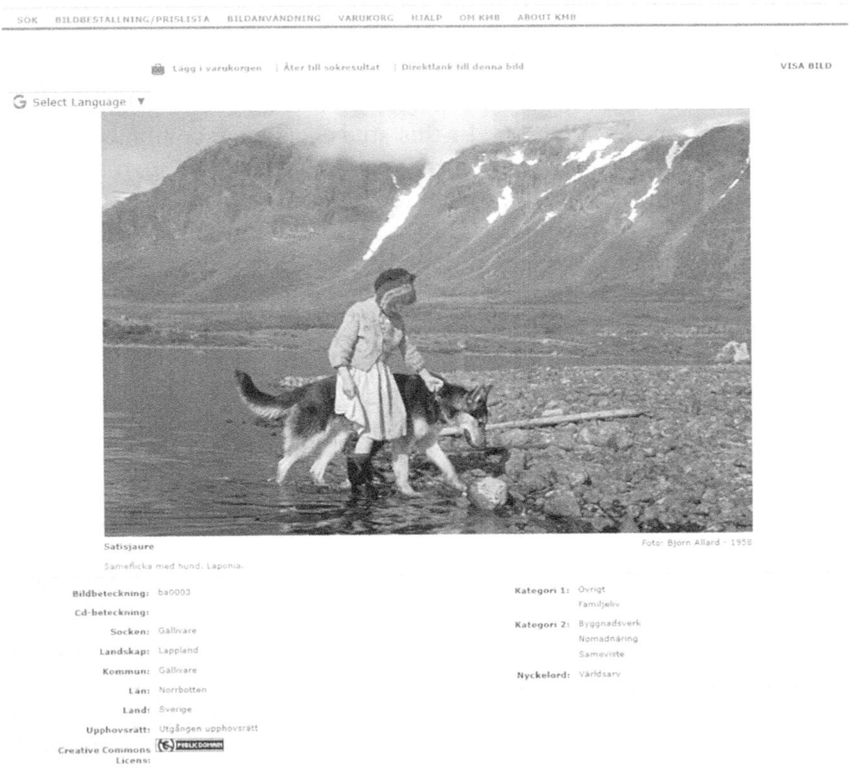

Figure 10.8 Björn Allard: *Girl and dog, Satisjaure (Satihaure), Gällivare, Lappland, Sweden* (1958). Screenshot. SNHB, Flickr Commons 2020 (public domain).

names when specifying the location at the world heritage site Laponia. In Kulturmiljöbild, we find the image in a search on the photographer (Figure 10.8). While the categories hide a Sami lifeworld under emphasised as "world heritage" – restoring a Sami identity. As our entry-point to the Sami material in the SNHB archive, the image thus exemplifies both problems and potentials regarding diversity as it conveys a mismatch between image and metadata that reveals multiple narratives and diverging metadata practices across Flickr and Kulturmiljöbild.

Conclusion: Working around curatorial workarounds

This chapter discloses how metadata shapes the conditions of cultural heritage representation, with a focus on Sami cultural heritage in the online image archive of the Swedish National Heritage Board. By tracing images across the in-house database Kulturmiljöbild and the social media platform Flickr Commons, we uncover how different metadata structures and practices create different narratives through tags, categories, captions, and comments.

A lesson learnt from this case study is that digital technologies for storage, retrieval, and display of images as cultural heritage need to be addressed with mixed methods. In this study, we have combined quantitative and qualitative analysis, focusing on both visual and textual aspects of the image archive. Our approach adds granularity to broader critical research on the archival apparatus (e.g., Bonde Thylsdrup *et al.* 2021) and on photographic documentation of the Other (e.g., Smith 2013; Turner 2016) as well as research focused on Sami heritage (Swensen 2017; Horsberg Hansen 2020). This method for studying image archives can be applied to analyses of similar cases which encompass complex social and representational dynamics. A problematic "authorized heritage discourse" (Smith 2009) can thus be confronted from inside and outside, thereby safeguarding against biases also within the paradigm of normative criticism (Bernsand and Narvselius 2018). Our initial claim, that metadata establishes and maintains the integration of technical and social norms, is substantiated as it confirms the falsity of data neutrality (Gitelman, 2013; Mauthner and Gárdos 2015). We stress the importance of open negotiation about who is included in a cultural heritage archive and in which way through both textual and visual markers – e.g., if identity specifics need address, where to place them in the metadata structure, and how to do so with historical accuracy and contemporary concern.

In this study of SNHBs image archive, we have identified four workaround strategies in how the institution selects, publishes, and labels images in relation to diversity. The strategies are used to resolve or bypass limitations to the spectrum of perspectives expressed in both textual descriptions and image contents. These workarounds are omission, abstraction, translation, and hyperbole. Omission implies not recognising the Sami at all, a stance of representational politics that consolidates absence despite inclusionary intentions. Abstraction implies pointing to similarities rather than differences, i.e., not differentiating whether a dwelling is a Sami hut or a farmstead but labelling both with the more abstract generic term "house". A third strategy used is translation, where outdated or derogative terms are systematically translated into modern terminology – e.g., Sami rather than *lapp* – and thereby whitewashing historical downgrading and discrimination. Finally, there is the hyperbole strategy which implies an exaggeration of the historical visibility of a discriminated group by showcasing and highlighting these few examples, making them more visible than they were in earlier times and in the collection's holdings at large.

This typology of strategies illuminates both visual and verbal biases in collections management and metadata practices, and how they comply with each other. In effect, this study discloses that the pursuit of diversity is a complex challenge when it comes to historical image collections.

As such, our study contributes to the ongoing scholarly discourse on metadata, representation, and diversity in relation to digital classification systems and specifically to identity politics that characterise diversity descriptors (e.g., Clarke and Schoonmaker 2019: 20). Based on this typology, it is possible to synthesise the disparate implications of previous research on metadata and diversity where descriptors are shown to resist biases as well as to reinforce them (e.g., Liew 2016; Miltenburg 2016; Alemu 2018). For future research and information management in the heritage sector, we believe that a raised awareness of these four strategies could make practices of online and offline display and metadata production more conscious, transparent, and diverse. Every little step taken to resolve the mismatch between image and metadata, and the gap between the analogue archive and the online display, is important. The above cases and analysis underline the significance of these small steps as they reveal layers of metadata that both confirm and contest the dominant narrative that frames the images – layers that call for future scientific and technical efforts towards social inclusion in cultural heritage contexts.

Summary

With the consistent media usage that follows the SNHB's metadata strategy, the curator and manager Anna Boman is correct in claiming: "We succeed in reaching out" (2020). Yet, the institution's mission comprises a cultural heritage that points beyond any default borders of nationality while its archival infrastructure risks to reduce a plurality of cultures to monoculture. By articulating this tension, and by pointing out the four workaround strategies as ways in which this tension can be identified also in other cultural heritage archives, this study contributes key insights into the rhetorical dynamic between interface and infrastructure in archives where dominant narratives are limiting claims to diversity. With an innovative combination of visual and textual analyses that show how metadata both enables and complicates diversity ambitions, this mixed-media study on representational politics goes beyond the "awareness-raising" scope of the UNESCO diversity plan (2001: §2) through its empirical, methodological, and analytical contribution. Building on these insights, both professionals in the cultural heritage field and the broader community of online archive users can gain leverage to explore how cultural heritage representations are framed by metadata – and how metadata may be changed to reframe these representations, inviting multiple possible frames for multiple narratives.

Acknowledgement

The research for this article was conducted within the project *The Politics of Metadata*, at the Department of Culture and Aesthetics, Stockholm University, funded by the Swedish Research Council (grant no. 2018-01068).

References

Alemu, G., 2018. Metadata enrichment for digital heritage: users as co-creators. *International Information & Library Review*, 50 (2), 142–156.

Andrews, J., 2011. The photographic stare. *Philosophy of Photography*, 2 (1), 41–56.

Austin, J.L., 1962. *How to do things with words: the William James lectures delivered at Harvard University in 1955*. Oxford: Clarendon Press.

Barthes, R., 2000. *Camera lucida: Reflections on photography*. London: Vintage Books. (1980). Translated by R. Howard.

Baylis, G., 2014. A few too many photographs? Indexing digital histories. *History of Photography*, 38 (1), 3–20.

Bernsand, N., and Narvselius, E., 2018. Cultural heritage in Sweden in the 2000s: contexts, debates, paradoxes. *Politeja*, 1 (52), 57–94.

Boman, A., 2020. Interview with Anna Boman, antiquarian at the Swedish National Heritage Board, curator and manager of the Flickr commons account. Skype, 2 September 2020 and e-mail, 1–10 June 2021. See HDR 2021.

Bonde Thylsdrup, N. *et al.*, eds., 2021. *Uncertain archives: critical keywords for big data*. Cambridge, MA: MIT Press.

Butler, J., 1988. Performative acts and gender constitution: an essay in phenomenology and feminist theory. *Theatre Journal*, 40 (4), 519–531.

Cairns, S., 2013. Mutualizing museum knowledge: Folksonomies and the changing shape of expertise. *Curator: The Museum Journal*, 56 (1), 107–119.

Clarke, R.I., and Schoonmaker, S., 2019. Metadata for diversity: identification and implications of potential access points for diverse library resources. *Journal of Documentation*, 1–24, DOI 10.1108/JD-01-2019-0003.

Dahlgren, A. *et al.*, 2020. The politics of metadata, special issue of *Journal of Digital Culture & Society*, 6 (2).

Ellcessor, E., 2016. *Restricted access: media, disability, and the politics of participation*. New York and London: New York University Press.

Eriksen, K.G., 2018. The indigenous sami citizen and Norwegian national identity: tensions in curriculum discourses. *Human Rights Education Review*, 1 (2), 25–45.

Flickr, web a, 'The Commons', https://www.flickr.com/commons (accessed 30 June 2021).

Flickr, web b, 'The App Garden', https://www.flickr.com/services/apps/about (accessed 30 June 2021).

Flickr, web c, 'The Developer Guide', https://www.flickr.com/services/developer (accessed 30 June 2021).

Flyvbjerg, B., 2011. Case study. In: N.K. Denzin and Y.S. Lincoln, eds. *The sage handbook of qualitative research*. Thousand Oaks: Sage, 301–316.

Fraser, N., 2005. Reframing justice in a globalizing world. *New Left Review*, 36, 69–88.

Freire, N. *et al.*, 2020. Cultural heritage metadata aggregation using web technologies: IIIF, sitemaps and schema.org. *International Journal on Digital Libraries*, 21, 19–30.

Gitelman, L., ed., 2013. *'Raw Data' is an oxymoron*. Cambridge and London: MIT Press.

Gräslund Berg, E. *et al.*, 2013. Praktiker som gör skillnad: Om den verb-inriktade metoden. *Historisk Tidskrift*, 133 (3), 335–354.

Hansson, K., and Näslund Dahlgren, A., forthcoming, Choice, negotiation, and pluralism: a conceptual framework for participatory technologies in cultural heritage, *Computer Supported Cooperative Work (CSCW).*

Harding, T., 2020. World culture, world history, and the roles of a museum: a conceptual study of the Swedish museums of world culture, debates concerning them, and their roles in cultural politics. *International Journal of Cultural Policy*, DOI: 10.1080/10286632.2020.1752684, 1–14.

HDR, Harvard Dataverse Repository, 2021. All data referenced in this article is available in compiled format here: 10.7910/DVN/RPMZNO. Individual datasets are also available here: https://dataverse.harvard.edu/dataverse/samitraces (accessed 29 January 2022).

Horsberg Hansen, H., 2020. The sámi art museum: there is no – or is there? *Nordlit*, 46, 222–241.

Iversen, M., 2007. Following pieces. On performative photography. In: J. Elkins, ed. *Photography theory*. New York and London: Routledge, 91–108.

Kember, S., and Zylinska, J., 2012. *Life after New Media: mediation as a vital process*. Cambridge and London: MIT Press.

Kitchin, R., and Lauriault, T.P., 2014. Towards critical data studies: Charting and unpacking data assemblages and their work. *The programmable city working paper 2*. Programmable City: Social Science Research Network.

Kvale, S., and S. Brinkmann, 2014. *Den kvalitativa forskningsintervjun*. Lund: Studentlitteratur.

Liew, C.L., 2016. Social metadata and public-contributed contents in memory institutions: 'Crowd Voice' Versus 'Authenticated Heritage'? *Preservation, Digital Technology & Culture*, 45 (3), 122–133.

Loukissas, Y.A., 2017. Taking big data apart: local readings of composite media collections. *Information, Communication & Society*, 20 (5), 651–664.

Marks, L.U., 2002. *Touch: sensuous theory and multisensory media*. Minneapolis and London: University of Minnesota Press.

Mauthner, N.S., and Gárdos, J., 2015. Archival practices and the making of 'Memories.' *New Review of Information Networking*, 20 (1–2), 155–169.

McRuer, R., 2006. *Crip theory: cultural signs of queerness and disability*. New York: New York University Press.

Miltenburg, E. v., 2016. Stereotyping and bias in the Flickr30K dataset. Proceedings of the *Workshop on Multimodal Corpora: Computer Vision and Language Processing*, 1–4.

Mirzoeff, N., 2006. On visuality. *Journal of Visual Culture*, 5 (1), 53–79.

Noble, S.U., 2018. *Algorithms of oppression: how search engines reinforce racism*. New York: New York University Press.

OED, Oxford English Dictionary. Search terms: diversity, workaround. https://www.oed.com/ (accessed 30 June 2021).

Overud, J., 2019. Memory-making in Kiruna – Representations of colonial pioneerism in the transformation of a Scandinavian mining town. *Culture Unbound: Journal of Current Cultural Research*, 11 (1), 104–123.

Pinto-Guillaume, E., 2017. The sami people's cultural heritage in Swedish EIAs. *Impact Assessment and Project Appraisal*, 35 (3), 227–239.

Porsanger, J., and Virtanen, P.K., 2019. Introduction – A holistic approach to indigenous people's rights to cultural heritage. *AlterNative: an International Journal of Indigenous Peoples*, 15 (4), 289–298.

Rubinstein, D., and Sluis, K., 2013. Concerning the undecidability of the digital image. *Photographies*, 6 (1), 151–158.

Saini, G., 2018. How to use Flickr API to collect data for deep learning experiments? *Towards Data Science*, https://towardsdatascience.com/how-to-use-flickr-api-to-collect-data-for-deep-learning-experiments-209b55a09628 (accessed 30 June 2021).

Saleh, E.I., 2018. Image embedded metadata in cultural heritage digital collections on the web: An analytical study. *Library Hi Tech*, 36 (2), 339–357.

SIC, web a, Samiskt informationscentrum (Sami Information Centre), 'Sápmi', http://www.samer.se/1002 (accessed 30 June 2021).

SIC, web b, Samiskt informationscentrum (Sami Information Centre), 'Mission among the Sami', http://www.samer.se/missionen (accessed 30 June 2021).

Schneider, R., 2011. *Performing remains: art and war in times of theatrical reenactment*. London and New York: Routledge.

Schwartz, J.M., and Cook, T., 2002. Archives, records, and power: from (Postmodern) theory to (Archival) performance. *Archival Science*, 2, 171–185.

Smith, L., 2009. Class, heritage and the negotiation of place. In: Missing Out on Heritage: Socio-Economic Status and Heritage Participation. Conference, English Heritage, London.

Smith, S.M., 2013. *At the edge of sight: photography and the unseen*. Durham: Duke University Press.

SNHB, The Swedish National Heritage Board, 2016. *Kulturarvsarbetet i samhällsutvecklingen. Redovisning av regeringsuppdrag om omvärldsanalys och kunskapsöversikt avseende kulturarvsområdet*. Report.

SNHB, The Swedish National Heritage Board, web a, 'Our History', https://www.raa.se/in-english/swedish-national-heritage-board/our-history/ (accessed 30 June 2021).

SNHB, The Swedish National Heritage Board, web b, https://www.flickr.com/people/swedish_heritage_board/ (accessed 30 June 2021).

Swensen, G., 2017. Objects as identity markers – Ways of mediating the past in a south sámi and norse borderland. *Museum & Society*, 15 (2), 236–258.

Turner, H., 2016. Critical histories of museum catalogues. *Museum Anthropology*, 39 (2), 102–110.

UNESCO Universal Declaration on Cultural Diversity, 2001. UNESCO, Paris, 2 November 2001.

UNESCO, 2004. Universal Declaration on Cultural Diversity [online]. Available from: https://www.ohchr.org/en/instruments-mechanisms/instruments/universal-declaration-cultural-diversity[Accessed 17 October 2022]

Waterton, E., and Smith, L., 2010. The recognition and misrecognition of community heritage. *International Journal of Heritage Studies*, 16 (1–2), 4–15.

Were, G., 2015. Digital heritage in a Melanesian context: authenticity, integrity and ancestrality from the other side of the digital divide. *International Journal of Heritage Studies*, 21 (2), 153–165.

Wu, T., 2019. Automated web scraping using Flickr API with dynamic dashboards for analysis. *Medium*, https://medium.com/@wutianhao910/automated-web-scraping-using-flickr-api-with-dynamic-dashboards-for-analysis-9df5501d2107 (accessed 30 June 2021).

11 Reading, play, and critical engagement with cultural heritage: Associating children with Orientalist paintings through an interactive picturebook

Betül Gaye Dinç, Özge Subaşı, and Ilgım Veryeri Alaca

Introduction

This study focuses on the potential of a picturebook prototype that is tailor-made for the Suna and İnan Kıraç Foundation's Orientalist Painting Collection permanent exhibit in the Pera Museum, in Istanbul, to nurture children's interaction with artworks in a museum. Museums, one of the primary institutions preserving and displaying cultural heritage artefacts, have been crucial informal learning settings studied by the Human-Computer Interaction community due to the opportunities to test and experiment with different interaction types, technologies, and devices in a public environment with a diverse audience (Hornecker and Ciolfi 2019). Inclusive experimentation with museum content needs careful consideration of several aspects in order to appeal to each visitor in an eloquent and fulfilling way. Smith (2006, p. 30) conceptualises power dynamics in cultural heritage studies through "Authorised Heritage Discourse" (AHD) that signifies a single hegemonic voice valuing particular identities while alienating others. Critical perspectives in museum and heritage studies, such as New Museology or critical heritage studies, challenge professionals in museums to review their discourses, decolonise their collections and create accessible, inclusive, and dialogic places aiming for social change (Marstine 2006, Witcomb and Buckley 2013). Similarly, according to Galani *et al.* (2020), digitisation in museums and cultural heritage institutions goes beyond using an assemblage of technologies; it is a dynamic process of negotiations of self and alterity where constant recreations of reciprocal relationships with communities through dialogic practices occur. Digital technologies concerning the plurality of cultural heritages offer material, embodied, and aesthetic experiences that challenge the authoritative narration via polyvocal and participatory features (Schofield *et al.* 2019, Claisse *et al.* 2020, Galani et al. 2020).

Despite the cultural splendour that a museum collection aims to offer, children's perspectives can easily get lost in the complexity of these

DOI: 10.4324/9781003277606-11

presentations. Smith (2006, p. 26) explains that the authorised heritage discourses consider heritage properties as valuable assets to preserve for future generations.This concept of heritage assigns a passive role to children who are expected to take patrimonial responsibilities in the future by undermining children's agency in the present time. However, studies in childhood theories, such as Gubar's (2013, p. 453) "kinship model", reject the idea of children as "becoming" or "adults in the making". Accordingly, Gubar's idea positions them as "beings" having differences yet kinship to adults' perspectives; therefore, as coproducers of cultural texts with them.

Children's interactions with cultural heritage objects and artworks vary according to the museum types and prescribed museum education programs. While studies on child-technology interactions in science and maritime museums (Beheshti *et al.* 2019, Hershman *et al.* 2018, Hogan *et al.* 2017, Long *et al.* 2019) are more common, there are studies on facilitating children's learning through interactive technologies in art and history museums as well (Thom-Santelli *et al.* 2006, Yiannoutsou 2009, Apostolellis and Bowman 2015, Roussou and Katifori 2018, Vayanou *et al.* 2019). Art museums provide child–adult/peer interactions (e.g., storytelling activities), child–environment interactions (e.g., hands-on activities), and combinations thereof (e.g., playful and multisensory experiments) (Andre *et al.* 2017). As such, the technologies in art museums often take the form of mobile museum guides, games, and interactive installations and apply different museum education approaches (namely Active Learning, Contextual Model of Learning, etc.) as it is suitable to their institution (Thom-Santelli *et al.* 2006, Apostolellis and Bowman 2015, Hornecker and Ciolfi 2019). In some cases, art museums employ technology that integrates participatory design aspects to create an art education program for children (Roussou *et al.* 2007).

Museums use diverse approaches to facilitate children's interactions with an exhibit through mobility (Thom-Santelli *et al.* 2006), playfulness (Yiannoutsou 2009), and active participation (Roussou *et al.* 2007), and most interactions are carried out through storytelling (Roussou and Katifori 2018; Vayanou *et al.* 2019). Furthermore, these studies reveal that significant design elements of tools such as games are attuned to education approaches through active learning (Apostolellis and Bowman 2015). Unfortunately, few of the studies we reviewed discuss how they helped facilitate interactions that would clearly explain art terminology, employ narratives in such a way that the artwork would be memorable, or discuss the curation process of similar works, which would give a historical context. To rectify this oversight, we have addressed these frequently disregarded aspects through a case study of our own.

These issues led us to draw knowledge from picturebook studies where children's engagements are built on multimodal narratives, material, aesthetic, and cultural explorations that may be beneficial in specialised contexts. A picturebook, mainly "the interaction between written text and image and where both have been created with a conscious aesthetic intention" (Arizpe and Styles 2016), is often the earliest object to introduce artistic sensibilities and multimodal literacies to children. Scrutinising the illustrations in picturebooks is comparable to observing the artworks as both evoke aesthetic sensations through their affordances. Thus, picturebook interactions offer a degree of intimacy for children through their handling in close proximity to the child's body, thus triggering tactile explorations (Nodelman 2018). Since material interactions at times heighten the multimodal reading opportunities of picturebooks, this study finds merit in using the picturebook's capacity to narrate and facilitate hands-on and bodily engagement to encourage art appreciation at museums. Thus, according to the findings of this case study, picturebooks may also be used for further surface interactions supported by (simple to complex) technologies.

To examine how this interplay of Picturebook studies and HCI benefits museums, we have chosen to study Pera Museum due to its extensive experience in children's learning programs and eagerness to blend low- and high-technology interactions in exhibitions. The corresponding collection that displays Orientalist paintings is challenging for children since many of the themes are unfamiliar to them, such as the historical context, terms, traditions from earlier eras, people's occupations, hierarchical roles, and a regime type different from today. Based on the first author's experience as a museum educator for this collection, we decided on creating a narrative background supported with action questions to transform these subtle but culturally loaded themes into enjoyable ones. Our observations of children's reflections on their experience and use of picturebooks helped define the elements that would support interactive museum learning for the Orientalist Painting Collection. These elements include historic, multi-cultural context supported with narrative, aesthetic, and cultural engagements with the artworks.

Previous works

To support dialogues in museums and cultural heritage institutions, Galani *et al.* (2020) suggest practices focusing on the *polyvocality* achieved through inviting visitors to construct multiple histories and *civic listening* by reflecting on challenging sensitivities with openness. Similarly, Claisse *et al.* (2020) create polyvocal, dialogic, and spatio-temporal interactions in a house museum by underlining key aspects of the materiality of the tools, the aesthetic experience of viewing the craftsmanship, the value of individual stories, rather than the AHDs and constructivist heritaget. Similarly, Schofield *et al.* (2019, p. 4) assert that design for cultural heritage should focus on *plural heritages* signifying the encouragement of individuals and communities' stories and *future-oriented* practices resisting prescribed methods of building "past" and memories. They designed cultural probes for participants to discuss Istanbul's Historical Peninsula (e.g., Theodosian Walls), a UNESCO World Heritage Site, and they asked participants to first imagine giving a tour of the place to someone who passed away, point out areas where the walls witnessed conflicts, write a letter to the walls, and create a flipbook. Hence, sensorial, embodied, and open-ended activities help participants reflect on the past while covering different perspectives on the same cultural heritage assets in Istanbul.

Since Pera Museum is neighbouring the Historical Peninsula, the cultural probes explained by Schofield *et al.* are significant in this study. Embodied activities centred on participants' creative responses can address adults and children as coproducers of cultural heritage in Istanbul. This section presents a broad cross-section of previous works under the following categories: we critically introduce how the museum context augmented by interactive elements enriches children's engagement, then we introduce the technological possibilities that come with interactive book formats. Lastly, we give an overview of children's experiences with interactive books and children's interactive engagement with artworks supported by certain activities in the museum space.

Interactive technologies and children's engagements in museums: A critical stance

Organising interactive events in museums for child visitors poses many challenges based on their ages and education. Science, technology, engineering, maths, and sometimes arts disciplines are integrated into the education of older children and teenagers. For instance, in science museums children try haptic devices to learn about the electric circuit related to the exhibit (Beheshti *et al.* 2019), and they engage with stories presented through a multimodal installation (auditory, projected graphics, thermal and haptic wall), which enhance their curiosity in the story and delight them through the physical engagements (Hogan *et al.* 2017). Gamification and storytelling are popular tools incorporating mobile devices, as various gaming elements (clues, treasure hunt, quiz, collection, simulation, and timeout strategy) are fused with storytelling elements (plots based on adventure or emotions). Studies (Yiannoutsou *et al.* 2009, Thom-Santelli *et al.* 2006) on mobile games and hand-held systems in an art museum context show that playing team-based games designed with a socio-constructive learning approach in museums encouraged children to view the artworks attentively as they communicated with their peers on artworks. The playful storytelling elements in these studies provided a trajectory compiled of different interactions that benefit and support our case study.

Although these interactions facilitate gaining familiarity with the artworks, the increased engagement with the technology on offer may overshadow the museum experience and create several challenges. To give an example, Hornecker and Ciolfi (2019) underline the popularity of these treasure-hunt games but mention at the same time the danger of focusing on achieving the tasks instead of reflecting on the content. Similarly, research on children's playing C-Olive, a collaborative museum game, suggests that playing a game about art in the museum space fosters a "play mode" where children merely focus on gaining high scores and not concentrating on the art (Apostolellis and Bowman 2015). Although this game is developed according to Falk and Dierking's *The Contextual Model of Learning* (CML), it addresses children's context (e.g., motivation and expectations; prior knowledge, interest, and beliefs; choice and control) and socio-cultural context (e.g., within-group sociocultural mediation; facilitated mediation by others) rather than the physical context (e.g., advance organisers and orientation; design; reinforcing events and experiences outside the museum) (Apostolellis and Bowman 2015). They also added that any tool for children should be culturally informed, which implies addressing the children's background, prior knowledge, and learning (Apostolellis and Bowman 2015). Therefore, offering a suitable scenario in which children reflect on their opinions about the artworks is yet another challenge to creating dialogic space.

Human-Computer Interactions in Museums (Hornecker and Ciolfi 2019) is significant for our study since it presents a diverse range of interaction types supported by different interaction modalities, from stand-alone installations, tangible and digital assemblies, mobile devices to Extended Reality works. Hornecker and Ciolfi (2019) emphasise the necessity of considering the aspects of different types of museums such as their vision, the exhibition's content and space, curatorship, the audience and learning outcomes when selecting a suitable interaction type or technology. They borrow Jenny Kidd's term "artistic narrative interpretation" (2018 cited Hornecker and Ciolfi 2019) exemplifying the interactivities evoking the historical and cultural context of the art through the combination of fact and fiction as well as storytelling techniques. Less descriptive and static narratives on artworks challenge the participants' imagination, evoke their attention, and encourage them to discuss art with their peers (Vayanou *et al.* 2019, Roussou et al. 2018).

Picturebook affordances for imagining new interactions

Picturebook affordances such as narration, incorporation of knowledge and facilitating critical, hands-on and bodily engagement are broadly used to counterbalance these challenges since the applications of sociocultural theories to museum environments emphasise "the power of narrative" (Allen 1997) and make museums venues for dialogue between children and artworks. Therefore, in addition to CML, which is also rooted in sociocultural theories, we built on other applications of them in the museum environment (Allen 1997, Piscitelli and Weier 2002) to foster better interactions and provide children with the tools for dialogue on artworks' content through subtle technological intervention/integration. Piscitelli and Weier (2002) suggest that museum guides should utilise directive (e.g., instructing), non-directive (e.g., encouraging), and scaffolding (e.g., reinforcing, focusing attention, posing problems, prompting, clarifying, reading, recalling, co-constructing) elements to guide children in art criticism (Piscitelli and Weier 2002). Picturebook interactions theoretically have some parallels with aspects of these interactive behaviours, for instance, picturebook interactions can be based on dialogic reading and have the potential to extend our understanding of artwork on a critical level through scaffolding in the narration. A tool developed from the social interactions with the artworks' content and culture, especially those like Orientalist Painting Collection that presents a challenging and controversial topic in history and art, can offer children entry points to discuss everything from the aesthetic and artistic value of the artworks to its significance in the past or its cultural relevance today. In conveying these sensibilities through creative and inquisitive methods, picturebooks can narrate through malleable material engagements that foster children's interactions with the historic content without dwarfing the original artworks.

Children's material experiences with interactive picturebooks

Traditional picturebooks where only images and text through paper surfaces play a role diverge from HCI-integrated ones. In HCI-related picturebooks, modalities multiply although the tangibility of physical books in reading still retains its importance. Researchon the book format (Cesário *et al.* 2016) reveals that children find it preferable to other formats because its physicality allows for bonding with the object due to handling the book and exploring page surface qualities. It also provides autonomy of reading without anyone's help and without any restrictions over the time spent, enabling a pleasant and discreet reading routine (Cesário *et al.* 2016). Touching and especially turning a page can be one of the most important movements in the kinaesthetic repository of reading. Paper as a material has a physical significance for children's engagements. This issue has been revisited by recent research (Sim *et al.* 2016) that compared children's interaction with the prototype played on paper or an iPad, revealing that although the form did not affect their enjoyment, the paper version they played elicited more comments on the aesthetic aspect of the game. Moreover, the increase in the attention to paper crafting tradition that combines low and high technological elements such as Paper mechatronics with Led circuits and circuit stickers encourages a reconsideration of the physical interaction opportunities of a print book (Qi *et al.* 2015; Oh *et al.* 2018). Similarly, "Hello World" is an interactive touch-and-feel book using e-textiles with inserted electronics that react with haptic, audio, and visual feedback to the children's actions. Observations of children's tactile experiences through materials and texture in the story show that their imagination is engaged in a positive way (Moorthy *et al.* 2017). In the "Light it Up" project (Hershman *et al.* 2018), children utilised different paper recording buttons to guide a voice-controlled rocket to go on a mission to

Mars. Children's increased interest highlights the importance of the narrative in using light, a strong abstract concept suitable for this story for various reasons (Hershman *et al.* Hershman 2018). These studies showed us that the materiality of picturebooks and paper is being widely investigated by researchers from diverse disciplines and that these books are not being abandoned for their digital counterparts.

Children's narrative experiences with picturebooks on museums

Museums aim to provide accessible information for children starting with free guidebooks and tailor-made children's books often found in the museum space, its shops and at times in the museum libraries. Conceptually, these resources are closely related to picturebooks (Lechner 1993, Sipe 2001, Nodelman 2018, Yohlin 2012). Lechner (1993) considers picturebooks as "portable art galleries" that go beyond the function of the paintings hanging on the walls since they train children to consider the illustrator's choices, understand a different point of view, recognise compositions and details, grasp the impressions and emotions, and follow the visual storyline. Since picturebooks with or without the art history content are "aesthetic objects" (Sipe 2001), even analysing and questioning the design choices of the artists in these books and reflecting upon them orally or in written format enhance children's creativity and critical thinking (Pantaleo 2017). Sipe (2001) examines picturebooks on art history and categorises them as fictive stories of famous artists, appropriating an artistic style and displaying a museum visit. He asserts that these picturebooks are not just teaching art history to children but liberating them to experiment with different techniques, critique styles, and even take this critical stance further in their cultural life. Similarly, children's reflections on reading picturebooks related to the original artwork in an art institute proved that picturebooks may be regarded to form a threshold to enter the artistic realm while easing the complexity of understanding as well as talking about the artworks as they are often authored, illustrated, and designed in such a way as to create an intimacy for the selected age group (Yohlin 2012). Since children frequently question the protagonists' behaviours in the museum and compare them with their own behaviours, the picturebooks provide critical thinking and a deeper level of engagement with the painting when entwined around a story. Furthermore, children also evaluate the illustrations in the picturebooks with the artworks in terms of reinterpretation and authenticity to further the initial engagement (Yohlin 2012).

Moreover, reading narrative accounts in picturebooks builds empathy in children towards the characters and among the reading group (Kucirkova 2019) and generates familiarity with the complex information just as picturebooks with science themes do (Mantzicopoulos and Patrick 2011). For example, inspired by the socio-cultural theories in museum studies, Hapgood and Palinscar (2002) create a fictional narrative of a scientist whose notebook for an art museum is presented to children. This way, their meaning-making is mediated by the text with first- and second-hand investigations as follows. The first investigation is to look at the artwork purposefully to find a detail or understand the function of the machine, and the second one is to critically understand the context that scientists and curators envision. They suggest referring to the source of questions directly, using traditions in the scientific community, exemplifying expert reasoning, representing data in different ways, and more importantly creating a fictional narrative to give it a framework (Hapgood and Palinscar 2002).

On the other hand, picturebooks created for museums also articulate physical activities. Reading fiction with less movement helps the reader suspend their disbelief which means the reader's interrogations of things from the character's perspective but not one's own. However, hands-on or bodily movements disrupt this inactive immersion and impact the meaning-making of a work's content energetically. Therefore, books for art museum education can integrate movement, enriching children's experience and cognition in the selected period and setting. Analysis of the interactive aspects of children's nonfiction picturebooks on art history demonstrates that children can benefit from these books in sensorial, hands-on, bodily, and spatial ways (Dinc and Veryeri Alaca 2021). Picturebooks can provide a meaningful sequence among the artefacts through a map and physical activities that can be varied from designing an object inspired by the artefact to acting out the artwork. These picturebooks can engage children in exercising different professions in relation to museums such as curatorship and allow children to unfold the pages to form museum space/walls. Decision-making via stickers or sketching can be some of the many interactions to grasp the curatorial aspects of an exhibition. Hence, a picturebook which is "the cultural artifact" (Kim and Short 2019) supports children's museum learning to develop art appreciation and sustain inquiries on the culture represented in the artworks and surrounding them in real-life experiences with their physical affordances.

Bringing these studies together gives us insights into different engagements with the artworks via picturebook interactions that allow historic, multi-cultural context supported with narrative, aesthetic, and cultural engagements . Whether sensorial, spatial, hands-on, or bodily interactions, the learnings from our case study are numerous. Our picturebook prototype inspired interactions while creating new opportunities to foster children's responses to sophisticated cultural and artistic content. Hence, our study opens up a space for rethinking the polyvocal museum by inviting children for subjective interactions and material exchanges, by not merely utilising concepts but also senses and spaces. In sum, this study investigates engagement types with children via a picturebook prototype tested in a museum, using the elements from picturebooks: historic, multi-cultural context supported with the narrative, welcoming artistic and cultural engagements with the artworks. This work uncovers future potentials of picturebooks for special collections mediating a specific period in art history with tangible interactions and customised technology integration. It also facilitates the children's experience in the museum setting proposing activities entwined with stories.

Designing a picturebook enhanced with paper circuitry for Pera Museum's Orientalist Painting Collection

Suna and İnan Kıraç Foundation's Orientalist Painting Collection in Pera Museum covers three centuries of Ottoman and European relationships (Pera Museum 2021). Starting in the late 17th century, the Ottoman Empire sent envoys to European countries to develop diplomatic relations and commercial exchanges. This, for instance, introduced the Ottoman fashion to the West and initiated the Westernisation movement in the Ottoman Empire in return. As Ottoman artists studied in the West and Western artists visited Istanbul and served the ambassadors of the Ottoman royal court, this instigated a considerable cultural exchange. Since travel to Eastern countries was becoming quite popular, the emergence of studies in relation to Orientalism inspired the subject matter of numerous art forms such as paintings. The *Intersecting Worlds: Ambassador and Painters* exhibition highlights Ottoman and European relations and the ambassador's art patronage with selected artworks from the Orientalist Painting Collection (Pera Museum 2021). There are more than 30 artworks from the collection on display, some of them being high points of the museum's collection. These artworks are the subject of our study since they reflect the cultural, economic, and artistic life in that period, aiding a comparative look from the past to the present. Rather than focusing on every single work in the collection, we took our cue from the experience and knowledge of the museum educator and first author by focusing on a range of paintings based on the inclinations of child visitors' during general guided tours. We aimed to keep the theme of ambassadors at the centre of our picturebook and emphasised a meaningful path of visiting the artworks in the exhibition with the LED interactions in the picturebook.

Considering all artworks highlighted by the Learning Programs primarily, six artworks were selected based on representing diversity in subjects, their distribution in the exhibition space and their popularity among the public. The first artwork is *The Welcoming of Venetian Balios to Ottoman Lands* (1725) by Jean Baptiste Vanmour and it is a series of paintings narrating the story of the Venetian ambassador Francesco Gritti's arrival to Istanbul to present a letter from the Venetian King to the Ottoman Sultan (Inankur 2014). In some of these paintings, the ambassador accompanied by his regiment is riding his horse to the Topkapı Palace, where he is welcomed with a special performative event called "the sacking the bowl", in which the Jannisary, the court soldiers, are searching for gold in the bowls of rice. Children are helped to identify the ambassador by his unique attire and position in the space and how to distinguish local and foreign officials from each other. Since being an ambassador is not a common occupation, children often need an explanation for what an ambassador does. They also often query the act of the soldiers, since they cannot see the gold and are not familiar with this type of performance.

Mehmet Said Efendi and his Retinue (1733) by George Engelhardt Schröder depicts the envoy Mehmet Said, who was responsible for collecting monies owed by Sweden but returned home unsuccessful and empty-handed (Renda 2014). This painting is perhaps the one the generic guided tours spend the least time on, as the diplomatic story might be perceived by some as dry, but it is one that could be enlivened with the support of the picturebook reading process. Hence, some of the paintings reflected the social life in Istanbul, including the portrait of *The French Ambassador Comte de Vergennes in Turkish Attire* (1762) painted by Antoine de Favray that illustrates how foreign ambassadors at times dressed in culture-specific attire to depict the fashion and culture of the time (Renda 2014). At times, the sultans would present special caftans called hilat to ambassadors as a gift exchange. These paintings provide a wealth of information for discussions with children that focus on the identity of these figures, foreign or not, through the accessories, the clothes as well as body positionings. *A Scene from the Turkish Harem* (1654) (Figure 11.1) painted by Franz Hermann, Hans Gemminger, and Valentin Muller displays a scene that envisions the entertainment Ottoman women indulge in, a popular artwork

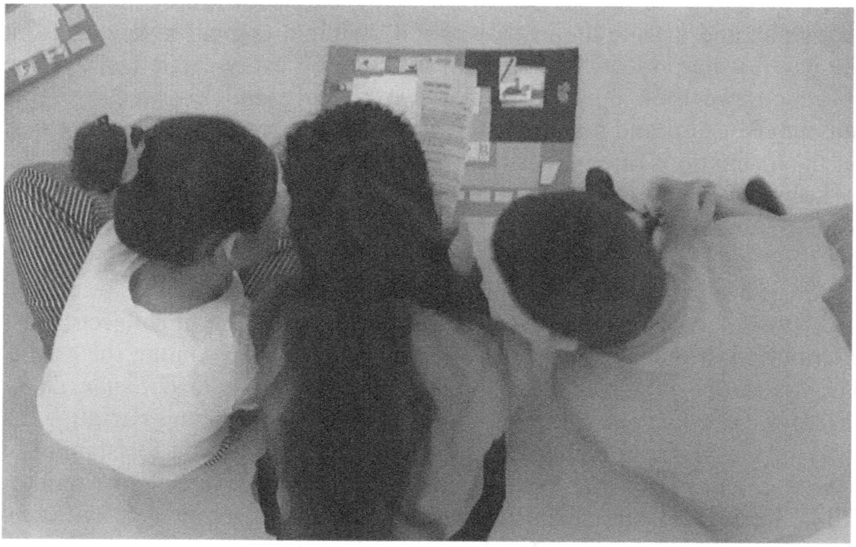

Figure 11.1 *A Scene from the Turkish Harem* (1654) by Franz Hermann, Hans Gemminger, and Valentin Muller, with the permission of Suna and İnan Kıraç Foundation Orientalist Painting Collection, Pera Museum.

of the Orientalism genre that imposes suppositions on Ottoman people and pastimes (Inankur 2014).

The only contemporary artwork in the exhibition, Horror Vacui (2017) by Alejandro Almanza Pereda catches children's attention in an incongruous installation half comprises a cement slab overlying the bottom half of an 18th-century landscape painting from Turkey (Pera Museum Blog 2017). While it is interpreted by the children as representing the environment trapped between nature and men, it also highlights how values and art are transformed across time and artistic preferences are deviating from hand-crafted paintings to modern conceptualisations made of concrete that blatantly indicate fine art being abandoned (Pera Museum Blog 2017). A leading figure of Turkish art and diplomacy, Osman Hamdi Bey's painting the *Tortoise Trainer* (1906) (Figure 11.2), which displays a man captivating tortoise with a special flute, ney, is one of the primary attractions for visitors to the museum.

Ultimately, these paintings present a retrospective look at different aspects of culture and related performances such as historical versions of fashion, entertainment, travel, and international dialogue that allow children to position Istanbul in a global setting. Our work simplifies complicated concepts, explaining new ideas via the narrative and related activities of a picturebook (ambassador, Orientalism, implications of variety in fashions like caftan). These explanations also give children a chance to view the paintings as a political and cultural medium between different countries.

In our case, children experience the collection with the guided tour enriched with play-acting as they are asked to perform one of the scenes from Vanmour's painting. Here, children re-enact the Venetian ambassador's presentation of the letter to the Ottoman Sultan by wearing the attire of a sultan, a vizier, and an ambassador. Children, in front of the Harem scene, imitate the figures in pairs. Children's engagement in this role-playing gives an insight into less descriptive and more interactive acts in the museum space. Since the theme of the guided tour and workshop focuses on the ambassador's role, the picturebook aims to complement it in numerous ways.

Designing the picturebook prototype

The picturebook is designed by selecting the story of the ambassadors to narrate and allow hands-on, bodily, and material engagements in the museum space. It introduces children to historical and cultural vocabulary and provides prompts that help children discuss the painting's content while synthesising the basic electric circuit embedded in certain parts of the content to inform, attract, and reason. Furthermore, the picturebook has two sides, one for interactions in the exhibition space and the other one for reading. The prototype, which is a 35 × 50 cm duplicate of the exhibition on

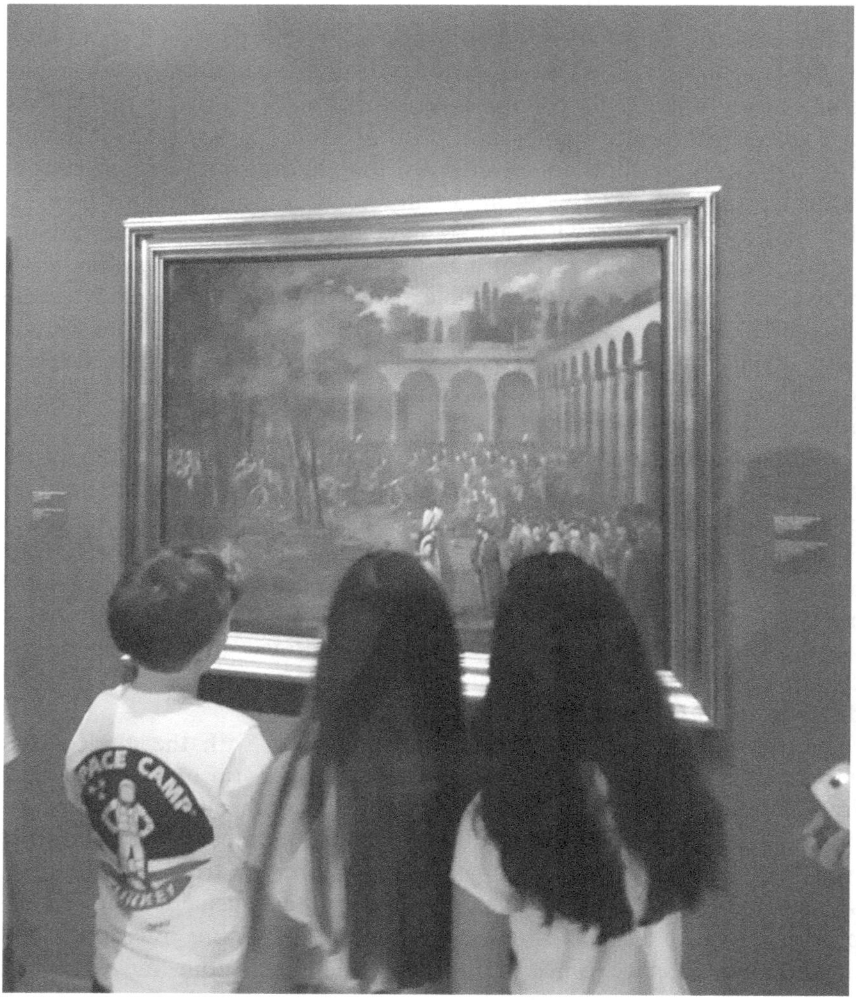

Figure 11.2 *Tortoise Trainer* (1906) by Osman Hamdi Bey, with the permission of Suna and İnan Kıraç Foundation Orientalist Painting Collection, Pera Museum.

one side by referring to its floor plan, is a large single-page version of the picturebook, providing a guided tour of the collection (Figure 11.3) and a map along with activity cards (Figure 11.4). It aims to provide hands-on, bodily, material, and critical engagements with artworks through different tasks (Table 11.1).

As part of the narration, children are expected to embark on a journey as the ambassador on a mission to find the message and carry it to the king. It is inspired by treasure hunts, and as such children are expected to read the

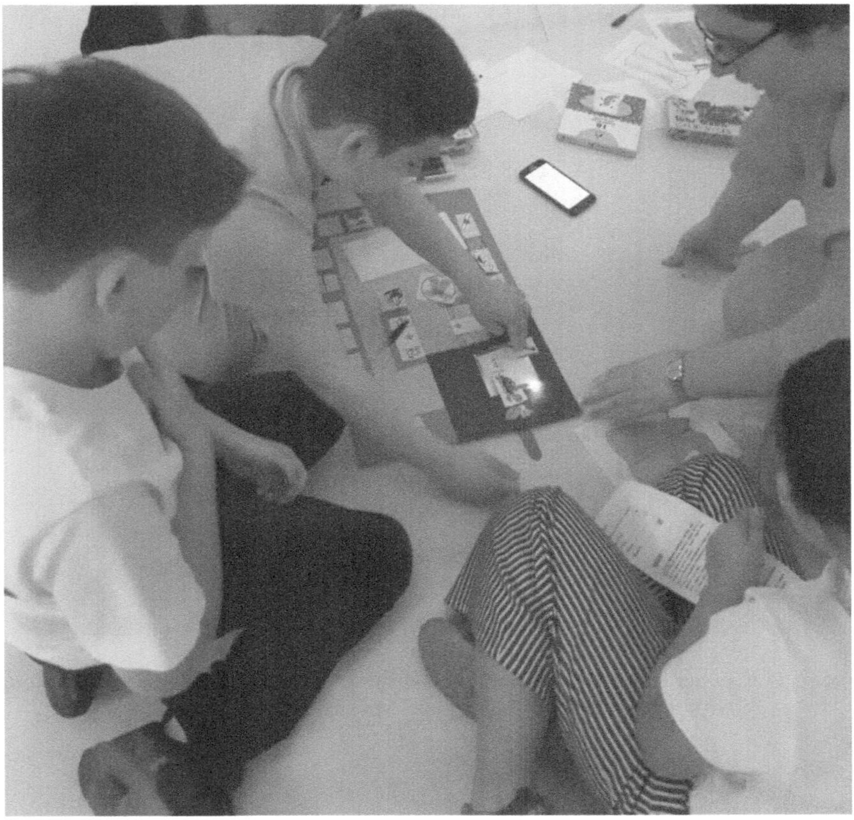

Figure 11.3 One side of the picturebook presents unfolded pages. Image by the first author.

clues, find the artwork, and experience it through specific performances (e.g., dancing, discussions, or drawing), check the additional information in the reading part, and find the next artwork. To help complete this task, there are small symbols that resemble objects or animals in the selected artworks left as clues to help the children identify the correct painting.

By incorporating LED lights in the narrative inspired by paper-circuits-related works, we utilised the circuit system to refer to the tasks carried out by ambassadors, carrying information between different parties to make the clues more playful and meaningful. Interacting with circuits hints at the location of the artwork in the space, but also reveals an important path between the artworks. For instance, pressing on the inside of a gold bowl lights up the next painting with a story on diplomacy and finance. The circuit system also highlights the historical tradition such as the training of tortoises by flute to carry candles while walking at night in the garden. By

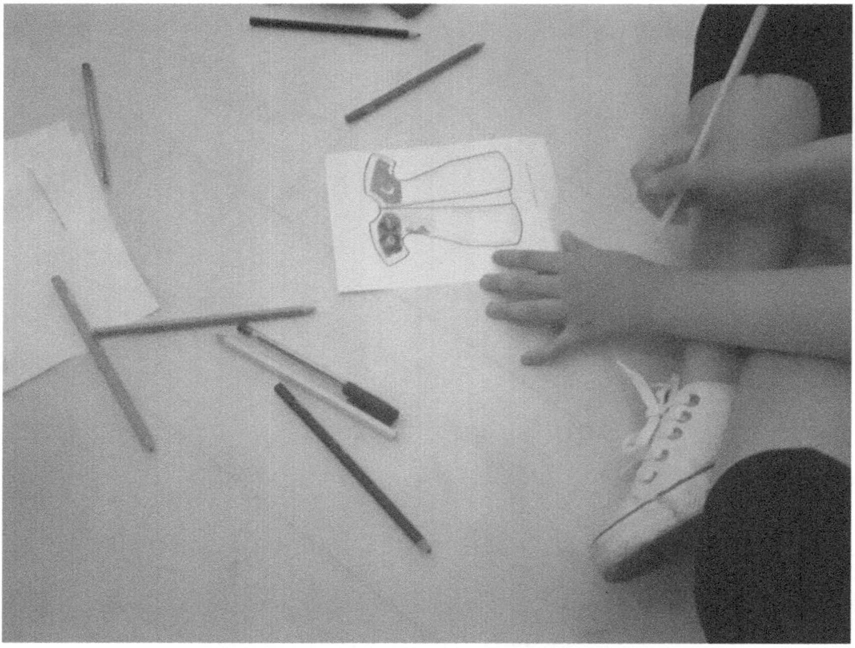

Figure 11.4 Other side of the picturebook displays the plan of the exhibition along with a mission card and a name sticker. Image by the first author.

Table 11.1 Activities that are in relation to paintings provide different engagement types

Painting	*Task*	*Engagement type*
The Welcoming of Venetian Balios ... (1725)	Whispering game, pressing the gold symbol in this painting to light up the next one related with money	Hands-on, bodily, Material
Mehmet Said Efendi (1733)	Thinking as an ambassador for financial negotiation	Narrative
The French ambassador in Turkish attires (1762)	Designing a caftan and exchanging it with a friend as a gift	Hands-on, Narrative
A Scene from Turkish Harem (1654)	Imitating the dancing scene	Bodily
The Tortoise Trainer (1906)	Sliding the tortoise, lighting the candle, a number appears.	Hands-on, Material
Horror Vacui (2017)	writing a letter to the future as an ambassador of today	Narrative

swiping a bar with the tortoise image and pressing the flute image, children light up the candle, re-enacting a historical tradition of the use of candles at night through circuitry. We allowed the copper strips linking the light from one side to another to be visible since there were concerns that the children might not readily make the connection.

Thus, the picturebooks offer comparisons between at least two things: paintings at the museum and illustrations in the picturebook that represent the culture in the paintings and the children's own culture. In connection, the cards supporting the mission and the picturebooks' map/guide first explain the duty of ambassadors in that period on one side and then ask children to accomplish a similar task but one that is familiar to them in their daily life. Thus, these cards make children go back and forth to paintings to observe and evaluate what the ambassadors did and then later figure out what they could do and set criteria in this specific theme in a pleasurable way. Informative materials are offered in cards to explain and engage in activities as well as to describe certain terminology unique to the exhibition. Considering that children utilise the picturebook as a map of the exhibition floor, and follow the route through the instructions and games, the tasks provide embodied engagement and interaction as they move from one work to the next. The children would play a whispering game (or telephone) to pass the ambassador's message along, orally similar to the circuits carrying energy but offering sensorial and bodily engagement. For further engagement, children offer the caftan that they designed to a friend as a symbolic gift. To embrace the ambassador experience, they wear the ambassador's name tag and negotiate between countries about various issues. Finally, as they craft a letter to the future as an ambassador of today, all these activities coalesce to form the creative parts of the picturebook. experience, they wear the ambassador's name tag and negotiate between countries about various issues.

Testing the picturebook prototype with the children

In Turkey, museums tend to produce activity books for schoolchildren since one of their primary audience groups is students. Because these activity books target mostly 9- to 12-year-olds, the participants of this project were seven children aged between nine and ten from a volunteer program. In this program, children who are studying at a public school attend a course taught by university students who volunteer over the weekends. The group of children never visited the Pera Museum before, making this their first exposure to the selected collection. In the selected exhibition area, we explained to them that we are designing an interactive picturebook about the exhibition and wanted to investigate its potential outcome with them. During the project, four volunteer university students with whom the children were already familiar were present to assist. The children were divided into two groups and each group was given one of the two copies of this prototype. Both books aid in a dialogic reading of the content as well as of the instructions for certain activities. The first group consisted of three children and the second group consisted of four children. To understand in what ways children's interactions with the artworks can be strengthened by the help of picturebook, we paid attention to several criteria: to what extent children are making comparisons (e.g., the culture presented in the artwork with real life), having inquiries on the artwork and beyond it (e.g., picturebook, or daily life); recalling the narration and historical information during the activities; reflecting themselves within diverse ways.

To be a part of the narrative, they each wrote their name on a sticker as "Ambassador ..." and then stuck it on their clothes to identify themselves as an ambassador fostering collaborative working, reading, and negotiating acts. This was the first step in adopting the role of an ambassador and engaging in active dialogue about the museum content. They read the first card about the ambassador's mission and their first task began with the whispering game: to whisper the message to their friends and in doing so give them the next clue. It was quite a challenging task as it was a long sentence making it hard to remember. This stage of the game taught the importance of accuracy in communication and the duty of the ambassador to deliver a message carefully. Thus, whispering worked as an icebreaker and eased the social tension of introductions. Although they do the activity together as a group, they shared roles (e.g., reading the map, mission cards, dictionary, and picturebook) among each group's members. Therefore, the activity and novelties facilitated feelings of togetherness and collaboration as a group in the exhibition space. After reading the sentence in the whispering game, they started to search for an ambassador on a white horse and they found two paintings that faced each other. Since the clue hinted at the Venetian ambassador, they discussed which one appeared foreign and which one was from the Ottoman Empire. One child pointed out the very tiny flag on the horizon of a painting that distinguished the ambassadors.

Another mission required them to analyse the portraits of Comte and Countess de Vergennes dressed in Ottoman clothing and design their own caftans that they would later swap with one of their friends. Children were expected to reflect upon the accessories and attires as well as the reason for depicting a foreign ambassador in Ottoman clothes. However, they went beyond the aspects of fashion in that era to develop inquiries on today's diverse understandings of fashion. They first discussed among themselves why a foreign ambassador would wear Eastern clothes. Then, one child questioned why the male ambassador would wear clothes decorated with a flower pattern as he considered it unusual, opening up new discussions for instance on the pattern in relation to gender in different eras. This was useful in terms of comparing the past and present and engaging in critical dialogue on cultural and personal norms. When they were invited to decorate a caftan (Figure 11.5), some children decorated caftans with different patterns, one child drew the Ottoman flag to show that this caftan belongs to an Ottoman

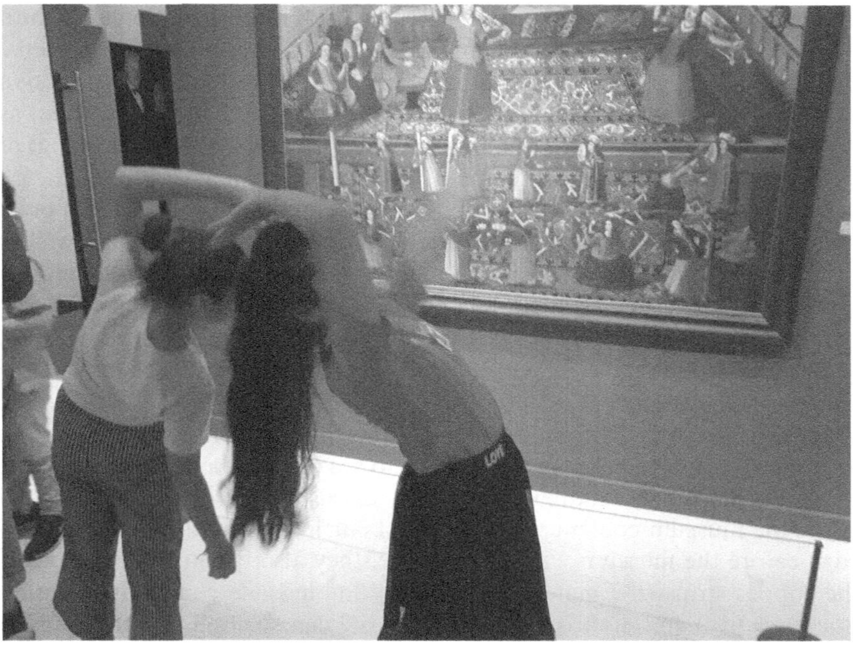

Figure 11.5 Children's engagement with the artworks and the picturebook. Photographs by the first author.

ambassador, and one child explained that her drawing of Turkish and British flags together on a caftan implies the peace among countries. Thus, some children recalled the story of the ambassadors and visualise an abstract concept, diplomacy, in their drawings. This diversity in children's reflections on the same activity hinted us how the narrative account about ambassadors offered children different meaning-making opportunities.

Another task involved action. First, they were asked to select figures in the Harem Scene and then dance in pairs, which led them to guess that the dance the figures were involved in was unusual even for the time (Figure 11.5). Bodily interaction in this task paved the way for critical thinking because they questioned the feasibility of the dance figures in real life. After they read the definitions of Harem and Orientalism, they discussed how the artists could paint this scene from their imagination which might cause these unusual dance figures.

Although in guided tours, the attention is on the individual animals as main attractions, such as the dog figure in Mehmet Said's painting, during our run-through with our prototype picturebooks, children paid less attention to single details. Instead, they could ponder upon the artwork's story as a whole with the support of the picturebook that is illustrated in the following instances. They discussed financial negotiations between an ambassador and the representatives of Sweden such as offering to split the money owed or accept a ship in lieu (Renda 2014) and agreed to find a third way to keep the peace since the ambassadors' duties were also to preserve diplomatic dialogue. At this moment, they remembered the first mission card about the features (e.g., being diplomatic, polite, and constructive) as well as responsibilities (e.g., fulfilling the duty given by a sultan or a king) of an ambassador so they build empathy towards the ambassadors.

Another task involved using circuitry in a meaningful way. Children press a detail from the painting and slide the tortoise to light the candle as well as to uncover the next clue which is a number (Figure 11.5). They added this number to the painting's production year to find the year of the next painting. In this task, they noticed that they could utilise the artwork labels to check the dates as well as the time difference between a historical and contemporary artwork. Therefore, they navigated themselves not only in the space but also in the chronology. One of the children confessed that among all the tasks, he liked sliding the tortoise to see the number (111) appear the most. Furthermore, children could easily discuss the circuit's function and relate the museum content to their school curriculum and previous knowledge before the museum visit. In this case, they also questioned the role of the copper strips (the materiality) visually linking one concept to another (the narrative) and discuss what this material can symbolise in this ambassador theme. After viewing the one piece of contemporary artwork and completing the task of writing as today's ambassador to a future ambassador, they settled down to discuss issues using the ambassador as a metaphor. They discussed how copper is a bridge between different energies, how an ambassador is a bridge between countries, and how art is a bridge between humans and nature. Thus, they once more recalled the narration on ambassadors to understand how the material (the circuitry) is in relation to the story. Moreover, they interpret this metaphor to understand today's world (e.g., the role of art in protecting nature).

Children had discussions on the aesthetic and technological features of the picturebook. A child started to inquire about the medium itself and proposed additional features by stating that the tortoise could move further or perhaps even walk by itself. Many of them commented that it would be enriching to hear the barking of the dog and the singing of the bird. Unexpectedly, one child questioned the missing paintings on the map and commented that there could be more paintings placed on the map. Although she likes that the book is informative, she prefers to see the names and exact images of the paintings on the map. Although children received a toy at the end of reading the picturebook, one proposed that the gift-giving could be even more physically engaged if it involved the exhibition space and the gift and some materials could be hidden in the exhibition area. Therefore, their criticality in this whole experience was not limited to the artworks, nor the narration in the picturebook, they prolonged their inquiries on the medium through material engagement.

Based on a set of criteria, testing children's interactions with the artworks through the prototype showed how each engagement type and the rationale behind the designs invited children for a more inquisitive museum experience. For example, (1) *narrative engagement* offered comparisons (the artworks and real life, the culture in a historical period and today's), inquiries on the artwork, developed empathy towards the ambassadors and other figures, and sought strategies to build peaceful dialogues among different cultures. Similarly, (2) *hands-on* and (3) *bodily engagements* provided diverse comparisons, inquiries on power dynamics in society, and questions about the norms. (4) *Material engagement* (paper circuitry and the picturebook) was efficient to recall the narration and historical information, build metaphorical relationships, and setting discussions on the role of their generation and art in creating future societies and environments. Ultimately, the (5) totality of these engagements revealed children's initial realisation of the discourses surrounding them and reflections to challenge these constructions.

Discussion

Critical heritage involves perceiving heritage as a process and constant re-creations that reject authorised discourses with the help of various disciplines and underrepresented groups (Witcomb and Buckley 2013, p. 569), such as children who might be expected not to acknowledge the complexities of "heritage". By working with children who are less likely involved in museums as coproducers (Roussou *et al.* 2007), we aspire to integrate them in heritage-making as agents with interactive tools (picturebooks) designed specifically for their development and interest through narrative, material, hands-on, and bodily engagements.

Plural heritages and polyvocal imagination across time and space

The Orientalist Painting Collection at Pera Museum presents abstract, cultural as well as historic concepts that challenge children while displaying a valuable resource for imagining thought-provoking heritages. Diplomacy for instance is a difficult concept even for adults because it requires geographical and historical knowledge to understand what Venetian and Ottoman relations signified in different centuries. Although children were already aware of the geographical location of Istanbul and its pre-Republican history in general through their school curriculum, they still had a hard time grasping the diplomatic relationships that could occur and the main actors, the ambassadors, responsible for continuing constructive relationships between the countries. However, they overcame these challenges through the picturebook narration about the ambassadors which made material and bodily interactions meaningful. Hence, the picturebook as an interactive artifact and narrative contextualised the cultural heritage and provided material, metaphorical, and informative entanglements that help children step into critical heritage. In line with previous studies offering participants polyvocal narratives, multisensorial interactions, and spaces to reflect themselves (Schofield *et al.* 2019, Claisse *et al.* 2020, Galani *et al.* 2020), we underscore the possibilities of valorising heritage discourses with children's participation through several factors: considering other studies that also specialised in museum education during design, creating embodied interactions through a material familiar to children, and providing imaginative narratives that help children to think different historical perspectives.

As conveying pluralistic narratives via digital technologies in heritage demands participants' acknowledgement of the self-other relationship and active listening (Galani *et al.* 2020), the children in our study imagined similar identity negotiations through different key figures in history. Because of the narration in relation to the historical facts, children did not only ponder the diplomatic relationships but also experienced the responsibilities of an ambassador, the sultan and some underrepresented groups, such as women at that period, thereby realising that cultural heritage is not singular. While trying to solve ambassadors' problems, children experienced the concepts of negotiation, compromise, sanctions, and communicating their message in a formal setting. Children challenged themselves to find a creative way to represent diplomatic relationships via images as well. For example, although the attires in the paintings feature floral designs, children re-interpret the symbolism of caftan in order to design their own caftan with flags of different countries. Hence, creative activities through narration help children interpret "past" and cultural heritage as a dynamic process in a flow affecting present social issues. The picturebook married the past to the present by using the activity cards that first gave them the duty of the ambassador in the past and then related it to the children's duties today. Although the picturebook facilitated a comparison of past and present cultures, drafting a letter to a future ambassador at the end was meant to open their minds to the fact that similar issues to occur at any time. Since this activity as a cultural probe help participants to reflect on histories based on their community (Schofield *et al.* 2019), it provided children with a tool to consider the discrepancies in the future of cultural and natural heritage and their own role to bridge between past and future in cultural heritage.

Embodied and material assemblage of criticality

Similar to the studies that pave a path to participants through artworks and activities or offer treasure hunt-themed engagement with artworks in museums (Yiannoutsou *et al.* 2009, Thom-Santelli *et al.* 2006), children were supported by the map and the narrative of the picturebook to connect them and orient them within the space. Both reading the map and then finding the corresponding artworks within the actual space was sometimes demanding for children however clear clues combined with tasks about the paintings were helpful. The circuit lights on the map further assisted children in finding their way around in the museum space. Children also experienced reading the museum's sources (e.g., labels, boards) in a fun way; therefore, a picturebook can benefit children by providing a sense of agency in visiting the museum with their friends. As children were walking, running, zigzagging, pathfinding, stopping each other (while considering other visitors), and dancing in the space together through guided prompts, "they created shared embodied ways of being in the space" (Hackett *et al.* 2018, p. 177).

By capturing children's attention by giving the picturebook enhanced with circuitry and light (Qi *et al.* 2015, Hershman *et al.* 2018) and then assigning them a meaningful role related to the stories of the artworks, the paintings that once were found to be less attractive and maybe even dull became more engaging as children critically reflected upon them. Sometimes bodily challenges raised awareness as well as interest. The whispering game, for instance, allowed them to experience how difficult it was to deliver a message from one person to another, let alone from one country to the other. In addition, children could socialise among themselves and feel comfortable about moving around the museum space even though some of them did not know each other and the museum at the beginning. The book provided numerous benefits supported by the symbolic interpretation of artworks through social gestures while still making the centre of the artwork of attention. Children exercised deictic gestures (such as pointing out the details on the paintings) and mimicked the figures on the paintings. While they were doing this, they compared today's dance movements with the old ones and discuss Orientalism. Since children were mostly interested in developing the interaction through guided tasks, picturebooks in relation to museums can benefit from basic craft paper enhanced with circuits to draw attention to the details in the artworks (e.g., the dog or a candle on the tortoise), certain traditional acts (e.g., training the tortoises), and to link children's school curriculum with what they were learning at the museum.

Since being guided by a museum expert provides greater learning gains in comparison to children independently playing in museums (Weisberg *et al.* 2016), we underscore that guidance and structure are important in children's museum learning for two reasons. First, children benefit from the assistance adults can offer to understand the directions in the narrative. Secondly, after the workshop, a concluding guided tour was provided to children upon their request, which helped us to evaluate how much they recalled. Even without the tasks, they were still interested in Van Mours' painting and willingly engaged in the activities from the book. Besides retelling the story about the characters and ceremonies based on the picturebook reading experience, they were also interested in discovering additional details in the paintings on their own. This proves that guided learning is significant in museum learning and how this activity supported by the picturebook prototype could enrich the museum guide herself.

Comparison of interactions of children in the general tours (according to the earlier experience of the first author) and in the picturebook workshop shows how the picturebook complements the other. The first painting on welcoming the Venetian ambassador in the Ottoman lands was explained through the drama activity by imitating the scene by describing the traditions in the guide tours. Similarly, the picturebook provided a bodily engagement but this time it focused on experiencing the challenges of being an ambassador. For the portrait of Mehmet Said Efendi, the discussions in the guide tours focused on mostly the dog which is more compelling to children in addition to mentioning the historical story. Through the narration in the picturebook, children discussed the historical story, tried to think like an ambassador, build empathy towards him and therefore, spend more time solving the challenge. While children in general tour guides can discuss the diplomatic and cultural reasons for painting the portraits of the French ambassador and his wife in Ottoman clothes and the richness in the attires, the utilisation of the picturebook helped children to visualise this abstract concept of diplomacy as well as make a comparison of the history with the real life. As embodied activities in design practices encourage participants to reflect on cultural heritage (Schofield *et al.* 2019), engagement with the Harem scene through dance provides efficiency in evoking children's responses. Also, the picturebook narration emphasised the concept of Orientalism which children critically think about historical and contemporary cultures. The symbolism, animal and human figures in the tortoise trainer painting are widely explained during the guided tour after storytelling about who the painter is. The picturebook, however, mostly focused on cultural tradition. In general, contemporary artwork guided tours can offer more detailed explanations on a range of artworks than a picturebook reading. Also, art and historical concepts can be reinforced in the creative workshops led by the Learning Programs. However, testing the picturebook with children showed that critical thinking about culture via bodily, hands-on, material, and narrative engagements can be encouraging in order to grasp the artwork's essence.

Conclusion

This study explored ways to hone children's interactions with cultural heritage in museums by considering research in HCI-museum interactions and then synthesising them with picturebook studies. Children's participation in heritage-making encompasses several layers; learning about the artefacts, examining the details in the artworks, playing with the tools, and critically reflecting on the concepts, implied in the paintings, through embodied activities and active discussions.

Firstly, our study recommends professionals in museums and cultural heritage studies to benefit from interdisciplinary environments of museums with a focus on children's narratives and preferences. As an example, picturebook studies back artistic and educational outcomes such as learning new concepts, easing the challenges of understanding historic concepts, and synthesising physical actions to new vocabulary via utilizing the circuitry.

Furthermore, these narratives foster children's experiences and evaluation of curatorial decisions by giving them agency in a storytelling path that builds dialogue and winds between the artworks and real life.

Offering interactive prototypes to children suits their motivations for interaction and their related curricular content at school. Rather than just presenting them bare descriptions, posing questions in relation to material engagement inspire children to explore the paintings with language arts and support their vocabulary. For instance, circuitry opens up new topics related to the school curriculum, but this technology can be utilised in museum learning programs in a metaphoric way. What we found useful was to familiarise the new terms with activities that could be meaningful for the selected age group (e.g., designing caftan, casting the children as the ambassador). Finally, utilising visual materials derived from the collection and referring to the most attractive details highlighted with interactions facilitate the children's attentive observations.

To foster children's museum experience, inquiries on the cultural practices in past and present, and participation in the heritage making as a stakeholder, this research suggests the importance of utilising narrative, playful, and embodied interactions that include activities urging children to think from the figure's perspective and generate their personal reflections. Revisiting objects and practices, such as reading picturebooks, in new and creative ways, and supporting children through prototypes would benefit practitioners to make the stories of the paintings more memorable and questionable. This way, the terminology is more accessible and the museum engagement is dialogic. There is an interplay between the content in the picturebook and the social interaction in the museum setting that makes it easier for children to process historic content, imagine how certain events in the past could have been explored in more peaceful and inclusive scenarios, and reflect on individuals' responsibilities for a better future.

Our study also recommends considering technologies (such as circuits) not only through their educative and aesthetic aspects but also due to their potential cultural and historical entwinements. By embedding technologies (in our case circuits) in an appropriate narrative, children can engage with metaphorical concepts (e.g., transmitting energy like ambassadors delivering messages), revealing a way to process allegorical interpretations through novel systems. This case can be expanded by discussing visual to conceptual metaphors if desired according to the age of children involved as well as the guide or instructors' choices. Besides metaphors, differing verbal devices may also be used to trigger debates and further interactions. How these may support a different modality beyond the visual can be a bridging experience and even be tested out at more experimental levels by children themselves. Hence, this study demonstrated in a nutshell that the integration of paper technologies with picturebooks has a significant potential to ease the perception of these complex concepts. Further sensorial and embodied explorations of picturebooks and paper-based counter surface technologies can support the co-existence of material, hands-on and narrative experiences to encourage children's contribution to the heritage field while facilitating enjoyable musings.

References

Allen, S., 1997. Sociocultural theory in museums: insights and suggestions. *Journal of Museum Education*, 22 (2–3), 8–9.

Andre, L., Durksen, T., and Volman, M.L., 2017. Museums as avenues of learning for children: a decade of research. *Learning Environments Research*, 20 (1), 47–76.

Apostolellis, P., and Bowman, D.A., 2015. Small group learning with games in museums: effects of interactivity as mediated by cultural differences. In: Proceedings of the *14th International Conference on Interaction Design and Children (IDC'15)*. New York: ACM Press, 160–169.

Arizpe, E., and Styles, M., 2016. *Children reading picturebooks: interpreting visual texts*. 2nd ed. New York: Routledge.

Beheshti, E., Borgos-Rodriguez, K., and Piper, A.M., 2019. Supporting parent-child collaborative learning through haptic feedback displays. In: Proceedings of the *18th ACM International Conference on Interaction Design and Children (IDC '19)*. New York: ACM Press, 58–70.

Cesário, V., *et al.*, 2016. Children's books: paper vs digital, what do they prefer? In: Proceedings of the *15th International Conference on Interaction Design and Children (IDC '16)*. New York: ACM Press, 625–630.

Claisse, C., *et al.*, 2020. Crafting critical heritage discourses into interactive exhibition design. In: Proceedings of the *2020 CHI Conference on Human Factors in Computing Systems (CHI '20)*. New York: ACM Press, 1–13.

Dinç, B.G., and Veryeri Alaca, I., 2021. Interacting with nonfiction picturebooks in art museums. In: N. Goga, S. Hoem Iversen, and Teigland, ed. *Verbal and visual strategies in nonfiction picturebooks*. A. Scandinavian University Press, 236–249.

Falk, J.H., and Dierking, L.D., 2018. *Learning from museums*. 2nd ed. Lanham: Rowman & Littlefield.

Galani, A., Mason, R., Arrigoni, G. (Eds.), 2020. European heritage, dialogue and digital practices. Routledge.

Gubar, M., 2013. Risky business: talking about children in children's literature criticism. *Children's Literature Association Quarterly*, 38 (4), 450–457.

Hackett, A., Procter, L., and Kummerfeld, R., 2018. Exploring abstract, physical, social and embodied space: developing an approach for analyzing museum spaces for young children. *Children's Geographies*, 16 (5), 489–502.

Hapgood, S. and Palinscar, A., 2002. Fostering and investigatory stance: using text to mediate inquiry with museum objects. In: S.G. Paris (ed.) *Perspectives on object-centered learning in museums*, Routledge, 171–190.

Hershman, A., *et al.*, 2018. Light it up: using paper circuitry to enhance low-fidelity paper prototypes for children. In: Proceedings of the *17th ACM conference on interaction design and children (IDC '18)*, New York: ACM Press, 365–372.

Hogan, T., Hayes, S., and O'Keeffe, M., 2017. Piecing together the past: constructing stories with jigsaw puzzles in museums. In: Proceedings of the *2017 ACM conference companion publication on designing interactive systems (DIS '17 companion)*, New York: ACM Press, 79–83.

Hornecker, E., and Ciolfi, L., 2019. *Human-computer interactions in museums*. Morgan & Claypool Publishers, 12, 2, i–171.

Inankur, Z., 2014. Ambassadors and their patronage of the arts. In: *Intersecting worlds: ambassadors and painters*. Suna ve Inan Kıraç Vakfı, Pera Museum, Istanbul.

Kidd, J., 2018. "Immersive" heritage encounters. *The Museum Review*, 3 (1).

Kim, H.Y., and Short, K.G., 2019. A picturebook as a cultural artifact. In: Johnson, H., Mathis, J. and Short, K., ed. *Critical content analysis of visual images in Books for young people: Reading images*, New York: Routledge, 245–264.

Kucirkova, N., 2019. How could children's storybooks promote empathy? A conceptual framework based on developmental psychology and literary theory. *Front Psychol*, 10, 121.

Lechner, J.V., 1993. Picture books as portable art galleries. *Art Education*, 46 (2), 34–40.

Long, D., *et al.*, 2019. Trajectories of physical engagement and expression in a co-creative museum installation. In: Proceedings of the *2019 on creativity and cognition (C&C '19)*, New York: ACM Press, 246–257.

Marstine, J. (Ed.), 2006. New museum theory and practice: an introduction. Malden, MA: Blackwell.

Mantzicopoulos, P., and Patrick, H., 2011. Reading picture books and learning science: engaging young children with informational text. *Theory Into Practice*, 50 (4), 269–276.

Moorthy, P., *et al.*, 2017. Hello world: a children's touch and feel books enhanced with DIY electronics. In: Proceedings of the *16th international conference on mobile and ubiquitous multimedia (MUM '17)*, New York: ACM Press, 481–488.

Nodelman, P., 2018. Touching art: the art museum as a picture book, and the picture book as art. *Journal of Literary Education*, 1, 6–25.

Oh, H., *et al.*, 2018. Paper mechatronics: present and future. In: Proceedings of the *17th ACM conference on interaction design and children (IDC '18*), New York: ACM Press, 389–395.

Pantaleo, S., 2017. Critical thinking and young children's exploration of picturebook artwork. *Language and Education*, 31 (2), 152–168.

Pera Museum, Orientalist painting collection [online]. Istanbul, 2013–2020. Available from: https://www.peramuseum.org/Collection/Orientalist-Painting-Collection/15 [Accessed 5 September 2021].

Pera Museum Blog, 2017. Horror vacui alejandro almanza pereda [online]. Istanbul: Pera Museum. Available from: https://www.peramuseum.org/blog/horror-vacui-alejandro-almanza-pereda/1308. [Accessed 17 October 2021].

Piscitelli, B., and Weier, K., 2002. Learning with, through, and about art: the role of social interactions. In: S.G. Paris (ed.) *Perspectives on object-centered learning in museums*, Routledge, 121–151.

Qi, J., and Paradiso, J. 2015. Crafting technology with circuit stickers. In: Proceedings of the *14th international conference on interaction design and children (IDC '15)*. New York: ACM Press, 438–441.

Renda, G., 2014. Diplomatic relations in the ottoman empire-ambassadors and portraits. In: Barış Barış Kıbrıs (ed.)*Intersecting worlds: ambassadors and painters*, Istanbul: Suna ve İnan Kıraç Vakfı, Pera Museum, Istanbul, 37–44.

Roussou, M., and Katifori, A., 2018. Flow, staging, wayfinding, personalization: evaluating user experience with mobile museum narratives. *Multimodal Technologies and Interaction*, 2 (2), 32.

Roussou, M., Kavalieratou, E., and Doulgeridis, M., 2007. Children designers in the museum: applying participatory design for the development of an art education program. In: Proceedings of the *6th international conference on interaction design and children (IDC '07)*, New York: ACM Press, New York, 77–80.

Schofield, T., *et al.*, 2019. Design and plural heritages: composing critical futures. In: Proceedings of the *2019 CHI conference on human factors in computing systems*, 1–15.

Sim, G., Horton, M., and McKnight, L., 2016. iPad vs paper prototypes: does form factor affect children's ratings of a game concept? In: Proceedings of the *the 15th international conference on interaction design and children (IDC '16)*, New York: ACM Press, 190–195.

Sipe, L., 2001. Using picturebooks to teach art history. *Studies in Art Education*, 42 (3), 197–213.

Smith, L., 2006. *Uses of heritage*. Oxon and New York: Routledge.

Thom-Santelli, J., *et al.*, 2006. Beyond just the facts: transforming the museum learning experience. In: *CHI '06 extended abstracts on human factors in computing systems (CHI EA '06)*, New York: ACM Press, 1433–1438.

Vayanou, M., *et al.*, 2019. How to play storytelling games with masterpieces: from art galleries to hybrid board games. *Journal of Computers in Education*, 6 (1), 79–116.

Weisberg, D.S., *et al.*, 2016. Guided play: principles and practices. *Current Directions in Psychological Science*, 25 (3), 177–182.

Witcomb, A., and Buckley, K.A.M., 2013. Engaging with the future of 'critical heritage studies': looking back in order to look forward. *International Journal of Heritage Studies*, 19 (6), 562–578.

Yiannoutsou, N., *et al.*, 2009. Playing with museum exhibits: designing educational games mediated by mobile technology. In: Proceedings of the *8th international conference on interaction design and children (IDC '09)*, New York: ACM Press, 230–233.

Yohlin, E., 2012. Pictures in pictures: art history and art museums in children's picture books. *Children's Literature in Education*, 43 (3), 260–272.

12 Afterword: Code-switching: Feeling the "emotional turn" in digital cultural heritage

Ross Parry

Introduction

From a horizon of perspectives and through an array of rich accounts, this volume helps us to appraise the evolving role that digital technology plays within the socially purposeful work of European cultural heritage organisations. Part compendium of case studies, and part gazetteer of impactful practice, the chapters here combine to evidence the opportunity (indeed, the responsibility) the culture sector has today in building provision in participatory and inclusive ways – aspirationally and ethically for everyone, everywhere. Here this mix of institutions and professionals cohere to form a tableau of reflective work and critical thinking – an image of what probably surrounds us *now*, of what is plausibly coming *next*, as well as what possibly might need to be *new*.

Strikingly, through these chapters, we notice the concepts of "cultural heritage", "digital technologies", and "social innovation" plotted in different ways – concurrently, but without contradiction. A complexity that speaks to the multi-dimensional way in which any discussion of cultural technology must always operate. We see, for instance, digital technology in one role as a catalyst – helping cultural organisations to confront whether they have societal relevance as an institution. (In those instances, digital provides the challenge of whether these organisations are apt and fit for purpose, questioning why they might need to adapt, and modelling what they might need to become – adapting from keepers to storytellers, from collectors to editors, and from initiators to partners, if not followers.) At the same time, we also see digital technology in the form of a tool – helping cultural organisations to act in relevant ways. (In those instances, digital technologies are not the provocation but rather the appropriate channels and platforms, signs, and behaviours, by which a cultural organisation might seek to be more relevant to the rhythms and codes of its contemporary society.) And yet, further, still we see digital technology operating as context – part of the cultural landscape and ways of thinking within which relevancy is constructed and framed. (In those instances, digital becomes the circumstance in which, and the criteria by which, "relevance" is

DOI: 10.4324/9781003277606-12

determined by the cultural organisation and its publics.) The discussions collected here allow us to identify these axes and layers of cultural technology, with cultural organisations attempting to: appraise their *relevance* as institutions in a digital age; communicate in a *relevant* way for a digital age; and define *relevancy*, culturally and societally, within a digital age. Digital technology – all at once – as a disrupter, as an enabler, as well as a subject.

However, as we note (and enjoy) this multi-dimensionality of cultural technology, we might also pause to notice another characteristic to the studies compiled here. For, weaving across the summaries and synthesises of the volume runs another theme – distinctive, sustained, and unavoidable. A theme that demonstrates both a distinctive maturity in professional practice, as well as a prevailing priority in cultural discourse. That theme is "emotion". We notice it, for instance, in the way these accounts of progressive inclusive digital cultural heritage practice are at pains to embrace the diversity of interests and cultural perspectives of stakeholders – recognising different contexts, reconciling different perspectives, and responding to different needs. It is seen in the shape of the creative approaches to inclusive digital storytelling, in the programming for locally-focused placemaking, and in the creative outlooks and educational priorities of particular users within specific locations and situations – be that a classroom, a stage, a screening, or a city tour.

Similarly, we also notice it in the way these projects and programmes have ensured agency within their partners, abdicated responsibility to their co-producers, and moved aside to assign leadership to the users and communities themselves. It is heard there in the beats of "bringing in", "stepping back", "lifting up" – the co-creative activities, the approaches that privilege marginalised voices and narratives, the processes ready to apply a "post-custodial" mindset to cultural heritage. Likewise, we notice it in the way these institutions and consortia have acknowledged the judgments and biases that remain inherent in professional practice, and systemic within organisational processes and culture. In this case, it is felt in those acts of enablement and empowerment (developing community-driven tools and inventive platforms constructed with social innovation in mind), and it is felt in those acts of exposure and reckoning (confronting prejudicing legacies within data models, coding, and systems). In each of these cases (whether the empathetic design, leaderful trust, or cultural respect), the language and priority of digital cultural heritage is distinctive. Rather than focusing only on operational efficiency or machine compatibility, instead, it is also the personal and human dimension to using, managing, creating, and understanding digital in/with/for/by cultural heritage institutions that comes vividly into view. More precisely put, it is the *emotionality* of cultural technology that starts to matter as much – if not, at times, more.

It is this shift in focus, energy and expectation that deserves our attention. This, after all, is a re-centring from "technology" to "people". A change in emphasis – in professional practice and in academic discourse – from (only) business processes and technical systems, to (also) the feeling and experience of digital work and the digital workplace of the museum. What we are witnessing (in this volume, and in our practice and scholarship more widely) is a growing emphasis on the affective dimension of using digital technology in the everyday work of the culture sector; a switch to emotionality.

Sensing the postdigital

To help us feel for the finer contours of this emotionality, there is value in first acknowledging the broader intellectual and professional context into which this discussion on disciplinary and operational sits. This, after all, is a moment in the academy and the culture sector in which digital technology is managed, articulated and conceptualised within some noticeable and distinct frames, namely: *digital maturity*, *mediatisation*, and the *metamodern*.

It has, for instance, become increasingly routine for cultural heritage organisations to deploy the nomenclature and the day-to-day business processes of digital management. Evermore, as cultural organisations continue to adopt digital technology and adapt to an increasingly digital society around them, the normative expectation within these organisational settings is for strategies, policies, systems, and tools to be in-place that embed digital thinking and digital working. Today, the starting point for digital leadership (inside the organisation) and digital scholarship (of, with and by the organisation) is to assume the presence of technology. To be a cultural organisation today is to be inherently information-rich, data-driven, multi-channel, and interaction-ready – with digital technology more commonly innate within the organisation's vision of itself, informing its business processes, characterising its workplace culture, and shaping the skills development of its staff. This, in business terms, is the culture sector's "digital maturity".

Alongside this maturing of business confidence, there has been a similar development in the language and framing of the distinct role of the cultural organisations within digital society. Many cultural organisations today find themselves within parts of society that are increasingly defined in media terms. Digitally speaking, the world in which these organisations sit, which they reflect, and which comes to them, is one that is expansively dataful, progressively connected, and relentlessly inventive. This is a society which not only proliferates its use of media technology, but escalates the ways it understands itself, its relationship with others, its sense of space and time, in media terms. And yet, as well as being confronted with a mediatised world, cultural organisations are uniquely mediatised spaces. They are media-rich landscapes, assembled in a choreography of interfaces and sensory channels, unlike most other (if not any other) public spaces.

As well as these business and academic points of maturity and development sits another, more profound, philosophical shift. At the same time as cultural organisations have adopted and adapted to digital technology, and alongside the new insights and lexicons that media studies have brought to cultural heritage studies, another (third) context demands to be noticed. Today, the thinking on which discussions around digital cultural heritage is predicated, the vocabulary through which it is articulated, and the logic through which it is reasoned, is affected by wider and deeper shifts in our cultural condition(s). Plainly put, whereas at its point of adoption cultural heritage technology was part of a distinctly 20th-century drive to use the power of the computer to systematise organisational practice and provision, the software and hardware of digital technology today have gone on to assume a more complex role within professional practice and academic scholarship. Similarly, whereas at the turn of the last century cultural heritage technology was experiencing a period of interrogation (both professional scepticism and academic critique), the discourse of cultural technology today has developed nuanced and layered forms of engagement. Across these decades of change, the shift can be read as from a modernist building project to a post-modernist questioning forum, to today a contemporary philosophical condition that is comfortable reconciling the two. To be a cultural heritage organisation today is to both embrace the mobilising potential of technology as an agent of positive systemic change, whilst also being able to challenge, expose and (if necessary, at times, decline) that same set of technologies. This, in conceptual terms, is the culture sector's new-found place within the "meta-modern".

And so, our discussion here of a "turn to emotionality" within museum technology practice and scholarship, is helped by (and perhaps even best understood within) these wider business, academic, and philosophical contexts. It is these concepts of "digital maturity", "mediatisation", and "meta-modernity", which together offer the co-ordinates within which we can notice and express the post-digital condition of the culture sector.

Nurturing the affective and emotional turn

Cultural technology's shift to "emotion" marks a poignant stage in its maturity – adding a vital (if not overlooked) human dimension to decades of technological and business development. After all, looking back on recent history of the adoption of (and adaption to) digital technology we see institutions that, understandably perhaps, were initially focused on making the systems and tools work effectively. This was the era of experimentation, of constructing the first data models and networks, and of charting and following where users (and the market) might take the new computing. After several decades of grappling with hardware and software, putting in place the systems and standards for interoperability, and assembling the case for the "new technology" in the culture sector, emphasis turned to businesses processes – and operationalising technology, steady-state, day-to-day into the working life of cultural organisations. This was the era of strategizing with digital, of developing the first policies around data use, social media and digital collecting, and of embracing the role that digital might play in the visioning of the culture sector.

The change we see today, however, is a further turn – and one towards the element that was perhaps always present in this story of development, but that never held the centre ground. It is the element which these initial experiments and adoptions with computers required, and on which the subsequent strategizing and operationalising was based, but was never brought to the fore. That final element, alongside "platforms" and "processes" on which all digital transformation relies, is, of course, "people". Through their long history of technological adoption, cultural organisations always knew that the technology was there to serve users and community. They always knew that new business processes were in place to ensure the effective mobilisation of their staff and delivery of its provision. But what professional practice (and academic discourse) did not do perhaps as much as it ought, was to look to the experience of its leaders, its workers, and its change makers, of initiating this adoption of technology. This is our moment of the affective and emotional turn.

Sensitised by the turn to emotion more generally within digital cultural heritage studies, but also profoundly affected (undoubtedly) by the experiences of a global pandemic and its impact on the emotional intelligence and literacy of the culture sector, our subject is now ready, to confront and consider the human experience of adopting digital. Now that the digital systems work, that the tools are reliable, and now that the strategies are mature and policies are in place, we are ready to look at ourselves and reflect – with care and insight – on the emotionality of digital transformation. We are ready to reflect upon how crucial people (workers) are to making a cultural organisation digital, but also what the emotional consequences are of taking a cultural organisation through a moment of digital change. It is time, in short, from this new perspective, to ask a new set of questions around the affective dimension of cultural heritage sector work with digital technology.

Feeling emotion in cultural technology

Excitingly, the concepts, vocabulary, and reasoning, as well as the practical tools, for understanding the emotional dimension of digital change are (as this volume attests) emerging from an array of contemporary projects. These are helping the sector and the academy to find where to start, how to talk, and in which direction to head when thinking through emotionality in a digital context, but also (more practically) how to lead and be part of digital change in the museum with empathy and emotional intelligence.

First, this emotional turn is helping us to see digital change as *contextual* and site-specific – rather than generic across the sector. Starting to take the perspective of individual cultural sector workers helps us to appreciate how much "place" and "situation" impact upon why and how digital change happens in an organisation. After all, cultural organisations are diverse in size, governance, funding, and subject focus. They are on different parts of their journey to digital maturation. Their ambitions and strategies (in who they serve, why and how) are unique to their circumstance, capacity, capability, and resource. Considered in this way, a person-centred and context-based approach to digital change in the culture sector becomes self-evident.

Second, the emotional turn is enabling us to think *holistically* about digital change – rather than just in technological or business terms. Beginning our thought process with people (rather than machines) helps us critically to notice the cultural, psychological, and personal characteristics of digital change in an organisation. Digital transformation relies upon vision, strategy, processes, and systems to justify, initiate, support, and enable its activity and purpose. However, it is leaders (and the behaviours they model, and the empathy they show), as well as individual museum workers (and the culture of work they build between them, and the agency and resilience they possess) that ultimately will drive any such digital activity and change.

Third, the emotional turn in digital cultural heritage is enabling us to think *purposefully* about digital change – rather than just in technocratic or deterministic terms. When the thought process on why to use digital technology begins from the assumption that it must always be to serve the social good to which the cultural organisation aspires, this immediately brings into focus a number of questions and priorities around equity, inclusion, diversity and access. Looking at people (and not just the technology), and listening to lived experiences of working with digital in cultural organisations (and not just the business processes), reveals another set of fundamental themes and challenges for both the profession and the academy. This perspective will help us to confront a number of germane questions, not least: the extent to which our digital workplaces are accessible to all that work there. What cultural assumptions (and prejudices) are embedded within working practices and processes? Who has agency and who leads (and who does not) in the culture sector's digital landscape? And what within the institutional delivery of digital transformation is not understood, not recognised, and (even) not seen?

Conclusion: "Code switching"

The double meaning of our title here denotes not just the literal change ("switching") towards digital technology ("code") we are witnessing in cultural organisations today, but then also the new emotional skills of empathy we will need to deliver this change effectively. This is not intended as a glib metaphor, but rather a careful acknowledgement of the business maturity, emotional intelligence, as well as layered and concurrent meta-modern thinking, that is beginning to characterise this emerging next generation of cultural technology practice and scholarship. In sociolinguistics, the idea of "code-switching" relates to "the alternating use of two or more 'codes' within one conversational episode" (Auer 1998, p. 17), an "alternation between the different varieties which people speak" (Gardner-Chloros 2009, p. 11). As such, whether moving between languages, dialects or the idioms of different communities, "code-switching" (as an area of study, but also as a linguistic act) is inextricably linked to questions of power, inequality, and rights (Auer 1998, p. 20). Deploying the term in our discussion here, therefore, signals an intentionality to notice how more than one discourse can exist (concurrently) within our practice and discourse of museum technology, but also how the movement between these discourses (between the technological, the managerial, and the emotional) is itself a meaningful act worthy of attention.

Perhaps more profound still, we note that when psycholinguistic studies first used the term "code-switching", the word "code" was originally appropriated from the practices and disciplines of communication technology, and the term "switching" was literally understood as "something similar to flicking an electric switch" (Gardner-Chloros, 2009, p. 11). And so, to use the term as we are here, back in a computing and technological context, is itself cyclical, if not (pleasingly) autological. Moreover, our continued "code switching" in cultural technology (reflecting on the emotionality of using technology, and the role of technology in shaping our emotional self), will remind us of the deep links that remain between technology and people – each always and inescapably shaped by the other.

References

Auer, P., 1998. Bilingual conversation revisited. In: P. Auer, ed. *Code-switching in conversation: Language, interaction and identity*. London: Routledge, 16–56.

Gardner-Chloros, P., 2009. *Code-Switching*. Cambridge: Cambridge University Press.

Index

Note: **Bold** page numbers refer to tables and *italic* page numbers refer to figures.

For Product Safety Concerns and Information please contact our EU representative GPSR@taylorandfrancis.com Taylor & Francis Verlag GmbH, Kaufingerstraße 24, 80331 München, Germany